THE UNKNOWN

Throughout the ages people have sensed the
existence of a benevolent force intervening
from time to time in their lives as if to offer
them help and protection – or to chasten them.
The good fairy of folklore and the guardian
angel of Christian tradition belong in this
category. Socrates said that he had heeded the
voice of his 'daemon' all his life, and it had
never let him down. Churchill sometimes had
'a strong feeling', he told an audience of
miners during the Second World War, 'that
some guiding hand has interfered'.

In *The Unknown Guest* Brian Inglis explores
the historical and present-day evidence of the
force. In perhaps its most familiar guise it
operates as the 'muse' for writers and artists.
And many of us have felt that chance and luck
can't explain away hunches, premonitions,
meaningful coincidences and extra-sensory
perceptions. Brian Inglis concludes that we
don't know enough to be sure about the
source of these promptings but the evidence
is impressive enough to be worth examining
afresh.

About the author

Brian Inglis was born in Dublin and grew up in Ireland, though he went to school in England, and to Oxford University. After war service as a pilot in Coastal Command, finishing with the rank of squadron leader, he joined the *Irish Times* as feature writer, columnist and eventually parliamentary commentator. He also obtained a Ph.D. at Dublin University. Coming to Fleet Street in 1953, he joined *The Spectator* the following year, and was editor from 1959 to 1962. As writer and presenter he launched the Granada programme *What the Papers Say* in 1956, and wrote and presented *All Our Yesterdays* from 1962 to 1973. Among his recent books are *Natural and Supernatural*, *The Diseases of Civilisation*, *Science and Parascience*, *The Hidden Power* and *The Power of Dreams.*

The Unknown Guest

Brian Inglis
With Ruth West and the Koestler Foundation

CORONET BOOKS
Hodder and Stoughton

British Library C.I.P.

Inglis, Brian, 1916–
   The unknown guest.
   1. Paranormal phenomena
   I. Title   III. West, Ruth, 1948–
   III. Koestler Foundation
   133

ISBN 0-340-49122-1

Printed and bound in Great Britain for Hodder and Stoughton Paperbacks, a division of Hodder and Stoughton Ltd., Mill Road, Dunton Green, Sevenoaks, Kent, TN13 2YA. (Editorial Office: 47 Bedford Square, London WC1B 3DP) by Richard Clay Ltd, Bungay, Suffolk

For Rosamond Lehmann

The Koestler Foundation, which will be receiving half the royalties from *The Unknown Guest*, was set up in Arthur Koestler's lifetime to promote interest and research in areas just outside conventional science's boundaries. He assumed that it would work in conjunction with the chair in parapsychology to which he left his estate. But the Foundation's role, he hoped, would be wider, including territory of the kind he had explored in *The Act of Creation*, *The Challenge of Chance*, and *Janus*. We are appealing for further evidence of experiences of the kind described in *The Unknown Guest*, with a view to encouraging research into the problems they raise. Contributions will be welcome from readers who have had such experiences, or come across fresh historical examples. They should be sent to

The Koestler Foundation
484 King's Road,
London SW10

RUTH WEST

Contents

Acknowledgments

In the spring of 1985, following up a suggestion made to us by Rosamond Lehmann, Ruth West, Director of the Koestler Foundation, and I began to collect case histories of episodes which – as we put it – 'to those who have known them, appear to transcend everyday realities'. We were not concerned with psychic phenomena as such, we explained, but with those 'which suggest design: as if some prompter in the wings is operating through our subconscious minds'.

I concentrated on accumulating the material from history, while Ruth dealt with cases which came in from all over the world to the Foundation; and we are grateful to all those who have contributed experiences, or have suggested where material can be found in biographies and other sources. Many more have reached us than could be used in *The Unknown Guest*; but, as we pointed out, the venture is 'no more than a pilot study, designed less to answer baffling questions than to show the need to ask them'. We hope to make use of the material collected, later; and in the meantime, we would like to thank all those who have sent in accounts of their experiences.

The author and publisher would like to thank the following for permission to quote copyright material from:
The Last Days of Socrates by Plato, translated with an introduction by Hugh Tredennick (Penguin Classics, 1954, 1959, 1969), copyright © Hugh Tredennick, 1954, 1959, 1969, p. 174: Penguin Books Ltd; *Siegfried's Journey* by Siegfried Sassoon: Faber and Faber Ltd; *Memories, Dreams and Reflections* by Jung: Collins Publishers Ltd; *Creative Imagination* by J. E. Downey: Routledge & Kegan Paul

Ltd; Maeterlinck (1914 edn): Methuen and Co.; *Life's A Circus*, the autobiography of Lady Eleanor Smith: Aitken and Stone Ltd and by Longman Green; *My Life* by Tito Gobbi with Ida Cook: Rupert Crew Ltd and Macdonald and James; *The Twins* by Oliver Sacks: John Farquharson Ltd and Duckworth and Co; *Jung and the Story of our Time* by Laurens van der Post: Chatto & Windus The Hogarth Press Ltd; *Yeats: The Man and the Mask* Macmillan Ltd.

The Open Question

In 1971 a young architect who was suffering from a nervous breakdown threw himself in front of a train entering a London underground station. The train pulled up just in time. Although he suffered severe injuries, he lived.

A strange twist to the story was related by a friend of the architect in a letter to Arthur Koestler:

Apparently Harold's life was saved not at all because the train driver saw him and applied the brakes in time. Quite independently, and with no knowledge of Harold or of what he intended to do, some passenger on the train had pulled down the 'Emergency' handle. And again independently of Harold's case, London Transport had interviewed this passenger with a view to prosecution on the ground that he had no reasonable cause for pulling the handle.

A friend of Koestler's, Tom Tickell, was working on the *Guardian* at the time, and offered to investigate. London Transport confirmed the story, but declined to divulge the name of the passenger, so that he could not be asked why he had acted as he did. Still, as Koestler's informant had noted, the facts were remarkable enough.

The passenger's pulling the handle must have saved Harold's life. They had to jack up the train to get him out, therefore he must have been well under it. On the other hand, a wheel cannot have passed over him, or he would have been killed. Pulling the 'Emergency' handle applies the brakes automatically. The difference between life and death must have been measured in nana seconds.

As there could have been no way, in a London underground train, in which the passenger could have *seen* what was about to happen, coincidence is the only possible explanation. Yet the odds against its having been a *chance* coincidence are formidable. Could it possibly have been a concatenation, the attempted suicide and the pulling of the handle being linked by some undiscovered causal process?

It is only within the last two centuries that the assumption has arisen that there is but *one* form of cause and effect, and periodically it has been disputed. Schopenhauer insisted that there were two, so that a single event, 'though a link in two totally different chains, nevertheless falls into place in both', owing to 'some most wonderfully pre-established harmony'. Recently the idea has surfaced again as the result of collaboration between Carl Jung and the quantum physicist Wolfgang Pauli. There are some coincidences which are connected so meaningfully, Jung argued, 'that their "chance" concurrence would represent a degree of improbability that would have to be expressed by an astronomical figure'. This suggested the existence of 'an interconnection or unity of causally unrelated events', a principle which he thought of as 'synchronicity'.

But there is more to it. Most people, at some time in their lives, have had the experience of what seems like a personal intervention, protecting them or prompting them. Belief in such intervention goes far back in history — further back, in fact, into legend. Sometimes it has been attributed to Fate, an inexorable force, controlling us in some predetermined way. But ordinarily it has been regarded as the work of 'beings': the good (and bad) fairies of folklore; the guardian angels (and resident demons) of Christianity.

Insofar as it implies predestination, Fate is understandably regarded with suspicion; and spirits of any kind are dismissed, except by believers, as a superstition. Yet the feeling that there is something, not yet accounted for and perhaps unaccountable in our present state of knowledge, which operates in the good-fairy or guardian-angel tradition is widespread, even if tentative. Is it perhaps possible to find some way of revising those beliefs, to bring them more into harmony with our present age?

Arthur Koestler embarked on this exploration in the 1950s, surveying what is known and what is surmised about a range of human faculties which lie just out of conventional science's territory. Some, like intuition and inspiration, are accepted and familiar, even if imperfectly understood. Others, such as divination – perception of things or events other than through the five senses – have remained unacceptable, at least in the academic world, but are widely believed in outside it. His findings can be read in his books, from *The Act of Creation*, published in 1964, to *Janus*, 1978. Disturbed by the reluctance of orthodox science even to investigate paranormal phenomena, he decided to insert a Trojan horse into one of its citadels, leaving his money to found the chair of parapsychology which has since been established in Edinburgh. The Foundation which now bears his name was set up in his lifetime with the wider aim of seeking to arouse interest in, and support for, research in those boundary areas which straddle orthodox and unorthodox territory; independently of, though in liaison with, the university chair.

One of the Foundation's projects has been the collection and analysis of evidence for the activities of the Unknown Guest – the Belgian Nobel laureate Maurice Maeterlinck's term, which I have adopted for convenience. At first informally, and later by a published appeal, we asked for accounts of experiences which had led people to wonder whether there may be another order of reality, occasionally overturning our established, day-to-day order. This was admittedly vague; the problem was to find any simple, clear-cut definition of what we were looking for. But there was no shortage of replies, from all over the world. Some, we realised, were more attuned to the parallel inquiry which had been initiated by the Alister Hardy Research Centres at Oxford and Princeton, into religious and transcendent experiences; there seemed little point in duplicating their valuable work. Others were accounts of psychical phenomena which, though often striking, did not suggest the kind of personal intervention which has become the theme of this book. But there have been plenty from which to select, along with the historical examples.

As this is a voyage of exploration, I have tried to avoid preconceptions; but it will be as well to explain the premise. A century ago the philosopher and psychologist Frederic Myers presented his hypothesis of the subliminal mind – the part of the mind lying below the threshold of consciousness. The idea of what is now accepted as the unconscious, or subconscious, mind had not then established itself, but it was attracting speculation. The model which was eventually to gain the public's attention was to be presented by Freud, who thought of the unconscious as a primordial reservoir of energy, completely unorganised, over which the ego has to do its best to exert control. Myers had a different idea. The subliminal, he claimed, was able to perform in many of the ways that the ego performed, so that it was permissible to speak of a subliminal *self* – part of the larger self, but capable of behaving as if it enjoyed independence.

Myers did not contend that his concept of the subliminal self could account for all the mysteries remaining. But it could help to clear up one mystery. The unconscious mind, breaking into consciousness uncontrolled, could produce the symptoms of neurosis, psychosis and hysteria. Under the control of the subliminal self, however, it could produce the symptoms of genius.

The subliminal mind, Myers believed, had access to information beyond the normal range of the senses, the most important being the communication of thought between people, to which he gave the name telepathy. He accepted, too, that there was good evidence for the action of mind on matter: telekinesis. The subliminal self has the ability to take this information, along with what we collect through the ordinary processes of learning, and fashion it for our benefit. We do not, after all, work out what we are going to say in ordinary conversation; something presents the words for us. If we are lucky, it may present wit, or wisdom.

Often, though, it has a struggle to get through to consciousness. It resorts to what we think of as intuition – 'the function that mediates perceptions in an unconscious way', as Jung was to define it. And it is this device that leaves the impression of a prompter, the Unknown Guest, at work in our lives.

It takes various forms. I have begun with the 'daemon' notion, as it has so distinguished a pedigree; the feeling that the prompter is a lifelong companion – though he may not be recognised as such until a succession of meaningful coincidences, premonitions, intuitions, inspirations (and sometimes setbacks) makes us feel that there is some form of guidance at work.

Next, I have considered what might be described as specialist categories of daemon: the muses, traditionally regarded as the sources of inspiration for writers, composers and artists; and the Eureka Effect, performing the same service for mathematicians and scientists.

For most of us, intimations of a daemonic influence reach us only occasionally and erratically. When they do, however, the impact can be such as to make us feel that we are the potential beneficiaries of a superconscious mind, capable of informing us not only through extra-sensory perception, but through the medium of vivid hallucinations of the senses – as if our subliminal selves, irritated at the difficulty of getting their messages across to us, have decided to dramatise some of them. This, incidentally, was one of Myers's most important, and most neglected, contributions to psychology: that seeing visions and 'hearing voices', though it can indicate mental disturbance, can also be the vehicle for inspiration.

Further possible indicators of the Unknown Guest's activities are certain manifestations of mind's powers over matter – easier to accept, now that the quantum physicists have, in effect, caused matter to dematerialise; the meaningful coincidences which support the case for synchronicity; and mystical experiences in the 'oceanic feeling' category. And, in conclusion, a brief survey of some of the ways which have been and are being experimented with to try to make better use of the superconscious mind's potential.

Daemon

SOCRATES

After his judges had found him guilty of corrupting the youth of Athens, Socrates explained why he did not intend to dispute their verdict:

In the past the prophetic voice to which I have become accustomed has always been my constant companion, opposing me even in quite trivial things if I was going to take the wrong course. Now something has happened to me, as you can see, which might be thought and is commonly considered to be a supreme calamity; yet neither when I left home this morning, nor when I was taking my place here in the court, nor at any point in any part of my speech did the divine sign oppose me. In other discussions it has often checked me in the middle of a sentence; but this time it has never opposed me in any part of this business in anything that I have said or done. What do I suppose to be the explanation? I will tell you. I suspect that this thing that has happened to me is a blessing, and we are quite mistaken in supposing death to be an evil. I have good grounds for thinking this, because my accustomed sign could not have failed to oppose me if what I was doing had not been sure to bring some good result.

From Xenophon as well as from Plato, the picture that emerges of Socrates' daemon is reasonably clear. He assumed that it was a minor deity, or a divine messenger, transmitting the gods' instructions to him through the medium of his inner ear by what is now known as clairaudience; he could listen to them in the same way as he could listen to conversation. And the instructions, he had found, had always been valuable.

The daemon had followed him since childhood, he told Theages; 'it always signifies to me the abandonment of what I am about to do;

it never incites me.' It also delivered warnings to him to transmit to his companions. When Timarchus had risen from a banquet, Socrates had not been aware that he was leaving to commit a murder; but he knew he must try to stop him.'

By no means, said I, rise up; for there has been to me the usual daemon signal. Upon this he stayed. And after a slight interval, he was again going away, and said – Socrates, I am going. And there was again the voice. Again, therefore, I compelled him to stay. The third time, wishing to escape me unnoticed, he rose up without saying anything to me, and escaped unnoticed, having watched me, while I had my attention otherwise engaged; and thus departing he perpetrated the acts, through which he went away about to die. Hence he told his brother, what I have now told you, that he was going to die, through his not believing in me.

Socrates was in no doubt, however, that other people had daemons which could provide them with inspiration. 'The authors of those great poems which we admire do not attain to excellence through the rules of any art,' he told Ion; 'they utter their beautiful melodies of verse in a state of inspiration, as it were possessed by a spirit not their own.' Only in this possessed state could they compose their poems, 'for whilst a man retains any portion of the thing called reason, he is utterly incompetent to produce poetry'; he must enter into a condition of 'divine insanity' to enable his muse to possess him. Although his daemon could interrupt his normal train of thought or conversation, Socrates himself used occasionally to enter a trance state in which he appeared to be unconscious of the outside world, rapt in contemplation.

Socrates' powers of divination – that is, of exploiting extra-sensory perception for the benefit of himself and others – were only slight, he told Phaedrus; but they were just sufficient for his own purposes, as they allowed him access to his daemon's instructions. And strongly though he disapproved of consulting auguries to obtain advice on everyday matters, such as choosing a driver, he told Xenophon that 'if any one desired to attain to what was beyond human wisdom, he advised him to study divination', because 'he who knew by what signs the gods give indications to men respecting human affairs, would never fail of obtaining counsel from the gods'.

ST GREGORY

Following their experience at Pentecost, when tongues of fire descended on them and they began to speak in languages they did not know, Jesus' disciples came to regard the Holy Spirit as their guide and protector; but the notion of a personal daemon filtered into Christianity from pagan sources, notably through Gregory 'the Thaumaturge', or wonder-worker, in the third century. In his *Panegyric* he described how he was the fortunate possessor of 'a certain divine companion, beneficent conductor, and guardian', who had been responsible for leading him to the theologian Origen – the crucial event of Gregory's youth, leading as it did to his conversion to Christianity. For this, he thanked 'that being who, by some momentous decision, had me allotted to him from boyhood to rule, and rear, and train – I mean that holy angel of God who led me from my youth', and who had continued to sustain him.

Being a part of the Judaic tradition out of which Christianity emerged, 'angel' was preferred to the pagan 'daemon', which was eventually to take on its wholly sinister connotation: an agent of the devil. But even angels, after a time, became suspect. They were acceptable when they appeared to holy and manifestly orthodox men and women in the privacy of their cells, and were not made the subject of boasts. But if their instructions conflicted with those of the church, or the authorities acting in the church's name, they could be condemned as indications of heresy. If the devil could cite scripture for his purpose, his demons could surely simulate angels, to delude the unwary – as, her accusers maintained, they did in the case of Joan of Arc.

JOAN OF ARC

Of all the men and women who have claimed spirit guidance, Joan of Arc presents the hardest case to explain away in rationalist terms. This has not been for want of trying; from Voltaire, with his 'poor idiot', to Anatole France, arguing that she was a simple, ignorant peasant girl, a pawn in the game played by unscrupulous courtiers and crafty clerics.

Initially in an article, later in *The Maid of France*, the shrewd historian, anthropologist and folklorist Andrew Lang showed that this version of Joan simply does not fit the known facts of her career. Simple she was, in many respects; but her defence of her actions at her trial displayed an enviable intelligence and resourcefulness, extraordinary for anybody of her age. By all her contemporaries' accounts, so was her grasp of military strategy and tactics. 'Come to the Salpêtrière hospital,' a sceptic told an abbé, according to Lang, after the war of 1870. 'And I will show you twenty Jeannes d'Arc.' 'Has any one of them,' the abbé mildly replied, 'given us back Alsace and Lorraine?'

Joan believed she had been selected by God as the instrument through which France would be freed from English domination. His instructions were transmitted by angels – St Catherine, St Margaret, St Michael – who were so real to her that at times she could actually see and touch them, though ordinarily they communicated to her through voices. How real they were to her was clearly demonstrated at her trial because her insistence upon their reality, as she well knew, could only ensure her condemnation as a heretic.

Although Joan had no way of proving that her information came from angels, she could show that it was sometimes of a kind which she would not have acquired except through extra-sensory perception. Again and again she demonstrated telepathy – she repeated the words of a prayer which the king had composed mentally; clairvoyance – she 'saw' where a sword lay hidden behind the altar at a Fierbois church; and precognition – she showed the place on her body where, she knew, she would be wounded by an arrow in the impending battle for Orleans; a correct prediction which was actually recorded before the event by a Flemish diplomat. A copy of his letter, Lang pointed out, has survived, lending confirmation.

In view of Joan's fate, Christians who had similar experiences were not likely to boast about them, and it became all the more necessary to keep silent about them after the publication in 1484 of *Malleus Maleficarum*, the witch-hunter's manual which was to lead to the persecution of those who heard voices or saw visions as the victims, or the exploiters, of diabolic possession. And although the rising tide of rationalism was eventually to spare them from being burned at the stake, it was only to put them at risk of the more protracted torment of incarceration, often for life, in a lunatic asylum; the voices and visions came to be diagnosed as symptoms of insanity. The concept of daemon would surface from time to time, as it did in *Antony and Cleopatra*, where the Soothsayer tells Antony

> Thy demon, that's the spirit that keeps thee, is
> Noble, courageous, high, unmatchable.

But gradually it faded away.

By the nineteenth century educated people in general were beginning to feel that they ought to dismiss the entire range of spirits as a superstition. Ghosts, fairies and the rest of the denizens of folklore inevitably had to go, too. The belief in 'powers that be' lingered; many a sceptic who professed to disbelieve in ghosts would not have cared to accept an invitation to sleep in a supposedly haunted room – just as many people who would have denied that they were superstitious continued to touch wood after a boast (and were uneasy if they could find no wood to hand for the purpose). But angels were relegated to heaven, there to play harps and sing hymns; demons to hell, to prod the damned with pitchforks. Although 'guardian angel' lingered on, it was most commonly used much as 'Thank the Lord' is used, without any religious connotation. The concept of daemon, in its Socratic usage, faded out: Goethe accepted it, in his rearguard action against advancing materialism, but by his time it was beginning to qualify for 'Obs.' in dictionaries. In our century some dictionaries had 'Daemon, *see* Demon'; others left it out. Few people, except those whose classical education had taken them up to the point of construing Plato, would have come across it.

The underlying concept of a guiding and protecting force, however, did not entirely disappear. Usually it has been attributed to divine intervention; but a few agnostics have preferred to leave the issue of its source open, contenting themselves with expressing the belief that such a force has played a positive part in their lives.

WINSTON CHURCHILL

The description of somebody as 'bearing a charmed life' has long

lost its impact, but it certainly applied to Churchill. He knew it, and
he attributed it to a protector. 'I sometimes have a feeling – in fact I
have it very strongly – a feeling of interference,' he told a gathering
of miners in 1943. 'I want to stress it. I have a feeling that some
guiding hand has interfered.'

In his youth he attributed the interventions to 'that Higher Power
which interferes in the sequence of causes and effects more often
than we are always prone to admit'; and in *My Early Life* he cited as
an example the way in which he managed to escape from captivity
during the Boer War. Foiled in his intention of clambering onto a
goods train going in the direction of Mozambique, he wondered
whether it would be safe to go to a place where he saw fires burning
at a distance, which he took to be a Kaffir kraal. The Kaffirs, he had
heard, loathed the Boers and might be friendly. But what if they
were hostile? He sat down, baffled.

Suddenly without the slightest reason all my doubts disappeared. It was
certainly by no process of logic that they were dispelled. It just felt quite
clear that I would go to the Kaffir kraal. I had sometimes in former years
held a 'Planchette' pencil and written while others had touched my wrist
or hand. I acted in exactly the same unconscious or subconscious manner
now.

When he reached the fires he found that they were from the
furnaces around a coal mine. There was nothing for it but to take a
chance. Some British subjects, he had heard, had been allowed to
stay to keep the mines working. He knocked at the door of a house,
explaining his dishevelled appearance by saying he had had an
accident, and he was let in. His host, who held a revolver, listened
sceptically to his tale, so obviously unimpressed that Churchill felt
compelled to reveal the truth.

My companion rose from the table slowly and locked the door. After this
act, which struck me as unpromising, and was certainly ambiguous, he
advanced upon me and suddenly held out his hand.
'Thank God you have come here! It is the only house for twenty miles
where you would not have been handed over. But we are all British here,
and we will see you through.'

His host hid Churchill down the mine until he could be concealed in a railway wagon destined for Lourenço Marques, where he regained his freedom.

In *My Darling Clementine*, the biography of Lady Churchill published in 1963, the story is related of an occasion during the Blitz when Churchill refused to go in the armoured car provided for him, because it was so uncomfortable, and instead commandeered a staff car. As he was about to get in,

a strange thing occurred. The nearside door of the car was opened for him – he always sat on the nearside. For no apparent reason, he stopped, turned, opened the door on the other side of the car himself, got in, and sat there instead.

This was something he had never done before. On his way home, a bomb fell near the car, lifting it up on two wheels.

If he had been sitting on the nearside, the car would have unquestionably turned over as the full force of the explosion lifted up the offside. Only Winston's extra weight had prevented disaster.

Although he didn't mention this escape to Clementine, she heard about it and asked, Why did you get in on that side?

'I don't know, I don't know,' Winston answered at first. Then he said: 'Of course I know. Something said to me "Stop!" before I reached the car door held open for me. It then appeared to me that I was told I was meant to open the door on the other side and get in and sit there.'

ARTHUR KOESTLER

Churchill recognised what he felt was a guiding hand; Arthur Koestler had several similar experiences, but did not accept a daemonic interpretation of them – or perhaps it would be closer to the truth to say that he would have been embarrassed to admit, even to himself, that such an interpretation could be put on them.

As a boy, Koestler was fascinated by mathematics and science. While still in his twenties, he was appointed science correspondent to the prestigious Ullstein chain of newspapers in Germany; and his delight in scientific rigour was reinforced by the philosophy of dialectical materialism which he embraced on joining the Communist Party. Yet at the same time, he had experiences which made it impossible for him to dismiss psychic phenomena out of hand. In his childhood he was regarded as being 'endowed with somewhat awe-inspiring potentialities' which meant he was 'much sought-after for table-lifting séances' – still, in the early 1900s, a popular pastime. The split between his intellectual beliefs and his occult encounters continued to trouble him almost to the end of his life. 'I know that these phenomena do exist,' he said in a television interview in 1966. 'At the same time my rational mind – my scientific mind, if you want – rejects them.'

In the two-volume autobiography, *Arrow in the Blue* and *The Invisible Writing*, Koestler managed to overcome his reluctance to discuss his personal experiences of what could be regarded as psychic or daemonic interventions, by relating some of them, and leaving it to the reader to decide what to make of them. One such episode occurred in 1934, when his failure as a writer, and the onset of disillusionment with Communism, decided him to end his life.

I stuck Scotch tape on the draughty slits of the door and window, and opened the gas tap. I had placed my bug-stained mattress next to it on the floor, but as I was settling down on it, a book crashed on my head from the wobbly shelf. It nearly broke my nose, so I got up, turned off the gas and tore off the tape. Of all one's failures, a failure in suicide is the most embarrassing to report. The book that fell on my head was the second Brown Book, *Dimitrov contra Goering*, with the story of the Reichstag Trial. A more drastic pointer to the despicableness of my antics could hardly be imagined.

In *The Invisible Writing* Koestler eased himself out of having to commit himself to an explanation with a quip: 'I must either have kicked the shelf, or it was a case of the dialectic producing a miracle.' Later, his research for *The Midwife Toad* was to provide another let-out. Paul Kammerer, whose tests with midwife toads threatened to restore credibility to the Lamarckian theory of evolution, had been fascinated by coincidences, which he meticulously recorded; many of them trivial, but some striking. In the course of his research, Koestler recalled in *The Challenge of Chance*, 'a whole series of coincidences seemed to descend on me – like a meteor shower on a summer's night. It was as if Kammerer's ghost were beckoning with a malicious grin: "I told you so." ' And some of the coincidences were daemonic, in the sense that they came to Koestler's help, providing him with information he needed.

Coincidences provided Koestler with a way to avoid the embarrassment of committing himself on the subject of some psychic phenomena. Whereas many scientists, including some he admired, rejected them out of hand, nobody could claim that coincidences do not occur. They are also clearly fascinating to people who experience them, as he found when hundreds of accounts poured in to him, following an appeal for them in the *New Scientist*. Some of them fell into the 'meaningful' category, as he showed in *The Challenge of Chance*, including one of his own. In 1972 the *Sunday Times* had invited him to report on the world chess championship which was being held at Reykjavik, and he went to the London Library to do some preliminary research.

I hesitated for a moment whether to go to the 'C' for chess section first, or to the 'I' for Iceland section, but chose the former, because it was nearer. There were about 20–30 books on chess on the shelves, and the first that caught my eye was a bulky volume with the title:

Chess in Iceland and in Icelandic Literature
by Williard Fiske

It was published in 1905, by – of all things – 'The Florentine Typographical Society, Florence, Italy.

The most remarkable case of a meaningful coincidence which Koestler personally encountered occurred after his release from the Seville gaol, during the Spanish civil war, where he had been under sentence of death. Following his experience there of the oceanic feeling, which relieved him of his fear of execution, he had recalled the episode in *Buddenbrooks*, in which Consul Thomas Buddenbrooks, with death approaching, found consolation in a book which had lain for years unread in his library, in which there was a passage explaining that death is not the end, only a transition. When he was freed, Koestler wrote to Thomas Mann to thank him for the comfort this recollection had provided. Mann replied, describing what had happened when the letter arrived, as he had recorded it in his diary. The entry ran:

Stirring letter from the journalist Koestler, writing from Gibraltar.

Sentenced to death and only saved at the last moment, he claims he was able to endure the ordeal with the help of my writings, specifically the Schopenhauer chapter in *Buddenbrooks*. When his letter arrived I was reading that very chapter in Schopenhauer, 'Concerning Death', which I had not looked at for thirty-five years.

For Koestler, the decisive episode in his career was the experience of the oceanic sense. Whiling away his time in solitary confinement, he took to scratching mathematical formulae on the wall of his cell; and one of them was Euclid's proof that the number of primes is infinite. He had always thought of it as aesthetically as well as intellectually satisfying, but on this occasion it overwhelmed him. It was as if, for him, 'I' had ceased to exist, in 'the draining of all tension, the absolute catharsis, the peace that passeth all understanding'.

When, three years later, *Darkness at Noon* was published, it was regarded as a political tract, with its devastating exposure of the methods used to extort the confessions of the old Bolsheviks in the Russian treason trials of the 1930s. Political tract it certainly was, one of the most immediately influential ever written. Yet this was not quite what Koestler had in mind when he was writing it. At the end of the book Rubashov, awaiting execution, recalls the 'queer sense of exaltation' he had felt after a prolonged bout of torture. But the oceanic sense, he knew, had been condemned by the Party as petty-bourgeois mysticism; and he had toed the Party line. So, for a few years, had Koestler. In *Darkness at Noon* he was, in a sense, explaining why, and at the same time trying to come to terms with the oceanic sense, which had finally banished his dialectical materialism, filling him with a certainty that a higher order of reality existed.

There were three orders of reality, he decided. The first was 'the narrow world of sensory perception'; the second, some related phenomena that the senses could not perceive, such as magnetic fields, which filled in the gaps 'and gave meaning to the absurd patchiness of the sensory world'. But it was the third order that was to him all-important. It not merely 'enveloped, interpenetrated and gave meaning to the second'; it also contained 'occult' phenomena which could not be explained either on the sensory or on the conceptual level, and yet occasionally invaded them, 'like spiritual meteors piercing the primitive's vaulted sky.'

This testament to the effect of his oceanic experience was written when he was still in his forties. His belief in the importance of occult phenomena, and the need to understand them better, was certainly not the aberration of a man in his dotage; and his decision to leave his capital to set up a chair of parapsychology had been taken long before his death. His reluctance to cite personal experiences as evidence – other than coincidences – would have made him wary of being classified as an example of a daemonic man; but those who knew him would agree that he would have been diffidently intrigued with the notion.

ROSALIND HEYWOOD

Of all the people whom Arthur Koestler met when he joined the Society for Psychical Research in 1956, Mrs Heywood was the one he most admired and trusted. He was to dedicate *The Roots of Coincidence* to her, as 'catalyst in chief'. She had smoothed his path in the Society – no easy task, as he found some of the council members irritating; and she was also, for him, a model of the way in which psychic faculties, for those who happen to possess them, should be employed.

Mrs Heywood's *The Sixth Sense*, published in 1959, was the first book for many years to provide a readable survey of the progress of psychical research since the Society had been formed in 1882. It attracted respectful, even enthusiastic, reviews from critics of the calibre of Sir Julian Huxley, Arnold Toynbee and Raymond Mortimer. It even won praise in the *New Scientist*. Emboldened by the reaction – or, more probably, as she was modest, pushed by her publishers and friends – she went on to write *The Infinite Hive*, about her personal experiences.

They were of two main kinds. One was the occasional telepathic or clairvoyant episode of the type that might happen to anyone. The other was frequent, and unusual: 'an inner prompting to action or comment on behalf of other people, which seems beyond my normal capacity, or absurd in the light of facts known to me at the time, but turns out to be relevant in the light of other facts learned later on'. She did not know how these 'Orders' – as she came to think of them, because they seemed more definite, more urgent, than simple promptings – came to her; but she was sure they did not come from her conscious self.

Although she called them 'Orders', she might have attributed them to her daemon, as they played so large a part in her life. In one respect, however, hers was different from others: it did not look after her, so much as look after her husband, family, friends and acquaintances, by compelling her to take some course of action which would help them, though at the time she might have no notion how, or why.

While she was with her husband in Washington, where he was working for the British embassy, they came to know and like 'Julia', whom they would occasionally meet at parties; and when Julia was killed in an air crash, Mrs Heywood felt she ought to write a letter of condolence to her mother. Before she could despatch it 'Orders' came, in the form of what seemed to be instructions from Julia. She was not to post it; instead, she was to go to Julia's mother, 'straight away, and tell her to stop all that ridiculous mourning at once'.

Mrs Heywood hardly knew the mother, and was understandably worried that if she were rebuffed, it could create a minor scandal, which might be embarrassing for her husband. Confident that his wife's 'Orders' were to be trusted, he told her to go ahead. She found the house, with all the blinds down, and was told that Julia's mother was conducting her mourning in bed.

That settled it. 'I must see her,' I insisted, and after much protest they let me up to her room. There, indeed, was the poor woman, alone, in the dark, in bed. Intensely embarrassed, for I supposed this was by her own choice, I got out my message, expecting to be thrown out at once as mad or impertinent. But her face lit up. 'I knew it,' she cried. 'I knew she'd hate it, and I didn't want it. I shall get up and stop it at once.'

For the most part, though, the 'Orders' related to mundane matters, prompting Mrs Heywood to ring friends without knowing why, only to find that they had need of her, often for some quite trivial reason, such as having forgotten a name which she was able to provide for them. This extra-sensory link was strongest with her husband. Out of numerous examples, a typical one related in *The Infinite Hive* was vouched for by friends who were staying with her at the time, towards the end of the Second World War.

Colonel Heywood, who was on the Allied staff at their Brussels General Headquarters, had written to say he was arriving at Victoria the following Wednesday at eight in the evening. A little more than an hour before the train was due, 'Orders' compelled her to check the arrival time of the train. It turned out to be 7 p.m. In her anxiety not to miss him, she told her friends what had happened, dashed out into the street, and begged a total stranger to drive her to Victoria – which, when he heard the reason, he did. As 'Orders' had told her, she engaged a porter. When her husband arrived, he told her that he had forgotten to allow for the hour's difference between Continental and British time; and as he was laden down with packages which had descended on him at GHQ, too many to carry, 'all I could do was to send you a mental message while I was coming up in the train.'

Although occasional telepathic contact between close friends or siblings is often reported, the ability to exploit it, as Colonel Heywood learned to do, must be very rare. He could even use it to the point of dispensing with the telephone if, for some reason, making a telephone call would be inconvenient. On occasion he picked up distress calls from her. She could not, however, tap *his* thoughts.

To outward appearances, the Heywoods were a conventional couple. His career took him through the army, the diplomatic service and eventually into business. She brought up their children, ran the local Women's Voluntary Service during the Second World War, and was a governor of the English-Speaking Union. She did not boast about her 'Orders'; she did not need to, as those who knew her soon came to think of them as natural, even mundane. That two such engagingly sensible, down-to-earth people should have enjoyed such a sensible, down-to-earth, extra-sensory communication, thanks chiefly to her ability to sense his needs, is yet another indication of the variety of ways in which the daemon's instructions get through – if not repressed (as she felt hers might easily have been, had not service as a nurse in the First World War liberated her from a stifling family background).

In the introduction to his *Blessings in Disguise*, Sir Alec Guinness recalls that when Hamish Hamilton suggested he should attempt to write an autobiography, 'Ego was immensely flattered and *I* was appalled.' The writing necessitated a compromise between him and his actor doppelgänger. Each contributed, from the time when Ego, 'now heavily disguised as a small, reddish-haired and very freckled child, makes his fearful entrance, upstage-centre; pursued by his infantile demons but greatly comforted by his good angels'.

The 'demons' and 'angels' turn out to be rather more than figures of speech. His earliest memories are of the house in St John's Wood where his mother had the top flat – 'the whole place was chilly and spooky, and to pass the empty flats, with their locked doors of peeling black paint, I found terrifying even if my hand was held' – and in New York during the war, when he had a brief respite from his naval duties to play in Terence Rattigan's *Flare Path*, he went almost nightly to fortune tellers. Only one of them, however, impressed him, using Tarot cards. Guinness had not seen them before; they made a disturbing impression on him, which was to revive after the war. 'If I hadn't had the good impulse, in about 1950, to chuck cards, books and all to do with the Tarot, into the fire, I might well be under their baleful influence today.'

Although obviously disinclined to make much of his psychic experiences, he relates a couple of examples of protective precognition. In 1943, when he was in charge of a landing craft, he received orders to proceed to a Yugoslav island. Knowing that he would be up all night, he took time off for a nap in the afternoon.

It was a heavy dreamless sleep I fell into until just before 1800 hours, when I woke with a start, the sweat pouring off me, and frightened as I had never been since childhood. I was wide awake when, as it seemed to me, a very unpleasant voice spoke close to my ear; just one word – 'Tomorrow'. It was penetrating, gloating, and undoubtedly evil. It implied that by the same time tomorrow I would be dead.

Turning it over in his mind since, Guinness feels that he cannot dismiss it as something purely subjective. 'There was a clarity and intention which I couldn't mistake; and whatever may have troubled me in my sleep, I know I was fully conscious when I had the experience.' That night a storm blew up, with winds estimated at up to 120 miles an hour. He and his crew were fortunate to survive it; they had to make a forced landing on the rocks at Termoli, leaving the landing craft a wreck.

In 1955 Guinness went to Hollywood to make his first film there. He was met by Thelma Moss, who had written the film script of *Father Brown*, and who invited him out to dinner. Three restaurants turned them away because she was wearing slacks; a fourth, which would have accepted them, was full. As they were leaving, 'I became aware of running, sneakered feet behind us, and turned to face a fair young man in sweat-shirt and blue-jeans. "You want a table?" he asked. "Join me. My name is James Dean."'

They followed him gratefully, but before entering the restaurant Dean wanted to show them his new sports car, which he had not even driven.

Exhausted, hungry, feeling a little ill-tempered in spite of Dean's kindness, I heard myself saying in a voice I could hardly recognise as my own, 'Please, never get in it.' I looked at my watch. 'It is now ten o'clock, Friday the 23rd of September 1955. If you get into that car you will be found dead in it by this time next week.' He laughed. 'Oh, shucks! Don't be so mean.'

Guinness apologised, explaining that it was from lack of sleep and food, and they enjoyed their meal together. But he continued to feel uneasy. 'At four o'clock in the afternoon of the following Friday James Dean was dead, killed while driving the car.'

Once, at least, Guinness's own good angel turned in a remarkable performance on his own behalf – though curiously, he does not relate it in *Blessings in Disguise*. Arthur Koestler happened to be present at lunch with him, on an occasion when he told the story; and Guinness wrote it out in full for inclusion in *The Challenge of Chance*.

When working in London, he used to get up at 07.20 on Sunday mornings to attend mass in Westminster Cathedral, before catching the 09.50 from Waterloo to his home in the country. His habit was to set *two* alarm clocks, to be on the safe side; but usually he woke up shortly before they rang.

On this particular morning I woke, glanced in the half light at the clock and thought 'My God, I've overslept!' It appeared to me the clock said 07.40 (I didn't refer to the second clock). I rushed through washing and so on, and hurried to the Cathedral. Very unexpectedly – in fact it had never happened before – I found a taxi at that early hour, so I thought I was at the Cathedral at 07.55. With time to spare I went to confession.

Although the attendance was considerably larger than usual, which surprised him, it was not until the sermon that he glanced at his watch, to find that he was at the 09.00, not the 08.00 mass; he would have to catch the 10.50.

When I arrived at Waterloo at 10.30 there was an announcement that all trains on the Portsmouth line were delayed for an unspecified amount of time. An inquiry gave me the information that the 09.50 train had been derailed a few miles outside London. Subsequently I found that it was the front coach of the train that had toppled on its side and that, although no one was killed, or even grievously injured, the occupants of the coach had been badly bruised and taken to hospital. My habit, when catching the 09.50 on Sunday morning, had been to sit in the front compartment of the front coach because, when in Waterloo station, the coach was in the open air, away from the roofing of Waterloo and consequently with more light for reading and less likelihood of being crowded . . .

As Koestler pointed out, not only had Guinness overslept, but he had also misread the time by an hour. Had he not done so, he might have decided to skip mass and catch the 09.50. 'If one opts for the ESP hypothesis – unconscious precognition – one must also assume that the unconscious cunningly persuaded the conscious self to misread the clock.' Or could Guinness's daemon have been the hidden persuader?

CARL JUNG

Of all the people in recent times who have acknowledged a daemonic component in their lives, the man who was most clearly aware of it, and who devoted most of his life to exploring its modes of communication and action and its significance, was Jung. From childhood, his daimon (the spelling he used) instructed him through dreams; but it also adopted an unusual method of prompting. It played paranormal tricks in his vicinity, as if determined to wean him from the materialist assumptions which had been instilled into him during his schooldays and his training as a medical student.

In 1898, realising that he did not have the financial means to fulfil his ambition to become a surgeon, he was thinking of settling for a post as a general physician in a local Zurich hospital when something occurred that was to have a profound effect upon him. He was sitting reading a textbook in a room adjoining the family dining room in which there was a walnut table.

Suddenly there sounded a report like a pistol shot. I jumped up and rushed into the room from which the noise of the explosion had come. My mother was sitting flabbergasted in her armchair, the knitting fallen from her hands. She stammered out, 'W-w-what's happened? It was right beside me!' and stared at the table. Following her eyes, I saw what had happened. The table top had split from the rim to beyond the centre, and not along any joint; the split ran right through the solid wood. I was thunderstruck. How could such a thing happen? A table of solid walnut that had dried out for seventy years – how could it split on a summer day in the relatively high degree of humidity characteristic of our climate?

'That means something,' his mother said; and Jung was disturbed, because he could think of no natural explanation.

Some two weeks later I came home at six o'clock in the evening and found the household – my mother, my fourteen-year-old sister, and the maid – in a great state of agitation. About an hour earlier there had been another deafening report. This time it was not the already damaged table; the noise had come from the direction of the sideboard, a heavy piece of furniture dating from the early nineteenth century. They had already looked all over it, but had found no trace of a split. I immediately began examining the sideboard and the entire surrounding area, but just as fruitlessly. Then I began on the interior of the sideboard. In the cupboard containing the bread basket I found a loaf of bread, and beside it, the bread knife. The greater part of the blade had snapped off in several pieces. The handle lay in one corner of the rectangular basket, and in each of the other corners lay a piece of the blade. The knife had been used shortly before, at four o'clock tea, and afterwards put away. Since then no one had gone to the sideboard.

There was nothing wrong with the steel, a master cutler told Jung after examining it. It could only have been broken, he thought, piece by piece, by sticking the blade into a crack and snapping off bits, a piece at a time; or it might have been dropped on a stone from a great height.

Jung was still not convinced that forces were at work which conventional science could not account for. But a few weeks later he had the opportunity to investigate a medium, and although occasionally she resorted to trickery, he was sufficiently impressed by some of the phenomena she produced to make his investigation the subject of his doctoral thesis. And although he did not immediately decide to become a psychiatrist, his anxiety to fuse such experiences with conventional science soon convinced him that this was to be his career.

It led him, a few years later, to become a disciple of Freud — Freud's chosen successor, in fact. But again, occult forces intervened. Freud warned him against taking psychical research seriously, 'in terms of so shallow a positivism that I had difficulty in checking the sharp report that was on the tip of my tongue'. Then,

I had a curious sensation. It was as if my diaphragm were made of iron and were becoming red-hot — a glowing vault. And at that moment there was such a loud report in the bookcase, which stood right next to us, that we both started up in alarm, fearing the thing was going to topple over on us. I said to Freud: 'There, that is an example of a so-called catalytic exteriorisation phenomenon.'

'Oh, come,' he exclaimed. 'That is sheer bosh.'

'It is not,' I replied. 'You are mistaken, Herr Professor. And to prove my point I now predict that in a moment there will be another loud report!' Sure enough, no sooner had I said the words than the same detonation went off in the bookcase.

To this day I do not know what gave me this certainty. But I knew beyond all doubt that the report would come again. Freud only stared aghast at me. I do not know what was in his mind, or what his look meant. In any case, this incident aroused his mistrust of me, and I had the feeling that I had done something against him.

Jung claimed that he never afterwards discussed the incident with Freud; but that it stuck in Freud's mind seems clear from the conversation they had the following year when Jung visited him in Vienna. Freud begged him never to abandon the sexual theory — 'the most essential thing of all' — which to Jung was bad enough.

But Freud went on to say, 'We must make a dogma of it, an unshakeable bulwark.' Against what? Jung wondered. 'To which he replied, "Against the black tide of mud" – and here he hesitated for a moment, then added "– of occultism."' It was this that finally destroyed their friendship. To Jung, 'what Freud seemed to mean by "occultism" was virtually everything that philosophy and religion, including the contemporary science of parapsychology, had learned about the psyche.'

Impressed by J. B. Rhine's research at Duke University in the 1930s, Jung adopted the findings for his own purposes. Telepathy, clairvoyance and precognition had previously been 'purely descriptive concepts'. The characteristic feature, he asserted, 'of all these phenomena, including Rhine's psychokinetic effect and other synchronistic occurrences, is *meaningful coincidence*, and as such I have defined the synchronistic principle'. ESP and PK, in other words, were two of the channels through which synchronicity operated. And he did not doubt that a daimonic element was involved. 'We know that something unknown, alien, does come our way,' he noted:

just as we know that we do not ourselves *make* a dream or an inspiration, but that it somehow arises of its own accord. What does happen to us in this manner can be said to emanate from mana, from a daimon, a god or the unconscious. The first three terms have the great merit of including and invoking the emotional quality of numinosity, whereas the latter – the unconscious – is banal and therefore closer to reality.

Jung preferred to stick to 'unconscious' for that reason, even to the point of asserting that 'daimon' was no more than a synonym for the unconscious – 'that is to say, we know just as much or just as little about them as about the latter.' But he conceded that 'daimon' had one great advantage; as a personification it had an emotional quality. And he had no hesitation about using it in connection with his own career.

There was a daimon in me, and in the end its presence proved decisive. It overpowered me, and if I was at times ruthless it was because I was in the grip of the daimon. I could not stop at anything once attained. I had to hasten on, to catch up with my vision.

For this reason, he admitted, he had made many enemies.

Reiterating, 'A creative person has little power over his own life. He is not free. He is captive and driven by his daimon', he went on to quote Hölderlin:

Shamefully
A power wrests away the heart from us
For the Heavenly Ones each demand sacrifice:
But if it should be withheld
Never has that led to good.

ADOLF HITLER

Where the daemonic power has not been withheld, can it be claimed that it has always led to good? Clearly, no. Some of the men who are remembered for their military conquests were clearly in the grip of daemonic forces. It is as if the forces themselves are neutral, capable of being put either to noble or to base uses.

If ever anybody had the devil's own luck, it was Adolf Hitler; and it helped to convert him from the preposterous figure he cut in the abortive coup of 1923 to the menacing Führer of the Second World War. The process apparently began during the first, when he was in the trenches: a nightmare warning of impending death woke him from sleep, and hardly had he scrambled out of the dugout when it was demolished by a direct hit from a shell.

From that time on, Hitler relied for guidance on intuitions, which he took to come from a divine source. In an article, 'Hitler: "psychic", shaman or paranoiac?', the psychiatrist Jan Ehrenwald cites a German industrialist as saying that the Führer had 'an antenna to tune him in directly to the Almighty', and his immediate circle came to regard him, as coup after coup came off successfully, as the 'supreme magician'.

Hitler's luck, or intuition, saved him again and again. Shortly after the outbreak of the Second World War, he went to deliver a speech to the Old Guard at their Munich beer-cellar meeting place. Ehrenwald happened to be listening to the speech on the radio; in retrospect he finds it intriguing that it was 'heavily laden with premonitions of impending death for some of those present. "None of us knows whether it is going to hit him next," was one of his concluding remarks.' Hitler had planned to stay on, talking with old colleagues, as he usually did. But a warning came that fog was expected, and rather than risk being held up, he decided to take a train back to Berlin, and consequently left early. A few minutes later a bomb exploded, killing eight of the old comrades and injuring scores of others who were in the cellar.

In March 1943 a more carefully designed plot was hatched by a group within the military which had ranged themselves against Hitler's dictatorship. Major General Henning von Tresckow, a Chief of Staff on the Eastern Front, and a junior staff officer, Fabian von Schlabrendorff, smuggled a delayed-action bomb onto Hitler's aircraft when he was about to fly back from the front, disguised as a present of brandy for an officer at Hitler's HQ. The detonator failed, and the aircraft landed safely; Schlabrendorff had to risk his life calling up to ask that the package should not be delivered, and flying over the same route to collect it. A few days later another member of the group, Colonel von Gersdorf, offered to undertake a suicide mission by accompanying Hitler round an exhibition with a time bomb in his pocket, to be exploded whenever a suitable opportunity occurred. Once again, the plot was foiled because Hitler decided to leave the exhibition early.

In the summer of 1944 Hitler was provided with even more striking proof, had he needed it, of destiny's protection. The culmination of the conspiracy to kill him was the placing of a briefcase carrying a bomb in the conference room where Hitler and his generals were meeting. Count Stauffenberg left the briefcase beside a table-support, next to which Hitler would be standing, and slipped out of the room. When he heard the explosion he assumed Hitler must have been killed, and left to alert the conspirators to take over. One of the generals, however, had moved the briefcase so that the table-support – a heavy wooden plinth – was between Hitler and the bomb. The bomb demolished the table, brought down the roof of the conference room and killed four of those who had been present, injuring many others; but General Fellgiebel, another of the conspirators whose task it was to telephone the news of Hitler's death to Berlin, to his dismay saw Hitler emerge. As Roger Manvell and Heinrich Fraenkel described the scene in *The July Plot*:

His hair was on fire, his right arm partially paralysed, his right leg burned, his ear-drums damaged, his uniform torn by blast and falling debris, and his buttocks so bruised that, as he described it himself, he had a 'backside like a baboon'

— but he was alive.

A few months later Hitler was to foil yet another assassination project. His armaments minister Albert Speer, one of his favourites, discovered that Hitler had settled for a scorched earth policy in the last winter of the war, and was giving orders that the retreating Wehrmacht should destroy cities, dams, bridges and factories to provide a Wagnerian conclusion if the tide of the war could not be turned. Speer decided that the Führer and his ministers ought to be wiped out, a feat which he thought could be accomplished with surprisingly little difficulty, as they met in Hitler's underground bunker which was ventilated through a funnel in the Chancellery grounds. Poison gas, Speer worked out, could quite easily be introduced into the air-conditioning system, leaving nobody in the bunker alive. When everything had been prepared, Speer found that Hitler had just decided to protect the funnel – perhaps against the risk of bomb damage – in a way which rendered the assassination project impracticable. It was as if destiny had determined not to be robbed of the final Götterdämmerung curtain.

In the course of his life, Goethe recalled in his *Poetry and Truth*, he had come across several people in whom the daemonic element was the distinguishing characteristic.

Such persons are not always the most eminent men, either morally or intellectually, and it is seldom that they recommend themselves to our affections by goodness of heart; a tremendous energy seems to be seated in them, and they exercise a wonderful power over all creatures, and even over the elements; and indeed, who shall say how much farther such influence may extend? All the moral powers combined are of no avail against them; in vain does the more enlightened portion of mankind attempt to throw suspicion upon them as deceived if not deceivers – the mass is still drawn on by them.

A century later, Hitler was to fulfil the specification with uncanny precision.

THE UNKNOWN GUEST

Scores of people, a few eminent, many obscure, have testified to their conviction that a mysterious power of some kind has watched over them, acting as guide, goad or prompter. Many of them have attributed their protection to an all-seeing and all-caring God. Some have come to the conclusion that it is the work of a spirit entity specifically charged with looking after them, as Socrates did. Some, Churchill among them, have accepted the existence of a higher power without committing themselves to assumptions about its source. Some have speculated about the existence of doppelgängers, as Goethe did: psychic doubles, having a partially independent existence. And some have regarded daemonic activity as, in effect, an evolutionary device, a kind of psychic concomitant to the genetic development of man. Maeterlinck presented his version – the Unknown Guest.

There is another, a more secret and much more active existence which we have scarcely begun to study and which is, if we descend to the bed-rock of truth, our only real existence. From the darkest corners of our ego it directs our veritable life, the one that is not to die, and pays no heed to our thought or to anything emanating from our reason, which believes that it guides our steps. It alone knows the long past that preceded our birth and the endless future that will follow our departure from this earth. It is itself that future and that past, all those from whom we have sprung and all those who will spring from us. It represents in the individual not only the species but that which preceded it and that which will follow it; and it has neither beginning nor end: that is why nothing touches it, nothing moves it which does not concern that which it represents.

Goethe, too, thought the daemonic power was in the service of humanity, rather than of the individual. 'Every extraordinary man has a certain mission,' he asserted in his autobiography.

If he has fulfilled it, he is no longer needed upon earth in the same form, and Providence uses him for something else. But as everything here below happens in a natural way, the daemons keep tripping him up till he falls at last. Thus it was with Napoleon and many others. Mozart died in his six-and-thirtieth year. Raphael at the same age. Byron only a little older. But all these had perfectly fulfilled their missions; and it was time for them to depart, that other people might still have something to do in a world made to last a long while.

Maeterlinck agreed. The Unknown Guest, he asserted, 'is always the winner, humiliating our reason, crushing our wisdom and silencing arguments and passions alike with the contemptuous hand of destiny'. But

suddenly a tiny shock, which our senses had not even transmitted to our brain, wakes it with a start. It sits up, looks around and understands. It has seen the crack in the vault that separates the two lives. It gives the signal for departure. Forthwith panic spreads from cell to cell; and the innumerous city that we are utters yells of horror and distress and hustles around the gates of death.

The term 'daemon', though, can be used in a looser sense, as Sir Julian Huxley clearly used it in his own case. As the grandson of T. H. Huxley, 'Darwin's bulldog', and the son of Leonard Huxley, one of the most eminent literary figures of the twentieth century, Julian was 'born with great advantages, genetic and cultural', as he put it in his autobiography. In his youth he had been too timid, too unsure of himself, to exploit them; yet he felt driven relentlessly, until he had overcome his timidity. 'Looking back, I seem to have been possessed by a demon, driving me into every sort of activity and impatient to finish anything I had begun.' It pushed him also into a great diversity of interests, to the irritation of some of his more specialist-oriented colleagues – but ultimately qualifying him to be offered the role of the first director-general of UNESCO.

Huxley may well have used the phrase 'possessed by a demon' in one of its colloquial senses, implying little more than that there was an unconscious determination to succeed in spite of diffidence – as in Bernard Shaw's case, when he felt compelled to get up and make speeches at meetings in order to banish his nervousness. In such cases, the prompting often appears to be similar to 'the voice of conscience' – childhood conditioning about right and wrong returning to nag. Yet in others, this explanation is unsatisfactory – as the nineteenth-century positivists clearly recognised. They did not dispute that Socrates and Joan of Arc heard voices; they simply diagnosed the voices as symptomatic of mental instability. In this, they harked back to Dryden:

> Great wits are oft to madness near allied
> And thin partitions do their bounds divide.

In 1837 F. Lélut, an alienist at the Bicêtre hospital in Paris, could claim that there were only three possible explanations of Socrates' daemon: that Socrates' description of it had been misunderstood; that he and his associates were frauds; or that Socrates was *un fou*. There could be no doubt, Lélut decided, that the last was the correct diagnosis. Socrates was insane.

Lélut was no lightweight; he was later elected to the Academy, and served for many years as a deputy in the National Assembly. His diagnosis, too, was endorsed by the much more influential Cesare Lombroso, inventor of scientific criminology. Genius, Lombroso asserted, was a morbid condition displaying almost all the characteristics of congenital mental abnormality. He had been horrified, he admitted, when his findings compelled him to identify 'those individuals who represent the highest manifestations of the human spirit' with idiots and criminals; but he had become reconciled to this view after studying research which had revealed that the phenomena of 'atavistic regression' – trances, visions, voices and so on – 'did not always indicate true degradation'. Often they appeared to be a form of compensation; just as giants often displayed mental weakness, 'so the giants of thought expiate their intellectual force in degeneration and psychoses'.

This view was powerfully reinforced by Dostoevsky in *The Idiot* (1868), with Prince Myshkin's reflections on the phenomena associated with his epilepsy. For a few moments, all his worry 'resolved itself into a superior harmony, a serene and tranquil gaiety', before he suffered the fit. Once, on recovering, the prince said to himself:

These fleeting moments, in which our highest consciousness of ourselves – and therefore our highest life – is manifested, are due only to disease, to the suspension of normal conditions; and if so, it is not a higher life, but on the contrary, one of a lower order.

Paradoxically, Dostoevsky continued, this did not prevent the prince from feeling that it might be worth having the disease, if its consequence included 'the very highest degree of harmony and beauty'. For Lombroso this made the explanation simple. A few individuals, including Socrates and Dostoevsky, were fortunate; although they suffered from 'degenerative psychosis, belonging to the family of epileptic afflictions', they happened to have a variety of the disorder whose symptoms included providing them with great thoughts, plays or poems.

That so grotesque a proposition could have been quite widely accepted can only be accounted for by the orthodox assumptions of the time about 'mind'. The existence of an unconscious – let alone a subliminal – mind was still unacceptable in conventional scientific circles; the only possible explanation for visions and voices breaking in was that they were pathological. It took courage for anybody in the scientific establishment to argue that in view of the historical evidence, this was nonsense; but Oliver Wendell Holmes, in addition to being professor of anatomy at Harvard, had established his reputation as a popular writer and homespun philosopher with his 'Breakfast Table' books, and felt he could afford to denounce the positivist creed in his *Mechanism in Thought and Morals*, published in 1871. 'We all of us have a double,' he contended, 'who is wiser and better than we are, and who puts thoughts into our heads and words into our mouths.' This double,

a creating and informing spirit, which is with us, and not of us, is recognised everywhere in real and in storied life. It is the Zeus that kindled the rage of Achilles; it is the Muse of Homer; it is the daemon of Socrates; it is the inspiration of the seer; it is the mocking devil that whispers to Margaret as she kneels at the altar, and the hobgoblin that cries 'Sell him, sell him!' in the ear of John Bunyan; it shaped the forms that filled the soul of Michael Angelo when he saw the figure of the great lawgiver in the yet unhewn marble, and the dome of the world's yet unbuilt basilica against the black horizon; it comes to the least of us, as a voice that will be heard; it tells us what we must believe; it frames our sentences; it lends a sudden gleam of eloquence to the dullest of us all.

Frederic Myers agreed. His *Human Personality* represented a filling-out, with case histories, of Holmes's idea. But it was Freud's version of the unconscious mind, instinctual and unorganised, that captured the market – such of it as was not appropriated by positivism's legacy to psychology, the behaviourism of John Broadus Watson and his followers, who sought to sweep away the mind, conscious or unconscious, as a concept; replacing it with a hail of neurophysiological conditioned reflexes.

Freud may no longer be so dominant a figure in the analytic school, and behaviourism is largely discredited; but in orthodox psychology circles there is little disposition to re-examine the teachings of Myers. Many psychological students graduate without even having heard of him. Major surveys of research into the human mind appear which do not so much as mention intuition, let alone explore its implications. Some of Jung's most devoted disciples shy away from the occult notions he propounded. Since the advent of the counter-culture, admittedly, there has been a greater willingness to explore territory previously shunned as irrational. Writers within the frontiers of academic respectability, as well as others outside them, have been examining intuition, creativity and related subjects. But the daemonic element has received little attention; and its use of hallucination, even less.

There is confusion, too, over another aspect of daemon: possession – 'not the loss of consciousness', as Julian Jaynes of Princeton defines it, 'so much as its replacement by a new and different consciousness'. Although certain that it represents another evolutionary device, he finds it disconcerting; understandably, because although it is not difficult to attribute the visions and voices which were taken to come from the gods to the workings of the central nervous system, a great deal of what the gods of the *Iliad* did (in *The Origins of Consciousness*, Jaynes cites them as a model) cannot be thus accounted for. Not merely did they protect their heroes by diverting spears thrown at them; they levitated them out of danger, and possessed them, where necessary, in order to be able to give instructions without identifying themselves.

In our time, possession is generally regarded as a form of mental disorder, dual or multiple personality; or, among Christians, as diabolic. But it also emerges in automatic writing, drawing and musical composition, either by allowing the hand to act without conscious control, or with the help of a planchette and a ouija board. The products rarely have more than curiosity value, but there may be an intimation that they are inspired, in the sense that they transcend anything which the writers can do when in their 'right' minds. They also occasionally provide information by what appears to be extra-sensory means. Possession, in this role, seems to be another evolutionary expedient; as if daemon is trying another way to make its presence felt. And it has achieved some of its most impressive results in the character of Muse.

The Muses

In *Creative Imagination*, published in 1929, June E. Downey recalled that it had once been the fashion to begin a poem

with an invocation to the Muse. However artificial such an opening would seem today, it was in its time a somewhat sophisticated recognition of an element in creative work which in earlier days was very simply reckoned with and attributed to divine inspiration. We no longer think of the hand of a poet being utilised as a tool by a power beyond himself; we no longer consider the ravings of madwomen oracular; we have transferred the whole drama to the mind itself. But the more extensive our survey, the more penetrating our analysis of the human mind, the more we realise its exceeding complexity; we become aware that daylight consciousness flickers over a voluminous and obscure mystery, and that we must look to the twilight or dark of consciousness for explanation of much that startles us on its sudden emergence into sunlit thought. To change the figure, we recognise that much of that which is most vital and significant in the mental drama is played off the boards or, at least, never succeeds in getting into the limelight.

June Downey's thesis is in retrospect the more interesting in that she was professor of psychology at the University of Wyoming; and psychologists at the time tended to be in one of two camps, both hostile to it. Freud had modified Lombroso's theory, to fit his own. The artist was not psychotic; but he was introverted, 'and has not far to go to become a neurotic', because he was urged on 'by instinctual needs which are too clamorous'. This line was to be developed by some of his disciples: one was even to link Leonardo's fascination with water to his bed-wetting in childhood.

By 1929, however, Freud's brief ascendancy, always shaky, was being challenged by the new behaviourism. The year before its leading exponent, John Broadus Watson, had claimed that there was nothing complex or mysterious about the human mind; 'mind' in fact was no more than a myth which mystics clung to, in order to mask their confusion. His experiments had shown that laboratory rats would learn how to get food when chance showed them how to go through the right motions. Poets, Watson argued, juggled words around until they fell into patterns which gave them similar gratification.

Far from bringing psychology as an academic discipline into ridicule and disrepute, behaviourism caught on. The elimination of mind, consciousness, inspiration and so on was a godsend – not that Watson's disciples would have given a god any credit for the way in which the human species had evolved, with the help of ever more elaborate conditioned reflexes. At Harvard, Professor B. F. Skinner took on where Watson had left off, rejecting 'mind' on the ground it had no basis in physical science, and clothing Watson's analogy in the latest jargon. Just as rats and pigeons learned how to get food by 'operant conditioning', with food pellets as 'reinforcers', and deprivation as 'negative reinforcers', Skinner claimed, 'the musician plays and composes what he is reinforced by hearing'; artistic creation is 'controlled entirely by the contingencies of reinforcement'.

Incredible though it now seems, behaviourism was widely taught for some years as if it *were* psychology. An opinion poll taken of psychology students in the United States in 1964 showed that Skinner was regarded as far and away the most influential living psychologist; his influence was strong in Europe, too. And though his brand of behaviourism has since fallen into some disrepute, a rat-infested, laboratory-based methodology remains widespread in the discipline because of a conviction that only material which can be objectively studied and rendered susceptible to statistical analysis is worthy of consideration. To explore the mind along the lines June Downey suggested would be to settle for the subjective and the anecdotal – two grave sins in academic eyes. Koestler, who attempted it in *The Act of Creation*, was jeered at for his unscientific approach.

Yet as he showed – and as Willis Harman and Howard Rheingold have since further illustrated in their *Higher Creativity* (1985) and

Nona Coxhead in *The Relevance of Bliss* (1985) – to brush aside imagination, intuition and inspiration (the three 'I's, as the psychiatrist Jan Ehrenwald has called them), on the ground that they are not susceptible to laboratory experiment or to statistical analysis, is as absurd as it would be to insist that because reports of dreams have never been confirmed by independent witnesses, they are unacceptable. Subjective the three 'I's certainly are, but in myth, legend, history and human experience they are of such profound importance that they merit fresh consideration, now that the theories suggesting they are pathological, or simply conditioned reflexes, can be thrown into the dustbin which holds the discards of science.

Of the three 'I's, imagination finds it easiest to slip into consciousness, because we can voluntarily conjure it up, when we want to. We use it all the time, in fact, making decisions like whether to watch a TV programme or read a book – so that when it breaks through unbidden we may be pleased or annoyed but we will not be greatly surprised. We cannot, however, summon intuition; often it nags at us from just below the surface of awareness, as if warning that it has a message for us, but lacks a channel to get it across. Inspiration is the most mysterious, coming as it sometimes does in the form of a blinding glimpse of the obvious, which we have been crass not to have recognised before; sometimes in a manner which appears utterly inexplicable, except on the assumption that it is a gift from the gods.

There is no shortage of speculation. Many great writers, composers, artists and scientists (and others who have not achieved greatness, but have believed themselves to be inspired) have tried to describe how they came to produce the work or works which brought them fame or wealth. Rudyard Kipling will serve as an introduction, because his inspiration – or so he believed – was in the hands of his Daemon (of which he stood in awe, always using the capital D).

AUTHORS

That the notion of a personal daemon and of a personal muse are, or can be, closely linked is clear from Kipling's fragment of an autobiography, *Something of Myself*, in which his daemon featured prominently – usually in the role traditionally assigned to a muse, except that, like Socrates' daemon, it figured as a protector as well as a source of inspiration, so consistently that he came to place total reliance on it.

At first glance this is surprising, in view both of his normal reticence and his dislike of occult dabbling.

> Oh, the road to En-dor is the oldest road
> And the craziest road of all
> Straight it runs to the witch's abode
> As it did in the days of Saul
> And nothing has changed of the sorrow in store
> For such as go down on the road to En-dor.

His attitude appears to have been that he should be content to be grateful for his gift, without allowing curiosity to lead him down dangerous paths; but he was not going to allow this to stop him from giving credit where, he felt, credit was due. 'Let us now consider the Personal Daemon of Aristotle and others,' he wrote.

> This is the doom of the Makers – their Daemon lives in their pen.
> If he be absent or sleeping, they are even as other men.
> But if he be utterly present, and they swerve not from his behest,
> The word that he gives shall continue, whether in earnest or jest.

Most men, he went on – some of them unlikely – kept their daemon under an alias which varied with their literary or scientific attainments; 'mine came to me early when I sat bewildered among other notions, and said: "Take this and no other." I obeyed, and was rewarded.'

Some of Kipling's recollections suggest that he believed his daemon actually possessed him, while he was writing. Living in America in 1892, through a winter 'of stillness, and suspense', he had an idea. After blocking it out, 'the pen took charge, and I watched it begin to write stories about Mowgli and animals, which later grew into the *Jungle Book*.' So popular were they, and so easy to write, that 'once launched, there seemed no particular reason to stop; but I had learned to distinguish between the peremptory motions of my Daemon, and the "carry-over", or induced electricity, which comes of what you might call mere frictional writing.'

Once, Kipling's daemon supplied him with a fact he could not have known about, 'a prized petty triumph' as he thought. 'I had put a well into the wall of Pevensey Castle, circa AD 1100, because I needed it there. Archeologically it did not exist until this year (1935) when excavators brought such a well to light.' This might have been a reasonable gamble, he admitted, on his part. Not so the way in which

if ever I held back, Ananias fashion, anything of myself (even though I had to throw it out afterwards) I paid for it by missing what I *then* knew the tale lacked. As an instance, many years later I wrote about a medieval artist, a monastery and the premature discovery of the microscope ('The Eye of Allah'). Again and again it went dead under my hand, and for the life of me I could not see why. I put it away and waited. Then said my Daemon – and I was meditating something else at the time – 'Treat it as an illuminated manuscript.' I had ridden off on hard black-and-white decoration, instead of pumicing the whole thing ivory-smooth, and loading it with thick colour and gilt.

On another occasion, when he could not keep the background to a story in key with the events, it was his daemon who told him to paint it first, 'as hard as a public-house sign'. This done, everything fell into place.

The daemon was with him, Kipling recalled,

in the *Jungle Books*, *Kim* and both *Puck* books, and good care I took to walk delicately, lest he should withdraw. I know that he did not, because when those books were finished they said so themselves with, almost, the water-hammer click of a tap turned off. One of the clauses in our contract was that I should never follow up 'a success', for by this sin fell Napoleon and a few others. *Note here*. When your Daemon is in charge, do not try to think consciously. Drift, wait, and obey.

Kipling did not go on to discuss the relationship between his own attitudes and beliefs and those which emerge in his writings. Although he claimed he was in no way psychic, and warned against taking the road to En-dor, in one sense he himself travelled along it again and again, and with quite extraordinary perception. This was in his short stories touching on reincarnation – 'The Tomb of his Ancestors', 'Wireless', and 'The Finest Story in the World'; on precognition – 'The Brushwood Boy'; and on spirit materialisations – 'They'. Little sympathy though Somerset Maugham had for their themes, he felt bound to include them in his *Choice of Kipling's Prose* as among the author's finest, and they have lasted better than some of the others in the collection. Unlike Dickens's ghost stories, where the supernatural is merely a device in the hands of another supremely gifted storyteller, they suggest not just that Kipling had a reader's familiarity with the disturbing environs of En-dor, but that he had often felt its pull, controlling it by putting it down on paper.

On at least one occasion, Kipling credited his daemon with paranormal protective powers. When he had made occasional slips, particularly over technicalities, he had been spared embarrassment; but this he could attribute to the fact that 'the men of the seas and the engine room do not write to the press'. The most striking protection he received was of another kind: it saved him from what could have been a very damaging accusation.

The nearest shave that ever missed me was averted by my Daemon. I was at the moment in Canada, where a young Englishman gave me, as a personal experience, a story of a body-snatching episode in deep snow, perpetrated in some lonely prairie-town and culminating in purest horror. To get it out of the system I wrote it detailedly, and it came away just a shade too good, too well-balanced, too slick.

Wanting reassurance from his daemon, Kipling put the tale aside. A few months later he had to go to the dentist in a small American town; and in the waiting room

I found a file of bound *Harper's* magazines – say six hundred pages to the volume – dating from the 1850s. I picked up one, and read as undistractedly as the tooth permitted. There I found my tale, identical in every mark – frozen ground, frozen corpse, stiff in its fur robes in the buggy – the inn-keeper offering it a drink – and so on to the ghastly end. Had I published that tale, what could have saved me from the charge of deliberate plagiarism?

Maddeningly, Kipling did not go into the question of what (or whom – he referred to his daemon as 'he') he thought his daemon might be. A literary conceit? A double? A split-off part of his personality? A spirit?

To have used a literary conceit would have been out of character; in any case, 'muse' would have been the more obvious choice. The way in which he emphasised the importance of his daemon suggests that whatever he may have thought about 'him', he took 'him' very seriously. That he did so has in fact been a source of embarrassment to some of his admirers – notably Lord Birkenhead, in what is regarded as a standard life of Kipling.

Birkenhead clearly shied away from *Something of Myself*. He used it only sparingly to illustrate episodes from Kipling's career; and when he came to describe the book, he gave it a single paragraph; 'We have already observed Kipling's reticence, and it is nowhere better exhibited than in this cautious, tantalising work. Vividly written, eminently readable, it yet masks every interesting detail of his past.'

It is hard to think of more interesting details than those Kipling actually gave – which otherwise might never have been known – of the way his daemon 'lived in his pen', and how he came to place such reliance on its promptings. The measure of Birkenhead's reluctance to face this, for him, uncomfortable revelation is that he mentioned the daemon only once, in passing, leaving the implication that he hoped it *was* no more than a literary conceit. Birkenhead's was a sympathetic and, in mundane respects, an understanding biography; but daemons evidently did not appeal to him, or surely he would at least have discussed what Kipling meant by 'the pen took charge, and I watched it write'.

The admittedly slender evidence suggests that Kipling was describing a form of automatism, of a kind which many celebrated writers have experienced and reported. Myers divided it, in humans, into two categories. In sensory automatism, he explained, we appear to pick up a flow of information *as if* it were coming through the five senses – Socrates 'hearing' his daemon's voice in his mind's ear, Joan 'seeing' and 'hearing' her angels. In motor automatism, the information is processed through us, either in 'automatic writing', which comes close to Kipling's description of the pen taking charge (the pen is held, but not consciously moved; it appears to write as if guided by another hand); or by what has sometimes been called psychography, in which a planchette, a pencil mounted on casters, is put on a ouija board. When a finger is placed on it, it will move to and fro among the letters on the board's edge, spelling out sentences.

Either way, the impression is often created that an invisible entity is giving the dictation, or moving the pen or the planchette. It is as if the writer is temporarily possessed. There are, however, other possibilities. Kipling might have had an exceptionally powerful imagination, ruled by an exceptionally acute intuition, which ferried material from his subliminal to his conscious mind so impeccably that he came to think of it as 'him' – either a double, an internal alter ego, or some external source feeding his imagination, using him as a medium.

Uneasy though psychic phenomena made him, Kipling could not reject such external influences. Apart from acknowledging his debt to his daemon for finding a way to save him from the charge of plagiarism, he had some paranormal experiences, notably a pre-cognitive dream. Although not dramatic in itself, it became so in retrospect when he watched it unfolding in real life, so accurately that he could not explain it away by coincidence. For the sake of the 'weaker brethren', he explained – those whose curiosity over such matters might lure them to En-dor – he had not written about the experience; 'but how and why had I been shown an unreleased roll of my life-film?'

For the present, the means are lacking to decide how far inspiration can be accounted for in terms of a particularly harmonious relationship in the subliminal mind between imagination and intuition, presenting the imagination's offerings to the fortunate writer *as if* they came from some external source; and those which can more plausibly be explained in terms *of* some external source. What *Something of Myself* does reveal is that a rather ordinary, and in some ways rather tiresome, individual in his everyday life was the medium, when inspiration struck, for some marvellous stories and some striking verses. Unless he was a liar of formidable proportions, it demolishes rationalist preconceptions about the nature of creativity, compelling attention to questions about the nature of the daemonic forces, even if it does not adequately answer them.

They are not satisfactorily answered in many other cases where it is clear that writing sometimes is assisted, or even controlled, by what seems to be a type of possession. George Eliot told the man she married following G. H. Lewes's death, J. W. Cross,

that, in all that she considered her best writing, there was a 'not herself' which took possession of her, and that she felt her own personality to be merely the instrument through which this spirit, as it were, was acting. Particularly she dwelt on this in regard to the scene in *Middlemarch* between Dorothea and Rosamond, saying that, although she always knew they had, sooner or later, to come together, she kept the idea resolutely out of her mind until Dorothea was in Rosamond's drawing room. Then, abandoning herself to the inspiration of the moment, she wrote the whole scene exactly as it stands, without alteration or erasure, in an intense state of excitement and agitation, feeling herself entirely possessed by the feelings of the two women.

In *The Lifted Veil*, too, George Eliot wrote a case history of possession which, though couched in fiction, gives the same powerful impression of daemonic intervention as Kipling's. The narrator, Latimer, describes how as a boy he was waiting impatiently for his father to return when, suddenly, there his father was, in the room, with a neighbour the boy knew and a young lady he did not know. 'Well, Latimer, you thought me long,' his father said – and all three vanished; it had been a hallucination. Alarmed, Latimer left the room to douse his forehead with eau-de-cologne. When he returned, there his father was in actuality, with the neighbour and the young lady, just as he had 'seen' them.

'Well, Latimer, you thought me long,' my father said . . .
I heard no more, felt no more, till I became conscious I was lying with my head low on the sofa . . .

Soon afterwards, Latimer became aware of a different form of his 'abnormal sensibility' – the intrusion into his mind of other people's mental processes; he describes how irritating this could be, when he picked up 'the vagrant, frivolous ideas and emotions of some uninteresting acquaintance', and the story goes on relentlessly to describe how Latimer is sucked into the grip of the evil lady in his vision.

It is an extremely powerful tale, as the disturbed reaction to it of George Eliot's admirers was to show (Her publishers' reaction, too.

It was offered to them after her successful first novel, *Adam Bede*, had appeared, and while *The Mill on the Floss* was being written. It would jeopardise the writer's future and their own prospects from her books, they felt, if *The Lifted Veil* came out in between.). And in an afterword to the Virago edition in 1985 Beryl Gray cites Marghanita Laski's predictable raising of rationalist eyebrows: 'a sadly poor supernatural story'.

If it *were* a supernatural story it would indeed be poor stuff compared to many. But George Eliot was writing from experience of mesmerism, and of the clairvoyance frequently reported in connection with it; she had herself been mesmerised, and she knew of Professor William Gregory's researches, which he described in his book on the subject in 1851 – Latimer's experiences, in fact, appear to have been adopted from Gregory. Far from being an experiment with occultism, *The Lifted Veil* is clearly *fact*, admirably portrayed in fiction. Henry James was near the mark when he called it 'the *jeu d'esprit* of a mind that is not often – perhaps not often enough – found at play'; and Jane Carlyle nearer still, with her description of it as 'this most beautiful human book'. It seems likely that it was George Eliot's mistrust of the growing influence of spiritualist mediums, fuelled by G. H. Lewes's detestation of them, that made her say, fourteen years later, that it would not be judicious to reprint it; but 'I care for the idea which it embodies,' she insisted; 'there are many things in it which I would willingly say over again.'

The feeling of being possessed, while writing, had been vividly described by the seventeenth-century mystic (and heretic) Madame Guyon. Questioned about a passage of scripture, she recalled, she would have no idea what it meant. Yet the explanation would present itself while she was writing,

with inconceivable quickness. Before writing I did not know what I was going to write; while writing I saw that I was writing things I had never known; and during the time of the manifestation light was given to me that I had in me treasures of knowledge and understanding that I did not know myself to possess.

Fate suggests ideas, Lombroso recalled one of the Goncourt brothers as saying: 'Then there is an unknown force, a superior will, a sort of necessity of writing, which command your work and guide your pen, so that sometimes the book which leaves your hands does not seem to have come out of yourself.' And Henry James marvelled at the steps by which *The Ambassadors* developed. 'They placed themselves with a prompt and, as it were, functional assurance' with the result that the events 'continued to fall together, as by the neat action of their own weight and form, even while the commentator scratched his head about them; he easily sees now that they were well in advance of him.' He was left with the feeling that 'from a good way behind', he had to catch up with them, 'breathless and a little flurried, as he best could'.

E. F. Benson, a novelist popular in the early years of this century and, unlike many of his more highly regarded contemporaries, still in print, left a detailed description of his daemon's domination:

I can still taste the relish of coming in out of a wet November evening, knowing that the characters in my tale would be waiting in my sitting room for me, and presently, with 'OUT' displayed on my door, I would immerse myself and see what they proposed to do. For, indeed, if the book, in my biased judgment, was going well, it seemed as if the persons I was writing about took charge of their own manoeuvres, while I, who held the pen, did little more than record their independent action. Often I would have planned, even with detail, what I meant to do with them, only to find that they had planned and now dictated something else.

When 'the mysterious workman was in possession', as Benson put it, 'he had to be obeyed'. 'He' was touchy: if Benson allowed his conscious mind to meddle, the workman would down tools. If all went smoothly, on the other hand, a dozen pages might be completed before the flow stopped – 'sometimes in mid-sentence'. Benson would take the hint and retire, 'wonderfully satisfied, to bed'. The next morning, he would have no recollection of what was on those twelve pages.

Again and again have I cudgelled my brains as I dressed, in the effort to remember what I had written and been totally unable to recollect it, so that I would read it over with surprised interest. Often these subconscious scribblings required correction and trimming, for sentences would be unbalanced and phrases needed the file or called for recasting; but the substance and general outline invariably met with the approval of my conscious self, who realised over his eggs and bacon that he had not and could not have devised the stuff. He might not think very highly of it, but he always passed it on those occasions when he had nothing to do with it.

More recently Thomas Wolfe, trying to get to grips with his own experience, recalled that in the year he spent in Europe while his first book was gestating he felt that he had inside him 'swelling and gathering all the time, a huge black cloud' like a storm about to break.

It broke that summer while I was in Switzerland. It came in torrents, and it is not over yet.

I cannot really say the book was written. It was something that took hold of me and possessed me, and before I was done with it – that is, before I finally emerged with the first completed part – it seemed to me that it had done for me. It was exactly as if this great black storm cloud I have spoken of had opened up and, mid flashes of lightning, was pouring from its depth a torrential and ungovernable flood. Upon that flood everything was swept and borne along as by a great river. And I was borne along with it.

In *Black Spring*, the final volume of the 'Tropic' trilogy, Henry Miller described what he called 'the genesis of a masterpiece'. For two days he had been blocked, 'like a cartridge that's jammed'. At ten the next morning the recollection of a past incident

shrieks at me. From this moment on – up until four o'clock this morning – I am in the hands of unseen powers. I put the typewriter away and commence to record what is being dictated to me . . . This continues and continues. I am exultant and at the same time I am worried. If it continues at this rate I may have a hemorrhage.

Trying to break out of the powers' grip, he went out to a restaurant, taking care not to bring a notebook; but by the time he started on the second bottle of Burgundy the tablecloth was 'covered with notes'. Later, in a café, he still could not extricate himself; 'someone is dictating to me constantly – and with no regard for my health'. Not until after midnight could he relax: 'The dictation has ceased. A free man again.'

Some writers have described how they have 'seen' their books in the mind's eye, as if on film – though in Harriet Beecher Stowe's case, before film had been invented. In 1851 she was attending a communion service when,

suddenly, like the unrolling of a picture, the scene of the death of Uncle

Tom passed before her mind. So strongly was she affected that it was with difficulty she could keep from weeping aloud. Immediately on returning home she took pen and paper and wrote out the vision which had been, as it were, blown into her mind by the rushing of a mighty wind.

Whatever may be thought of *Uncle Tom's Cabin*'s literary merits, few books have had so immediate and powerful an impact. Within a year, 300,000 copies had been sold. 'It is one of the greatest triumphs recorded in literary history,' Longfellow wrote to tell her. 'What a glorious work!' Whittier wrote ecstatically to William Lloyd Garrison, leader of the anti-slavery movement. Oliver Wendell Holmes offered a verse tribute, including the lines:

> Her lever was the wand of art
> Her fulcrum was the human heart
> Whence all unfailing aid is.
> She moved the earth! Its thunders pealed
> Its mountains shook, its temples reeled
> The blood-red fountains were unsealed
> And Moloch sunk to Hades.

Mrs Stowe's biographer was hardly exaggerating when she claimed that *Uncle Tom's Cabin* 'made the enforcement of the Fugitive Slave Law an impossibility'. Mrs Stowe, however, resolutely declined to take any credit for the book: 'I could not control the story,' she would reiterate. 'It wrote itself.' And as a devout Christian she believed it had been written by the hand of the Lord upon hers, 'to Him alone should be given all the praise'.

This ability to have the story unfold visually has been shared by some authors who are not high in the critics' esteem, but have acquired a formidable multitude of addicts. The 'Noddy' stories, anathema to many parents, have riveted millions of children. According to Enid Blyton all she needed to do was to sit, typewriter on her knees, make her mind a blank, and wait; then 'my characters would stand before me in my mind's eye'. The story would act itself out for her 'almost as if I had a private cinema screen there'. As she did not know what was going to happen, she was 'in the happy position of being able to write a story and read it for the first time at one and the same moment'. Sometimes

a character makes a joke, a really funny one that makes me laugh as I type it on my paper and think, 'Well, I couldn't have thought of that myself in a hundred years'; and then I think: 'Well, *who* did think of it?'

Enid Blyton claimed that she saw her characters 'as clearly as I could see real children', a form of visualisation which is ordinarily regarded as natural, though few people enjoy it to anything like the same extent. 'Hearing voices' is another matter; to a distressing extent they are still widely considered to be a symptom of impending mental breakdown. They may be – just as hallucinations may be the pink elephants of delirium tremens. Yet they can be both 'real' and informative.

This presents problems, as Leon Daudet realised when he was describing the creative processes of his father Alphonse (whose *Lettres de Mon Moulin* and *Tartarin de Tarascon* have reached a surprisingly large audience in Britain in their original language, thanks to their being regarded as suitable for schoolchildren).

When he wrote, he *heard*. A number of academics with new-fangled notions came down to ask him about this, and oversimplified, in their pedantic terms, a natural and complex method. We were endlessly lectured on the scholastic distinction between 'auditive' and 'visual', categories which have no absolute meaning and are useful only in a clinical sense.

A distinction can be made between seeing people in the mind's eye, knowing that they *are* in the mind's eye, and 'seeing' hallucinatory figures; or between hearing somebody in the mind's ear as if he were present, and 'hearing voices' when the initial impression is that the person really *is* present – aural hallucinations. It needs to be reiterated, though, that it is not necessary to think of the former as natural, the latter as paranormal. Both may represent the subliminal mind's ingenious expedient – sensory automatism – to get through to consciousness; a paranormal component enters into the calculations if the information turns out to be something which the recipient could not have known.

The distinction also arises in connection with motor automatism. Although automatic writing is accepted by psychiatrists as a symptom of dissociation, in the public mind it still is commonly regarded as paranormal – as, even more so, are the movements of the planchette around a ouija board. They, too, should be considered as purveyors of information from the subliminal mind. Only if the information turns out to be veridical can it be attributed to extra-sensory perception.

Whether the perception is veridical is not always easy to determine with any certainty; as in the numerous accounts of retrocognitive experiences where people have described what happened to them in what they believe were past lives. But a number of established authors have been quite sure about one thing: that the information provided for them cannot have come from their own source of knowledge.

Brian Cleeve is a contemporary example. The author of a number of conventionally written novels which had been well received, Cleeve began in 1977 to have a series of strange experiences – 'i.e. psychic, spiritual, subconscious; the label one attaches to them is unimportant – that had an intense and lasting effect on my mind, my way of thinking and living, on my ambitions and everything else I considered important'. The experiences arose from the fact that he became aware of 'a presence, invisible, intangible, but real', that wished to communicate with him. In 'the commonsense world of psychiatrists and greengrocers and politicians', this counted as madness; spirits of the kind do not exist. Priests, too, insisted that such experiences are unreal. (Cleeve rejoined the Catholic church after an absence of more than twenty years, 'the last thing I had ever expected'.) To Cleeve, they have been extremely real. They have produced no symptoms of mental instability; 'the visible results lie in several books that I have written under the influence and guidance of this "presence".'

In an epilogue to the first of these books, Cleeve described how the presence had told him to write a story about people living in Jerusalem at the time of Jesus' crucifixion:

I had no knowledge at all of the period, or the place, beyond what anyone may know from reading the Gospels. I imagined that I would need to spend months if not years researching and reading. In the event none of that was necessary and I wrote the entire story in ten days, in the interval between writing the two halves of another book. All that I needed to know, down to the names of obscure characters and details of the city and the landscape, was 'given' to me as I wrote. So was the story itself. Not word for word but thought for thought, if you are willing to make the distinction. As I wrote, I never knew what I had to write. I was never in doubt, never needed to hesitate or wonder what to write next. Yet each day I had no idea of how the story would unfold that day as I wrote, let alone how it would end.

Cleeve enjoys a form of sensory automatism, but not quite to the point of possession. Although he is told the story – 'or, rather, made aware of it' – he is aware of what he is writing, chooses the words, and sets them down in his own style. But in some cases authors are not aware of the nature of the material they are producing. It seems to be dictated through them, and has to be recorded and transcribed. A recent example has been the 'Seth' series of books, taken down by Robert F. Butts from what Seth, a 'nonphysical entity', said when speaking through Jane Roberts (Butts's wife) while she was in a trance.

Jane Roberts, an established author before the very successful 'Seth' books began to appear, did her best to explain how they were produced. In a way they were

the products of an inner psychic combustion – the spark that is lit in our world, as Seth's reality strikes mine – or vice versa. For me, this is an accelerated state. I would compare it to a higher state of wakefulness rather than to the sleep usually associated with trance – but a different kind of wakefulness, in which the usual world seems to be the one that is sleeping. My attention is not blunted. It is elsewhere.

As Jane, I am not discarded when I'm in such a trance. Yet I step out of my Jane-self in some indescribable way, and step right back into it when the session is over. So there must be another 'I' who leaves Jane patiently waiting at the shore while 'I' dive headlong into those other dimensions of experience and identity.

The most remarkable example of motor automatism and authorship is well documented and attested. In 1913 Pearl Curran, wife of a Missouri civil servant, was invited by a friend to try her luck on a ouija board; and as it was found that the planchette worked well for her, she continued to play. Soon, a 'communicator' emerged, calling herself Patience Worth and claiming to be the spirit of a British girl who had lived three centuries earlier. 'Communicators' were a common feature in ouija sessions; what was unusual about Patience was that she produced – to quote her investigator, Casper

Yost, the respected editor of the *Sunday St Louis Globe-Democrat*, founder and later president of the Society of Newspaper Editors – 'conversation that is strewn with wit and wisdom, epigrams and maxims; poems by the hundred; parables and allegories, stories of a semi-dramatic character; and dramas'.

Mrs Curran had neither written anything before, except letters, nor given any indication that she had the wealth of literary talent which Patience displayed. The nature-study verses which began to flow from her might have been the juvenilia of many a well-known poet.

> All silver laced with web, and crystal studded, hangs
> A golden lily cup, as airy as a dancing sprite
> The moon hath caught a fleeting cloud, and rests in her embrace
> The bumble-fly still hovers o'er the clover flower
> And mimics all the zephyr's song . . .

More startling material was to follow: a 60,000-word novel, *Telka*, about a girl growing up in Britain in Anglo-Saxon times. Sceptics, arranging for it to be vetted by experts, were disconcerted to be told that not merely did Telka speak in a way which she would have been likely to have spoken in the seventeenth century; the book was almost entirely written in Anglo-Saxon and Norman terminology, avoiding words which had entered the language subsequently. An expert would have had his work cut out to produce a similarly crafted book, avoiding anachronisms; yet *Telka* flowed out in thirty-six hours of ouija-board time.

It happened that novels in language of the 'soft-footed strideth Telka, bare toes a-sunk in soft earth' type were acceptable, then, and indeed popular, until they received their devastating come-uppance in Stella Gibbons's *Cold Comfort Farm. Telka* was quite well received. Its successors *The Sorry Tale*, a novel, based on the life and times of Jesus, and *Hope Trueblood*, set in Victorian England, were enthusiastically praised by respected critics; and to the end of Mrs Curran's life, Patience Worth continued to impress people such as the far from credulous Dame Edith Lyttelton, who paid her a visit out of curiosity and was startled to find that Patience not merely was gifted with second sight, revealing too intimate an acquaintance for comfort with Dame Edith's private life, but was still producing work which, 'difficult and obscure as much of it is', contained 'flashes of insight and passages of beauty, making her a good example of a medium who, had she produced a better-organised normal brain, would have been acclaimed as a genius'.

Mrs Curran's career presents a case for unexplained sources of information and inspiration which is hard to rebut. Numerous witnesses of standing testified to the fact that the poems and aphorisms continued to flow off the ouija board throughout her life, as if they were being dictated; and sceptics who tried to track down indications in her past, to suggest that she might have mugged up both the history and the dialects of the periods in which the novels were set, could only confirm that she had never had either the opportunity or the talent.

Her books, though, also mock the conventional spiritualist interpretation – that they were the work of a girl, Patience, who had lived in the seventeenth century, and who was returning in discarnate form. This might account for *Telka*, but not for *The Sorry Tale*, and still less for *Hope Trueblood*, unless it could be assumed that Patience was able to move around in time, spanning different incarnations, absorbing the culture of each era.

A more straightforward case of apparent spirit intervention was described by Maurice Collis in his biography, *Somerville & Ross*. When Violet Martin died in 1915 it was generally assumed that no further Somerville and Ross books – she had been the 'Ross' – would appear. For a while, Edith Somerville herself thought she would write no further stories without her collaborator. But the following summer she had a séance with a friend who was a medium, Jem Barlow:

Jem wished to see if she could communicate with Colonel Isherwood, who was killed in the war a short time ago. Jem held the pencil in her right hand and I put my left hand very lightly on hers. In a minute or two the pencil began to move and, without our asking any questions, wrote. The writing was very clear and legible, though sometimes it failed and became difficult to read. I can truly say that neither of us had any idea before or during the writing of what was being written, or who the writer was.

What had been written, they found, was at first confused; but then a message came through. 'You and I have not finished our

work. Dear, we shall. Be comforted. V.M.' In later sessions 'V.M.'
indicated that they could continue to collaborate through Jem –
eventually, she hoped, without the need for a medium; and on New
Year's Eve Edith recorded in her diary 'Wrote alone' – in other
words, without Jem being present. With *Mount Music* (1919),
'Somerville and Ross' reappeared as co-authors, as they were to
continue to do, with the help of automatic writing, for another
thirty years. 'In some ways,' their biographer Maurice Collis
remarked, 'Martin would be a more puissant collaborator than
when on earth.' Certainly there was no indication of any serious
break in the continuity of their partnership in some of the books,
notably, *Mount Music* and *The Big House at Inver*.

Victor Hugo also appears to have had a debt to the ouija board,
though of a different kind. All his life, according to his biographer
André Maurois, he had had visions of such intensity that they had
almost the quality of hallucinations; he had heard spirit 'rappings'
and had experienced premonitions – an overwhelming feeling of
sadness had engulfed him, one day, which he could not account for;
it turned out to have been at the very time his beloved daughter
Leopoldine was drowning. 'For him, the supernatural was natural.'
So when, during his exile in the Channel Islands, his old friend
Delphine de Girardin came to visit him and his family, and regaled
them with accounts of the table-turning craze which was sweeping
the capitals of Europe, she had an attentive listener.

When she came to dinner and suggested a séance, however,
Hugo was initially doubtful. The version of the pastime she offered
was table-rapping, in which the aim was to conjure up spirits who
would 'communicate' through the table's movements or noises. A
code could then be established, and the messages taken down. For a
time nothing happened, but in the first séance at which Hugo
agreed to participate, a single rap signified a spirit presence. Asked
who was there, the table replied, 'Leopoldine.'

Hugo was hooked. Soon, other 'communicators' were jostling
each other in the effort to get through to the Hugos; among them
Dante, Shakespeare, Racine, Molière and Byron. Often the messages were in verse, some of it showing considerable talent – but,
always, talent typical of Victor Hugo's own compositions. To

Maurois, it was astonishing that the poet 'should have failed to realise that the manifestations came entirely from himself'. Was Hugo's subliminal self shrewd enough to realise that he needed to *believe* he was guided by the great ones of history? Whatever the explanation, they did not merely deliver verses to him; they told him how he should shape his career. And after the months of table-rapping were over, 'never had Hugo written with such freedom, such power, such ease'. This was to be the period of his *Contemplations*, and of *Les Misérables* (1862).

The case for some form of psychic input is strengthened from time to time by evidence of precognition. Nobody would be likely to accuse Thackeray of occultist leanings, or of gullibility; yet he confessed to forces influencing him in his work which he could not account for. 'I have been surprised at the observations made by some of my characters,' he wrote in 'De Finibus', one of his *Roundabout Papers* (1860). 'It seems as if an occult power was moving the pen.' What was more, 'the imagination foretells things.' Some writers had an inflated style: 'What also if there is an *afflated* style – when a writer is like a Pythoness on her oracle tripod, and mighty words, words which he cannot help, come blowing, and bellowing, and whistling, and moaning through the squeaking pipes of his bodily organ?' He went on to cite examples of characters he had invented who had become realities: notably Costigan in *Pendennis*, written ten years before.

I was smoking in a tavern parlour one night – and this Costigan came into the room alive – the very man – the most remarkable resemblance of the printed skeleton of the man, of the rude drawing in which I had depicted him. He had the same little coat, the same battered hat, cocked on one eye, the same twinkle in that eye . . .

Of course, Thackeray went on, this Costigan (like his own creation) had been in the army, and spoke with an Irish brogue, and a few months later was in trouble with the law. 'How had I come to know him, to divine him? Nothing shall convince me that I have not seen that man in the world of spirits.'

An even stranger experience befell Morgan Robertson, a popular American writer of science fiction whose *Futility* was published in 1898. It described how a giant liner, designed to be unsinkable even if it struck an iceberg at full speed, was built for the transatlantic route; on its first voyage it struck an iceberg and sank with heavy loss of life. The liner was called the *Titan*; and in many of its details – tonnage, number of lifeboats, and so on – it bore a startlingly close resemblance to the *Titanic*, not then even on the drawing board, which was to meet the same fate in 1912.

The Denver psychoanalyst Jule Eisenbud has scrutinised the evidence in *Parapsychology and the Unconscious*, showing where it points to precognition rather than chance coincidence. Certainly Robertson was convinced of the reality of a psychic element in his writings. 'He implicitly believed that some discarnate soul, some spirit entity with literary ability, denied physical expression, had commandeered his body and brain for the purpose of giving to the world the literary gems which made him famous,' a contributor had written in *Morgan Robertson, the Man*, compiled soon after his death. 'He regarded himself as a mere amanuensis, the tool of a "real writer", whose shadowy fingers could not grasp the pen.' When the 'real writer' was uncooperative, Robertson simply had to wait, sometimes for weeks, as he was incapable of putting together as much as a sentence – except when 'commandeered'.

According to Richard Ellman, James Joyce had 'many examples' of what he took to be clairvoyance in his writings (as well as in his everyday life; his daughter's insanity seemed to nourish the faculty in her). Joyce was particularly impressed by the way in which Stephen Dedalus's prediction in *Ulysses* that the treacherous Lynch would come to a bad end was fulfilled when Vincent Cosgrave, the model for Lynch, committed suicide in the Thames. But Ellman relegates this feature of Joyce's authorship to a footnote; and it is only too likely that many a biographer of a famous writer has preferred to leave eccentricities like this – or those of Kipling and his daemon – on the equivalent of the cutting-room floor.

'Is imagination, either in part or whole, a sort of sixth sense?' H. E. Bates asked in his autobiography. 'The theory fascinates, and in the holding of it I am supported by certain strange things that have, from time to time, happened to me as a writer.' Many times he had invented characters for his stories, only to encounter them in real life in the same situations.

In a novella of mine called *Summer in Salamander*, where every incident and character is drawn exclusively by the power of imagination, a woman both rich and selfish sets out, having left her own husband, to destroy, rather after the manner of a spider with a fly, a young man she meets while on holiday on an island. Her name being Vane, I fitted her out, in the story, with an expensive set of matching luggage, each piece stamped with a V. Two years later, travelling by ship to the same island on which the story is set, I saw the set of matching luggage, each piece with its V, going aboard ahead of me and then watched, for the next three or four days, the woman of whom I had written, rich and selfish, proceed to her spider act of destruction.

Oscar Wilde, Bates recalled, had said that life imitates art.

Is it perhaps not also possible that imagination creates life, as it were, by some process of magical foresight, before life itself does? The temptation to say that all human life exists as a preordained pattern is one which has, for many people, a strong appeal. Are some of my stories, in some strange way, preordained? I wish I knew.

POETS

Could anybody, at the end of the nineteenth century, Nietzsche asked, 'possibly have any idea of what poets of a more vigorous period meant by inspiration?' His prose poem *Also Sprach Zarathustra* had come to him – 'perhaps I should rather say, *invaded me*' – through inspiration; but by the time it appeared the influence of positivism and materialism, he feared, had largely obliterated the notion, so he felt he had to describe it:

Provided one has the slightest remnant of superstition left, one can hardly reject completely the idea that one is the mere incarnation, or mouthpiece, or medium of some almighty power. The notion of revelation describes the condition quite simply; by which I mean that something profoundly convulsive and disturbing suddenly becomes visible and audible with indescribable definiteness and exactness. One hears – one does not seek; one takes – one does not ask who gives.

Many poets who would not have regarded themselves as the medium of some almighty power have nevertheless conceded that the production of a poem, at least in its initial stage, is 'less an active than a passive and involuntary process', as A. E. Housman described it. For him, it was a far from romantic process. He would drink a pint of beer – 'a sedative to the brain' – and go for a walk. While thinking of nothing in particular,

only looking at things around me and following the progress of the seasons, there would flow into my mind, with sudden and unaccountable emotion, sometimes a line or two of verse, sometimes a whole stanza at once, accompanied, not preceded, by a vague notion of the poem which they were destined to form part of. Then there would usually be a lull of an hour or so, then perhaps the spring would bubble up again.

If the spring failed to bubble up again, Housman would try to complete it 'by the brain, which was apt to be a matter of trouble and anxiety, involving trial and disappointment, and sometimes ending in failure'. He cited the case of a poem of which two stanzas came into his head, complete, as he was crossing a road; a third came 'with a little coaxing' after tea; but the fourth he had to rewrite thirteen times, and it was more than a year before he was satisfied with it.

It is impossible to make a clear distinction between inspiration in the loose sense of something leaping into consciousness from the subliminal, and the kind which suggests some form of outside intervention. In 'Un Spectacle dans un fauteuil', dedicated to Tennyson, Alfred de Musset claimed that at the moment of composition 'each nerve, each fibre, trembles'.

> *On ne travaille pas – on écoute – on attend,*
> *C'est comme un inconnu qui vous parle à voix basse.*

'The Unknown One', 'the Nameless' – like 'the Guest' – appear to represent the writers' attempt to make a distinction between the throwing up from the subliminal mind of an idea, a simile, a rhyme, a line, or even a couplet, and experiences less easily accounted for, like one which Milton described. 'I last week rendered this ode into heroic verse as I was lying in bed before the day dawned,' he wrote to tell Alexander Gill in 1643, 'without any previous deliberation, but with a certain impelling faculty for which I know not how to account.'

Longfellow had a parallel experience, in his case late one evening when he was sitting relaxed by his fireside, smoking. As he recorded the next day, 'Suddenly it came into my mind to write "The Ballad of the Schooner Hesperus", which I accordingly did.'

He then went to bed, but was unable to sleep; fresh ideas poured into his mind, and he felt compelled to get up to write them down. 'It hardly cost me any effort. It did not come into my mind by line, but by stanzas.'

Some poets have reported being compelled, against their intentions, to write something very different from what they had planned. In 1922 Rilke, then in his forties, sat down to complete some elegies which he was engaged upon. To his astonishment, he found himself writing what turned out to be the first twenty-six sonnets to Orpheus. A year later he recalled what had happened on this occasion, excusing himself in a letter to a friend for the 'lack of consideration' some of them might show for the reader.

Even to me, in their rising up and imposing themselves upon me, they are perhaps the most mysterious, most enigmatic, dictation I have ever endured and performed; the whole first part was written down in a single breathless obedience, between the 2nd and 5th of February 1922, without one word's being in doubt or requiring to be altered. And that at a time when I had got myself ready for another large work, and was already busy with it.

What can be additionally striking about this occasional uprush of inspiration is that on occasion, the poem thus presented has transcended any of the others which the writer has produced. The best-known example was related of Julia Ward Howe by her biographer. Returning from a review of the troops in Washington during the American Civil War, she and her companions sang 'John Brown's Body', and one of them asked her why she did not write some better words to that tune. She had often wished to do so, she replied.

Waking in the gray of the next morning, as she lay waiting for the dawn, the words came to her:
'Mine eyes have seen the glory of the coming of the Lord . . .'
She lay perfectly still. Line by line, stanza by stanza the words came sweeping on with the rhythm of marching feet, pauseless, resistless. She saw the long lines swinging into place before her eyes, heard the voice of the nation speaking through her lips. She waited till the voice was silent, till the last line was ended; then sprang from bed, and groping for pen and paper, scrawled in the gray twilight the 'Battle Hymn of the Republic'. She was used to writing thus; verses often came to her at night, and must

be scribbled in the dark for fear of waking the baby; she crept back into bed, and as she fell asleep she said to herself, 'I like this better than most things I have written.'

It was fortunate for Mrs Howe that she did write down the words. By the morning, she had forgotten them.

But for the 'Battle Hymn', Julia Howe would hardly now be remembered. Although Siegfried Sassoon would still feature in anthologies of World War One poetry, only one of his poems is still familiar. In *Siegfried's Journey* he was to recall that it came to him in a manner quite different from his other verse.

One evening in the middle of April I had an experience which seems worth describing for those who are interested in methods of poetic production. It was a sultry spring night. I was feeling dull-minded and depressed, for no assignable reason. After sitting lethargically in the ground-floor room for about three hours after dinner, I came to the conclusion that there was nothing for it but to take my useless brain to bed.

On my way from the arm-chair to the door I stood by the writing-table. A few words had floated into my head as though from nowhere. In those days I was always on the look-out for a lyric – I wish I could say the same for my present self – so I picked up a pencil and wrote the words on a sheet of note-paper. Without sitting down, I added a second line. It was as if I were remembering rather than thinking. In this mindless, recollecting manner I wrote down my poem in a few minutes. When it was finished I read it through, with no sense of elation, merely wondering how I had come to be writing a poem when feeling so stupid.

Sassoon thereupon went to bed; but next morning, he liked what he had written; and John Masefield, the Poet Laureate, confirmed his opinion of it. 'Everyone Sang' began to find its way into anthologies as soon as it appeared; Sassoon felt justified in claiming that it was almost as well known as Yeats's 'Innisfree'; and its opening, 'Everyone suddenly burst out singing', remains one of the best-known lines of poetry in the language. What continued to baffle Sassoon was that

there was no apparent mental process during its composition. Many of my shorter poems have been written with a sense of emotional release and then improved by revision – often after being put away for a long time. Others have been produced by mental concentration and word-seeking which lasted two or three hours. But there was usually a feeling of having said what I wanted to, with directness and finality. 'Everyone Sang' was composed without emotion, and needed no alteration afterwards. Its rather free form was spontaneous, and unlike any other poem I have written. I wasn't aware of any technical contriving.

And none of his other poems had come to him in the same way. Sassoon did not attempt to account for his experience; John Masefield, Poet Laureate for thirty-seven years, was too well aware of the importance of psychic influences on his life and work to evade admitting them. Once, depressed after a cold winter when snow-drifts were still lying deep in late April, he came across a bank of primroses. 'As I looked at them a voice within me that I did not know (a man's voice) said clearly, "The Spring is beginning."' Heartened, he walked home, 'feeling that the difficulties that beset me in what I was then trying to write would now clear away'. They did not clear away immediately, but a little later, unable to progress with what he was writing, he was crossing a country fence when he found himself saying, 'Now I will make a poem about a blackguard who becomes converted.'

Instantly the poem appeared to me in its complete form, with every detail distinct; the opening lines poured out upon the page as fast as I could write them down. I had written between fourteen and twenty lines before I reached home. I then lit the lamp and sat down to write some sixty-odd lines more.

Masefield was alone in the house at the time, deep in the countryside, and it was almost midnight.

Suddenly, as I wrote, the door of the room in which I wrote flung itself noisily wide open.

Do not think that I was scared: no, no; I was terrified, almost out of my wits.

Why the door had opened in that way, I do not know. It had never opened like that before, and never did again. The hint was not lost upon me: I packed up my writing and went to bed.

The voice that had told him, 'The Spring is beginning', Masefield realised, had told him the truth. He gave up the project he had been floundering on: 'since then, I have known that by instinct and aptitude I am a story-teller.'

Keats believed he had a spirit 'control' – a very eminent one. 'I remember your saying,' he wrote to Benjamin Haydon,

that you had notions of a good genius presiding over you. I have lately had the same thought, for things which I do half at random are afterwards confirmed by my judgment in a dozen features of propriety. Is it too daring to fancy that Shakespeare is this presider?

William Blake's verse was also, as he put it, written when 'commanded by the spirits'; often 'from immediate dictation, twelve or sometimes twenty or thirty lines at a time without premeditation and even against my will', so that a poem which might appear to the reader to be the fruit of protracted labour would in fact have been produced without effort. In her biography (1927) Mona Wilson was to point out that had Blake 'literally believed that he wrote every word by command of the spirits, correction would have been obviously a profanity'; the notion, therefore, was 'not only superfluous, but was clearly disproved by the existence of his corrections'. This was totally to misunderstand Blake, who would have assumed that he had misheard or misinterpreted the 'dictation' if he saw it needed correction.

In recent years, the poet most susceptible to psychic influences has been W. B. Yeats. Adequately to deal with Yeats's occultism, and its influence on his career, would require a book. In fact it has one: *Yeats and the Occult*, essays edited by George Mills Harper and published in 1976. It was also sympathetically surveyed in Richard Ellman's 1949 biography. Both works show why it is extremely difficult to separate the occult in his poetry from other influences – even his Irish nationalism.

The fairy tales Yeats heard as a child were not, to him, to be taken seriously only by children, like Father Christmas. Fairies, in Irish lore, are not the thistledown creatures of the English tradition, they are powers, for good or ill. Yeats felt able to fuse them into his theosophical beliefs as 'the lesser spiritual moods of that universal mind, wherein every mood is a soul and every thought a body'. In the 1890s he became a member of the Order of the Golden Dawn, and was introduced to the practice of magic by McGregor Mathers, becoming convinced that it ought to help him to find the secret of writing great poetry. 'All men, certainly all imaginative men, must be for ever casting forth enchantments, glamours, illusions,' he was to argue in his essay on the subject.

Have not poetry and music arisen, as it seems, out of the sounds the enchanters made to help their imagination to enchant, to charm, to bind with a spell themselves and the passers-by? Just as the magician or the poet enchants and charms and binds with a spell his own mind, when he would enchant the minds of others, so did the enchanter create or reveal for himself as well as for others the supernatural artist, or genius.

To the old Fenian John O'Leary, who understandably wanted Yeats to dedicate his talents – as his beloved Maud Gonne was doing – to the nationalist cause, Yeats pointed out that his poetry was the more important pursuit of his life, and the study of magic had been essential to it.

If I had not made magic my constant study I could not have written a single word of my Blake book, nor would 'The Countess Cathleen' ever have come to exist. The mystical life is the centre of all that I do and all that I think and all that I write. It holds to my work the same relation that the philosophy of Godwin holds to the work of Shelley and I have always considered myself a voice of what I believe to be a greater renaissance – the revolt of the soul against the intellect – now beginning in the world.

Although in the 1890s and in the Edwardian era Yeats immersed himself in magic, experimenting with formulae and ritual to conjure up spirits, having séances with mediums and examining alleged miracles, he had the good fortune to encounter one of the shrewdest and sanest of British psychical researchers, Everard Feilding, who became a friend and mentor, and Yeats always kept a critical eye on what he witnessed. His hopes of fusing poetry and magic were to be disappointed until at a séance in 1912 with an American medium, Mrs Etta Wriedt, 'Leo Africanus' came through to offer himself as Yeats's spirit control; and although Yeats was initially suspicious, 'Leo' offered enough information to convince him that his belief that magic and poetry might be fused had not been entirely an illusion. This was followed up with the help of Elizabeth Radcliffe, who passed messages to him which she obtained in automatic writing, and which he thought provided further valuable evidence for the reality of spirit communication. He had already affirmed his belief in the reality of daemons on the

Socratic model; 'Leo' not merely confirmed him in the belief, but as Ellman put it, gave him 'supernatural sanction for the pose he had built up since childhood'.

The fusion became complete for Yeats after his marriage in 1917 to Georgina Hyde-Lees. She tried automatic writing, and in the first attempt, after a few meaningless lines,

suddenly she thought that her hand was seized by a superior power. In the fragmentary sentences that were scribbled on the paper her amazed husband saw the rudiments of the system which he had spent his early life trying to evoke through vision, and his middle age trying to formulate through research. Here, in his own home, was miracle without qualification. The bush was burning at last.

Had Yeats died before his marriage, Ellman went on to surmise, he would have been remembered as 'a remarkable minor poet who had achieved a diction more powerful than that of his contemporaries but who, except in a handful of poems, did not have much to say with it'; had he not married Georgina, he might have continued to go to séances and to accept what emerged from 'controls' and 'communicators' without being able to adapt them for his own needs. As things worked out, he became a Nobel Prize winner in 1923 and, although that might have been taken by some literary figures of the time as a kiss of death, further rehabilitated himself in their eyes in the 'Byzantium' period which followed – over-heavily laced though some of his poems were with esoteric symbolism. 'Innisfree' holds its place in anthologies, and the Irish do not forget '1916'; but it is the later poems, spurred on by the nagging 'Plato's ghost', that have made his reputation secure.

'Do we delude ourselves in thinking we possess and command our own souls?' Jung wondered. The psyche, he felt sure, could not be arbitrarily confined within our heads:

Even in our midst, the poet now and then catches sight of the figures that people the night world – the spirits, demons and gods. He knows that a purposiveness outreaching human ends is the life-giving secret for man.

Contemporary poets, however, are reluctant to discuss the sources of their inspiration – except when their muse has departed, and they have gone on to make their names in other fields. 'I can point to several works of mine which were "given" to me, pretty well complete,' the journalist and novelist Philip Oakes claims – he was one of the members of 'the Movement' in the 1950s, along with Philip Larkin, Kingsley Amis and others.

My task was simply to sit still and listen to words which I could hear distinctly in my head, and then sometimes edit and arrange what I heard. It was not like dictation, but rather as though some other self was speaking the lines, often hesitantly, but always with a conviction that the verse would complete itself; that its form was already decided. There was also a visual accompaniment. I couldn't actually read the lines, but the shape of the verse on the page was clear. On most of the occasions that I recall the 'gift' of a poem (which, as far as I know, had not been touched off by any other reading or experience) it took place in the early morning when I felt rested and happy.

Age must have something to do with it, Oakes thinks. 'I was "given" poems in my twenties and thirties. No doubt I was more receptive then.'

MUSICIANS

Music, Frederic Myers commented in his study of 'The Subliminal Consciousness', appeared to have little relation to mundane requirements; it seemed to be a subliminal capacity, hard to account for on what had become the accepted Darwinian theory of evolution.

We know that it is like something discovered, not like something manufactured; like wine found in a walled-up cellar, rather than like furniture made in the workshop above. And the subjective sensations of the musician himself accord with this view of the essentially subliminal character of the gift with which he deals. In no direction is 'genius' or 'inspiration' more essential to true success. It is not from careful poring over the mutual relation of musical notes that the masterpieces of melody have been born.

The Tudor composer William Byrd acknowledged the existence of 'a mysterious hidden power', so that for anyone who carefully pondered over the divine mysteries, 'the most appropriate strains occur of their own accord in some strange way, and offer themselves copiously even when one's mind is sluggish and inactive.' The music of *Madame Butterfly*, Puccini claimed, 'was dictated to me by God; I was merely instrumental in putting it on paper.'

Richard Strauss felt he was being dictated to in his compositions, 'by more than an earthly power'.

Stravinsky in his autobiography recalled that to his surprise, as his mind at the time was full of other concerns, he had a 'vision' of what was to materialise as *The Rite of Spring*: he saw, in his mind's eye, 'sage elders, seated in a circle, watching a young girl dance herself to death' as a propitiatory sacrifice. (Diaghilev immediately recognised its ballet potential.) Later, the music came to Stravinsky when he was in a state of exaltation and exhaustion: 'I heard, and I wrote what I heard. I am the vessel through which the *Sacre* passed.' For Elgar, according to his biographer Basil Maine, composing was 'an almost unconscious process, so that he feels he can take no credit for what is going on and what ultimately happens'; of his greatest works, 'he regards himself as the medium – the all but unconscious medium by which they have come into being.'

A more elaborate account of the activity of a composer's muse was provided by Mozart, in a letter to 'Baron von P':

You say, you should like to know my way of composing, and what method I follow in works of some length. I can really say no more on the subject than the following. When I am, as it were, completely myself, entirely alone, and of good cheer – say, travelling in a carriage, or walking after a good meal, or during the night when I cannot sleep; it is on such occasions that my ideas flow best and most abundantly. *Whence* and *how* they come, I know not; nor can I force them. Those ideas that please me I retain in memory, and I am accustomed, as I have been told, to hum them to myself. If I continue in this way, it soon occurs to me how I may turn this or that morsel to account, so as to make a good dish of it, that is to say, agreeably to the rules of counterpoint, to the peculiarities of the various instruments, etc.

All this fires my soul, and, provided I am not disturbed, my subject enlarges itself, becomes methodised and defined, and the whole, though it be long, stands almost complete and finished in my mind, so that I can survey it, like a fine picture or a beautiful statue, at a glance. Nor do I hear in my imagination the parts *successively*, but I hear them, as it were, all at once [*gleich alles zusammen*]. What a delight this is I cannot tell! All this inventing, this producing, takes place in a pleasing lively dream. Still, the actual hearing of the *tout ensemble* is after all the best. What has been thus produced I do not easily forget, and this is perhaps the best gift I have my Divine Maker to thank for.

The actual committing to paper, the letter continued, would be done quickly, and rarely differed from what his imagination had provided.

In his biography of Mozart, Otto Jahn dismissed this letter as 'incontestably a fabrication' as it stood; 'as it is impossible to determine how far it is founded upon truth, it must remain entirely out of the question.' But Jahn gave no reason for his assumption that a letter which had long been taken to be genuine, and often cited, had been faked. The most likely explanation is that he was so deeply impressed by Mozart's skill as a composer, and so anxious to impress it on readers, that he could not bear to allow the entire credit to be taken away from the man and given, in effect, to his muse. Jahn was an archaeologist by profession, an academic at a time when positivism and rationalism ruled. To have allowed that Mozart 'heard' his music in the way described in the letter would have been tantamount to putting him in Lombroso's 'degenerative psychosis' category. At the time Jahn was writing the book, in the early 1880s, the scientific establishment had not even accepted the existence of an unconscious mind, let alone a subliminal mind with creative powers. Jahn, surely, was simply trying to do justice to his hero.

It is hard to think what anybody could have expected to gain from faking the letter. A forger, anxious to sell his wares, would surely have thought of something more spicy and scandalous. Its contents, too, fit well with what is known about Mozart's methods of composition from other sources. They also help to explain how such a phenomenal range of marvellous works could have flowed from the, in some ways, immature young man portrayed recently, and not unfairly, in Peter Shaffer's *Amadeus*.

The most detailed exploration of a composer's sources of inspiration are to be found in Tchaikovsky's letters in 1878 to Nadejda von Meck. When she asked him if he had a programme in mind, while composing a symphony, he replied that this was a hard question to answer.

How interpret those vague feelings which pass through one during the composition of an instrumental work, without reference to any definite subject? It is a purely lyrical process. A kind of musical shriving of the soul, in which there is an incrustation of material which flows forth again in notes, just as the lyrical poet pours himself out in verse.

The germ of a composition, he went on,

comes suddenly and unexpectedly. If the soil is ready – that is to say, if the disposition for work is there – it takes root with extraordinary force and rapidity, shoots up through the earth, puts forth branches, leaves and, finally, blossoms. I cannot define the creative process in any other way than by this simile. The great difficulty is that the germ must appear at a favourable moment, the rest goes of itself. It would be vain to try to put into words that immeasurable sense of bliss which comes over me directly a new idea awakens in me and begins to assume a definite form. I forget everything and behave like a madman. Everything within me starts pulsing and quivering; hardly have I begun the sketch ere one thought follows another.

Tchaikovsky described this state as 'somnambulistic'. Interruptions such as a ring at the bell had the shock effect from which sleepwalkers were traditionally supposed to suffer if abruptly woken; 'dreadful indeed'. The trance state lost, he would then have to resort to craftsmanship to do his best to join up what he had composed under its influence. Still, he realised that this was inevitable. 'If that condition of mind and soul, which we call *inspiration*, lasted long enough without intermission, no artist could survive it.'

A few days later Tchaikovsky elaborated on the theme – warming to it because, he claimed, he had never before 'had any opportunity of confiding to anyone these hidden utterances of my inner life'. Frau von Meck must not listen to those who claimed that composition was an intellectual affair; 'the only music capable of moving and touching us is that which flows from the depths of a composer's soul when he is stirred by inspiration.' Foreshadowing Maeterlinck, Tchaikovsky personalised his inspiration; to him it was 'the guest', who did not always respond to the initial invitation, and who always needed to be wooed by work, but who had to be waited for if anything worthwhile was to be accomplished.

That summer, Tchaikovsky returned to the subject. 'An artist leads a double life,' he told Nadejda, 'an everyday human life and an artistic life.' He went on to reiterate what he had told her earlier, with added emphasis on the trance condition necessary for the composition to flow. No effort of will was required.

It is only necessary to obey our inward promptings, and if our material life does not crush our artistic life under its weight of depressing circumstances, the work progresses with inconceivable rapidity. Everything else is forgotten, the soul throbs with an incomprehensible and indescribable excitement, so that almost before we can follow this swift flight of inspiration, time passes literally unreckoned and unobserved.

There is something *somnambulistic* about this condition. *On ne s'entend pas vivre.*

Again, he insisted, it was no use sitting back and waiting for the 'guest' to come; he had to work on, hoping it would come. But even if mundane distractions would normally drive the 'guest' away, he might stay unbidden.

Sometimes I observe with curiosity that uninterrupted activity, which – independent of the subject of any conversation I may be carrying on – continues its course in that department of my brain which is devoted to music. Sometimes it takes a preparatory form – that is, the consideration of all details that concern the elaboration of some projected work; another time it may be an entirely new and independent musical idea, and I make an effort to hold it fast in my memory. Whence does it come? It is an inscrutable mystery.

Mozart attributed his gift to his Divine Maker; Tchaikovsky to his 'guest'. Wagner believed in clairvoyance, of a kind which would now be described as extra-sensory perception, mediated by his daemon. There is only one state which can surpass the musician's, he wrote in his study of Beethoven,

the state of the saint; and that especially because it is enduring, and incapable of being clouded, whilst the ecstatic clairvoyance of a musician alternates with the ever recurring state of individual consciousness, which must be thought all the more miserable, as in the inspired state he was lifted higher above the barriers of individuality.

When Wagner was composing the *Ring* 'he must have seen and heard it all, with his inner eye and ear, very much as it would be at the finish', his biographer Ernest Newman considered, citing the way in which, dozing on a hard chair, Wagner 'fell into that cataleptic state that is the prime condition for all artistic creation of the highest kind'. Wagner himself described it:

The rush and roar soon took musical shape within my brain as the chord of E flat major, surging incessantly in broken chords: these declared themselves as melodic figurations of increasing motion, yet the pure triad of E flat major never changed, but seemed by its steady persistence to impart infinite significance to the element in which I was sinking. I awoke from my half-sleep in terror, feeling as though the waves were now rushing high above my head. I at once recognised that the orchestral prelude to the *Rhinegold*, which a long time I must have carried about within me, yet had never been able to fix definitely, had at last come to being in me.

Eighteen years later he recalled the episode. It had not merely given him the prelude; it had also shaped his future career by deciding him, in spite of his reluctance to leave Italy, to return home.

Be it a daemon or a genius that often rules us in hours of crisis – enough: stretched sleepless in a hotel in Spezia there came to me the prompting for the music for my *Rhinegold*; at once I returned to my melancholy home to carry out that immense work the fate of which now, above all else, binds me to Germany.

Other composers have spoken of occasions when they have been inspired through what they have come to believe have been telepathic premonitions. Absorbed in composing some new pieces in 1833, Schumann recalled, he began to feel haunted.

There is a certain passage which obsessed me, and someone seemed to repeat after me, from the depths of his hearth: 'Ach, Gott!' While I was composing I saw funereal things, coffins, despairing faces. When I had finished I sought for a title. The only one that came to my mind was *Leichenphantasie* (Funereal Fantasy). Wasn't it extraordinary? I was so much upset that tears came to my eyes; I really did not know why; it was impossible for me to discover a reason for this sadness. Then came Thérèse's letter and everything was explained.

The explanation was that his brother Edward had just died.

According to a friend, when Saint-Saëns was young 'he heard his own inspiration express itself and he had only to listen, like Socrates, to his genius'; and Saint-Saëns himself confirmed that one of his best-known compositions came to him as if it were a farewell from a dead friend.

It was in January, 1871, on the last day of the war. I was at the front lines, at

Arcueil-Cashan. We had just dined upon an excellent horse, of which we had made a good meat broth, and had gathered a great many dandelions, the roots of which, at that time of the year, are fully developed; in a word, a dinner that had satisfied us all, and we were on that day as gay as we could be in such circumstances. Suddenly I heard, running through my head, the musical dirge of melancholy chords which I have since made the beginning of my Requiem. I felt in the depths of my being the presentiment that a misfortune was happening to me. A profound anguish overwhelmed me.

It was at that very moment that Henri Regnault had been killed; I was bound to him by the closest friendship. The news of his death caused me such grief that I fell ill and was obliged to stay in bed for three days.

Relating the story to his friend Camille Flammarion, Saint-Saëns commented that he had 'experienced the reality of telepathy before the word was invented. How right you are in thinking that established science does not know the human being, and that we have everything to learn!'

In recent years the compositions of Rosemary Brown have attracted attention. She does not claim to be a composer herself; she is taken over, she feels, by celebrated composers from the past, who use her as a vehicle for works of their own. As a child, Mrs Brown 'saw' a man who appeared to come from a previous century, who told her that he would help to make her a musical celebrity. Dutifully she tried to learn to play the piano, until it became clear that she would never be even a competent performer; but years later, 'Franz Liszt', whom she recognised from his portraits as the man who had appeared to her earlier, appeared again, to be followed by Beethoven, Chopin and others, who dictated scores to her. Opinions vary about their musical merit, but it is not seriously contested that they sound like the work (or remarkably close to it) of whichever composer is involved; and they flow through her with extraordinary rapidity, as if by dictation.

The pianist John Lill puts a rather different interpretation on spirit influence. He feels sure, he said in 1980 in a BBC television programme (in which Rosemary Brown had taken down dictation from Chopin), that at its best, her composition 'gives off a spark of style which she could never create herself; it must emanate from a spiritual infusion from that composer.' But he does not believe that the composer's spirit is actually responsible for her compositions, or anybody else's. When composers die, their work ceases; but their inspiration may continue, 'an infinite thing', for those who have an affinity with them. When Lill gives concerts, he has found, he can play far better if he is able to empty his mind and let it be used by 'these benevolent forces'.

Ian Parrott, professor emeritus of music at the University College of Wales, Aberystwyth, agrees that there can be an extra-sensory input. Serving in the Middle East during the Second World War he managed to obtain leave to visit the temple at Luxor, which had a very powerful impact on him.

Subsequently I wrote a symphonic impression, 'Luxor', which was awarded the first prize at the Royal Philharmonic Society in 1949, and first performed by the London Symphony Orchestra under Sir Adrian Boult in 1950. The main theme had certainly 'come' to me – it even forced its way through – I feel it could never happen again. After it had been put on at the National Eisteddfod at Aberystwyth in 1952 Dr Frederic Wood, who was a music adjudicator there, came up to me and (with his knowledge of Ancient Egypt from a medium) said that the main theme, a Lydian mode melody, was almost certainly of the period of the 18th Dynasty, more than three thousand years ago – which I certainly did not know.

Parrott is impressed by some of Rosemary Brown's work – 'I think "Crübelei" from Liszt is stylistically outstanding' – and notes that it has also been praised by a leading Liszt expert, Humphrey Searle. 'The mind of man is surely not a container like a bucket,' Parrott concludes. 'It has no bottom, nor is it confined to the individual, like a personal possession. More likely, we are "plugged in" to the source of life, as a bulb is to the electric light supply.'

ARTISTS

When King David told his son Solomon, 'The Lord hath chosen thee to build an house for the sanctuary; be strong and do it,' he went on to give Solomon detailed plans for the whole building, from the porch to the upper chambers, the inner parlours, and 'the place of the mercy seat'. All this, David explained, 'the Lord made me understand in writing by his hand upon me, even all the works of this plan.'

William Blake had a different conception of 'the Lord'; but he, too, was in no doubt that he was the instrument of some higher purpose, assisted by the spirits of dead men and women who were still in the same service. After the death of his brother Robert, to whom he was deeply attached, William began to communicate with him; 'in hours of solitude and inspiration', as his biographer Alexander Gilchrist put it, Robert 'would appear and speak to the poet in consolatory dream, in warning, or helpful vision'. The most dramatic of these appearances occurred when the *Songs of Innocence* and the accompanying designs were ready, but William lacked the means to publish them. He could be his own engraver, but not his own compositor.

The subject of anxious daily thought passed – as anxious meditation does with us all – into the domain of dreams and (in his case) of visions. In one of these a happy inspiration befell, not, of course, without supernatural agency. After intently thinking by day, and dreaming by night, during long weeks and months, of his cherished object, the image of the vanished pupil and brother at last blended with it. In a vision of the night, the form of Robert stood before him, and revealed the wished-for secret, directing him to the technical mode by which could be produced a facsimile of song and design. On his rising in the morning, Mrs Blake went out with half-a-crown, all the money they had in the world, and of that laid out one shilling and tenpence on the simple materials necessary for setting in practice the new revelation. On that one shilling and tenpence he started what was to prove a principal means of support through his future life – the series of poems and writings illustrated by coloured plates, often highly finished afterwards by hand – which became the most efficient and durable means of revealing Blake's genius to the world.

In the catalogue to his 1809 exhibition of his pictures, Blake insisted that the spirits, to him, were as real as the angels had been to the Old Testament prophets. They were not, 'as the modern philosophy supposes, a cloudy vapour or a nothing; they are organised and minutely articulated beyond all that the mortal and perishing nature can produce.' He had found that, more and more, his style was being moulded by his angels; but 'though I call them mine, I know that they are not mine, being of the same opinion with Milton when he says that the Muse visits his slumbers and awakes and governs his song when morn purples the East.'

That some artists have appeared to produce their paintings through their muse having a hand upon them was commented upon by Hazlitt in his essay on 'whether genius is conscious of its powers'. The mystery of artistic inspiration has never been better expressed than in his discussion of the influence of the muse as an 'involuntary silent impulse' working through artists, notably Correggio and Rembrandt:

It is not known that Correggio ever saw a picture of any great master. He lived and died obscurely in an obscure village. We have few of his works but they are all perfect. What truth, what grace, what angelic sweetness are there! Not one line or tone is not divinely soft or exquisitely fair; the painter's mind rejecting, by a natural process, all that is discordant, coarse or unpleasing. The whole is an emanation of pure thought. The work grew under his hands as of itself, and came out without a flaw, like the diamond from the rock. He knew not what he did . . .

'And thou too, Rembrandt,' Hazlitt continued. 'Thou wert a man of genius, if ever painter was a man of genius!'

Did you know what you were about, or did you not paint much as it happened? Oh! If you had thought once about yourself, or anything but the subject, it would have been all over with 'the glory, the intuition, the amenity', the dream had fled, the spell had been broken.

The fact that Correggio knew not what he did was not intended to imply that he was a poor craftsman. On the contrary, Hazlitt contrasted the 'facility' of a Rubens unfavourably with 'the slow, patient, laborious execution of Correggio, Leonardo da Vinci and Andrea del Sarto'. Whatever role inspiration had in the making of an artist, the assumption then was that it needed to be subordinated to sheer professional skill in the actual putting of paint onto canvas. Flattered though George Moore was at being asked by Manet to sit for his portrait, he was disconcerted to find that Manet seemed to let instinct take over; he 'matched the tints without premeditation'. (The end product, making Moore look like a drowned man fished out of a river, must have confirmed his doubts.)

Manet's successors carried on the liberation movement. 'I take colours,' Cézanne explained, 'and they become objects without my thinking about them.' Picasso claimed: 'Painting is stronger than

I am; it makes me do what it wants.' At the start of each picture, he felt, 'there is somebody who works with me.' For Klee, his hand was simply a tool, 'remotely controlled. It is not my head which functions there but something else, something higher and more remote, somewhere. I must have powerful friends there, light ones but also dark.' The painter, he insisted, must not have an objective purpose; he might know a great deal, 'but he only knows it subsequently'.

The surrealists went further. 'The words "unconscious" and "automatic" were fundamental,' Klee's biographer Werner Haftman has recalled. To Breton, surrealism was 'purely psychic automatism, which sets itself the aim of expressing that which thought dictates, independent of every control by reason'. Stuck in a seaside inn in wet weather, Max Ernst looked at leaves, frayed sacking and whatever else was available, letting *frottage* conjure up visions from them. The drawings which resulted, he felt, were in a sense not his own.

The *frottage* process simply depends on intensifying the mind's capacity for nervous excitement, using the appropriate technical means, excluding all conscious directing of the mind (towards reason, taste, or morals) and reducing to a minimum the part played by him formerly known as the 'author' of the work. The process, in consequence, shows up as a true equivalent of what we now call *automatic writing*. The author is present as a spectator, indifferent or impassioned, at the birth of his own work, and observes the phases of his own development. Just as the poet's place, since the celebrated *Letter of a Clairvoyant*, consists in writing at the dictation of something that makes itself articulate within him, so the artist's role is to gather together and then give out that which makes itself *visible* within him.

Trying to reduce his own *active* participation 'so as to widen the active field of the mind's capacity for hallucination', Ernst found, 'I succeeded in being present *as a spectator* at the birth of all my works after 10 August 1925' – the day of the discovery of *frottage*.

Ernst claimed, 'I have done my best *to make my soul monstrous*.' Some critics have feared that Francis Bacon has taken the same road. He, too, has stressed that he does not feel entirely responsible for his paintings. They are not planned in detail – not, that is, in advance. 'I want a very ordered image,' he said in the course of a radio programme in 1966, 'but I want it to come about by chance.'

Of his friend Louis le Brocquy, Bacon has written that he belongs to a category of artists that has always existed 'who are aware of the vast and potent possibilities of inventing ways by which fact and appearance can be reconjugated'; an awareness which has led le Brocquy to adopt the technique (or perhaps it would be nearer the mark to say that he has allowed a technique to adopt him) which he described in an interview in 1957, after his 'The Family' had won an award at the Venice Biennale. He makes discoveries while he is at work; 'the painting itself dictates to an enormous extent, it may seem to others to be a deliberate act but in point of fact, it seems to me to be almost autonomous; it seems to me to emerge gradually under one's hands, not because of them.' This is a theme he has since returned to in an interview in *Art International*. 'Accident is extremely important to me,' he explains. Working on his heads of Yeats, Joyce and others, he would begin by making what he describes as 'gestures' with a brush,

and sometimes the suggestion of an image – a kind of *objet trouvé*, if you like – begins to emerge. Sometimes not. But those gestures almost always turn out to be significant if one is attentive to their possibilities. They seem to have a queer logic of their own. In my case, all I can say is that there has to be an element of accident, or discovery, or surprise all the way along, so that the emergent image is not so much made by me as imposing itself on me, accident by accident, with its own autonomous life.

'Accident by accident' might have been used by Jackson Pollock, to describe the development of his technique in the 1930s. 'To prepare a canvas he would put it on the floor and spatter it – that was the underpainting, spatter and drip – then let it lie there while he looked at it,' Mervyn Jules, the socialist realist painter who for a time worked in the same studio, recalled. 'Images began to appear for him. It was a stimulation, and he believed Michelangelo, who said he saw forms in clouds and such. Everything an artist sees becomes part of his visceral bank – exists in the subconscious. When the need arises it comes forward.'

Pollock believed he enjoyed psychic powers. On one occasion following a storm he warned Conrad Marca-Relli that they must go to his house, as it was going to be flooded. When they arrived, the sun was shining; but Marca-Relli allowed Pollock to bully him into taking all his paintings off the floor and putting them on tables. 'Do you know,' he told Pollock's biographer Jeffrey Potter, 'in about a minute there was a flash flood.' It left the floor of the house four feet under water. And in *Love Affair: A Memoir of Jackson Pollock* Ruth Kligman has described how she watched him walk in front of a hired tractor using the technique of a dowser, and every time he pointed down, a stone would be found and unearthed which could not have been detected by ordinary vision.

Pollock came to believe his hand was guided, when he was using the technique which bought him fame and notoriety. By the time the art critic Clement Greenberg named him among 'The Best?' in *Time* magazine in 1948, 'Jackson felt he had mastered the control of his pouring technique to the extent that he could honestly say the effect was not accidental, but directed,' Potter recalls; the technique came to be called 'action painting' but 'the most accurate (albeit undramatic) name was given to the style by James Brooks: 'direct painting'. 'Automatic painting' would have been even more accurate; 'direct', in this context, has ordinarily been used to describe cases where no human hand does the work – as in the writing on the wall in the Old Testament story of Belshazzar's feast.

Automatic drawing has been described by Matthew Manning in *The Link*, his account of the poltergeist disturbances which plagued him and those around him at home and in school: movements of objects, showers of pebbles, and so on. At the suggestion of a parapsychologist he tried allowing his hand to be taken over to produce drawings, and they began to provide such convincing imitations of the work of celebrated artists that they could have been mistaken for originals by all but the most experienced judges. Although he could only draw indifferently, when he was trying, these drawings flowed from him without effort, in minutes, rather than hours or days; and they relieved him of the poltergeist.

'I have a very odd story to tell,' the columnist Angus McGill of the *Evening Standard* wrote on 14 August 1985. It concerned Penelope James, 'a beautiful and cultivated woman', the wife of a London property developer. Sitting one day watching television with a pad on her knee, she found that she had covered it, without even realising that she was drawing, with horrendous figures. She was doing a painting course at the time in Atlanta, Georgia, and hurriedly reverted to straight painting: 'I was freaked,' as she put it in a radio interview. Then she thought she would try again, but observe what happened.

I was just watching what I was doing, and seeing these things come out. The hand would go from one side of the paper to the other. I actually had no idea what was going to come out at the end. At that time I think they were still pretty horrendous; so I said to myself, if something pretty comes out, then I won't mind. Having said that to myself, from then onwards whenever I held the pencil, pretty faces began to come out.

Penelope James has no idea why she should be able to draw – and, recently, paint in oils – in this way, different from what she would consider to be her own approach, and very much speeded up. 'I've tried to find a rational explanation,' she says. Imagination? Muse? Tuning in to some collective unconscious? In the autumn of 1986, visitors to the W. H. Patterson Gallery in Albemarle Street, London, were able to examine both her styles in an exhibition, and offer, if they wished, their own explanations.

THE CANDLE OF VISION

It is unusual, now, to hear echoes of Freud's portrait of the artist as a psychoneurotic, or of B. F. Skinner's view that art is produced by conditioned reflexes, or by accident. But it is by no means uncommon for people to accept that there is nothing to artistic inspiration that cannot be accounted for along rationalist lines; a view presented in such surveys as Professor Robert Weisberg's *Creativity: Genius and other Myths* (1986).

Weisberg's purpose, he explains, is 'to dispel some of the romance and mystery surrounding creativity by showing that many of the "facts" which the "genius" view assumes are true are not facts at all. They are really like myths, stories not based on fact which attempt to explain some natural phenomena.' But Weisberg's way with 'facts' can be judged by his comment on the letter Mozart wrote describing how compositions delivered themselves to him: 'There is strong evidence that he never wrote that letter.' Wisely, he does not disclose just how weak that evidence is. Mozart's 'excellent memory', he goes on to explain, 'might have enabled him to produce completed compositions on paper that had already been more laboriously worked out in his head'. How did they come into his head? 'A plausible answer is that they came from the unconscious.'

Well, yes; but *how* did Mozart's unconscious fashion such a profusion of marvellous symphonies, concertos and other works? What Weisberg is presumably trying to establish is that there is no need to invoke God, or daemon, or muse, or a superconscious self capable of tuning in to the music of the spheres. But he can establish this to his own satisfaction only by blandly ignoring the evidence which contradicts it.

Unquestionably creativity in music, art and literature can often be accounted for without recourse to belief in external sources, tapped by extra-sensory perception. But if it is conceded that ESP exists, we have to accept that music, pictures or stories which the imagination provides us with are not necessarily our own; as George Russell – Æ – felt compelled to recognise, early in his life. Before he established his reputation as author, playwright, poet and artist, he would seize opportunities to allow his imagination free rein.

Once in an idle interval in my work I sat with my face pressed in my hands, and in that dimness pictures began flickering in my brain. I saw a little dark shop, the counter before me, and behind it an old man fumbling with some papers, a man so old that his fingers had lost swiftness and precision. Deeper in the store was a girl, red-haired, with grey watchful eyes fixed on the old man. I saw that to enter the shop one must take two steps downwards from a cobbled pavement without.

Æ could have used it as the scene for one of his tales or verses, and neither he nor his readers would have regarded it as anything but the product of his imagination. But Æ happened to describe his vision to a young man who was working in the same office.

and I found that what I had seen was his father's shop. All my imaginations – the old man, his yellow-white beard, his fumbling movement, the watchful girl, the colour, the steps, the cobbled pavement – were not imaginations of mine in any true sense, for while I was in a vacant mood my companion had been thinking of his home, and his brain was populous with quickened memories, and they had invaded my own mind.

How many thousand times, Æ asked himself in *The Candle of Vision*, 'are we invaded by such images, and there is no speculation over them?' And if he *had* used his vision in a story, and gone on to describe what was happening elsewhere in the house, might he still not have been 'adventuring in another's life'? While a writer thinks he is imagining a character he may, 'so marvellous are the hidden ways, be really interpreting a being actually existing, brought into psychic contact with us by some affinity of sentiment or soul'.

Recalling this experience in *Song and its Foundations*, Æ pointed out that 'there was no "identity of emotion". It was only the transfer of images from an active to a vacant mind.' The fact that the vision came to him *ab extra* made it no more significant than if it had come from his imagination. But there could be more to it, he felt: the transmission may feed inspiration where there *is* identity of emotion.

I have often thought the great masters, the Shakespeares and Balzacs, endowed more generously with a rich humanity, may, without knowing it, have made their hearts a place where the secrets of many hearts could be told; and they wove into drama or fiction, thinking all the while it was imagination or art of their own, characters they had never met in life, but which were real and revealed more of themselves in that profundity of being than if they had met and spoken day by day where the truth of life hides itself under many disguises.

Certainly there are numerous indications in the plays and poems of Shakespeare's awareness of psychic forces at work, notably the eighty-sixth sonnet:

> Was it his spirit, by spirits taught to write
> Above a mortal pitch, that struck me dead?
> No, neither he, nor his compeers by night
> Giving him aid . . .

In Shakespeare, Æ believed, 'consciousness had transcended the dream state, and come to a magical awakening beyond which in India is called spirit waking'. It was in this state, 'higher than dream, that the supreme works of art are created'.

May it not also be that in the same state, lesser writers create lesser works, which transcend their normal capabilities? Again and again, they have described how they have been taken over as J. B. Priestley was, writing the second act of *Time and the Conways* (in it, one of the family dreams what they are going to be like in twenty years' time), widely regarded as the most impressive single act in all his plays. 'It seemed to cost me no more thought and trouble than dashing off a letter to a friend. Page after page, scene after scene, went off effortlessly, without a correction.' It took him only a couple of days, with no black coffee or wet towels around his head; 'and what I wrote then, with only two or three tiny alterations, was rehearsed, okayed, and afterwards printed'.

Is there any discernible difference between this and automatic writing? Only that Priestley was achieving what he wanted to achieve, an act in a play, whereas most automatic writing, even when the writer is conscious of what is appearing, is not to the writer's own design. But the link with what is commonly regarded as mediumship is surely close; as Gustave Geley, who gave up a brilliant scientific career to study psychic phenomena, was to find in the course of his research in the early 1920s. The state of mind of a poet, an artist or a philosopher composing under the influence of inspiration 'is, at bottom, identical with the secondary state of the medium', he maintained. 'Rousseau covering pages of writing without reflection or effort, in a state of rapture which drew tears, de Musset listening to the mysterious "genius" who dictated his verses, Socrates listening to his daemon, Schopenhauer refusing to believe that his unexpected and unsought postulates were his own work, all behaved exactly like mediums.'

The eminent philosopher/physicist Sir Oliver Lodge elaborated on this theme.

The process is called 'inspiration' in the higher stages, and sometimes 'possession' in the lower. Both the conscious and the subconscious part of the mind appear to be affected by the process; it is of all grades, and various degrees of value. To the higher grades of this phenomenon we owe most of the supreme works of art which humanity treasures. The lower grades we find exemplified in the peculiar condition which we have only recently begun to study under the term 'mediumship'. There are still lower grades, which call for the attention of psychiatrists, and which may be sum-marised under the contemptuous term 'lunacy'. But whatever their grade, or whatever their value may be, they are all examples of the inter-action of a spiritual world, or rather of a psychical influence of some kind, not commonly familiar in the ordinary experience of commonplace humanity.

As Lodge noted, 'possession' has ordinarily been used pejoratively, suggesting either some evil occupation of the mind, or a pathological condition. Yet there is a sense in which it could legitimately be used in those numerous cases where words, pictures or music flow forth in ways which indicate the influence of a personality distinct from that of the writer, artist or musician. Sometimes it seems likely that there is a secondary, resident personality which periodically takes over. Sometimes external influences appear to be at work. For the present, we lack the ability to pin down the sources of inspiration with any certainty; but the role of possession, in this sense, is indisputable.

Eureka!

PIERCING THE CATARACT

On 27 April 1802, André Ampère – his name still today a household word, thanks to its use as a unit of electric current – 'gave a shout of joy'. Seven years earlier he had found the solution to a problem which he knew was correct,

without being able to prove it. The matter often returned to my mind and I had sought twenty times unsuccessfully for this solution. For some days I had carried the idea about with me continually. At last, *I do not know how*, I found it, together with a large number of curious and new considerations concerning the theory of probability.

Ampère realised that what he had been presented with, when published, would be 'a good method for obtaining a chair of mathematics in a college'; and so it proved.

Ampère's account of his experience is one of many given by eminent scientists and inventors about the way in which their discoveries – usually, as in this case, unintelligible to lay readers, but vital for their reputation and for the advance of science – have been made not through the burning of midnight oil, but thanks to the 'Eureka Effect', first experienced – as every schoolboy once knew – by Archimedes. Asked by the ruler of his home city, Syracuse, to find whether a gold crown he had been given really was pure gold, and not adulterated, he could not think of any way in which to settle the issue except by melting it down. Getting into his bath, one day, he noticed the way in which the water level rose as his body sank into it, and in a flash it occurred to him that as the volume of water displaced was equal to the volume of his own body, the volume of the crown could be ascertained in the same way; and his glad cry of Eureka! has echoed down the ages.

As Koestler observed in *The Act of Creation*, Archimedes must have long been aware that the water level rose whenever he got into his bath. He had simply never consciously formulated that knowledge, because it had been hidden from his eyes 'by the blinkers of habit'. This, Koestler maintained, also applied to artists who see familiar objects in a new light, 'as if piercing the cataract which dims out vision. Newton's apple and Cézanne's apple are discoveries more closely related than they seem.'

The Act of Creation was not the first attempt at an exploration of the Eureka Effect and allied mysteries; but it was the most wide-ranging. In the popular imagination scientists 'appear as sober, ice-cold logicians', Koestler observed, 'electronic brains mounted on dry sticks'. But if one were shown an anthology of typical extracts from their letters and autobiographies, with no names mentioned, and then asked to guess their profession, 'the likeliest answers would be: a bunch of poets or musicians of a rather romantically naive kind'; and he listed examples of eminent scientists to illustrate the paradox that a branch of knowledge whose rationale is objectivity, verifiability and logicality 'turns out to be dependent on mental processes which are subjective, irrational and verifiable only after the event'.

A typical case of the Eureka Effect was the experience of Ampère's contemporary, Karl Gauss — his name, too, still in circulation (though not so familiar to householders) as a unit of intensity of a magnetic field. The solution to a problem on which he was working had eluded him for four years when suddenly it came to him, 'not by painful effort, but, so to speak, by the grace of God. As a sudden flash of light, the enigma was solved.'

Sir William Rowan Hamilton, professor of astronomy at Dublin University, had been baffled by a mathematical problem for longer — fifteen years. In the autumn of 1843 he was strolling with his wife along the Grand Canal in Dublin when, in his words,

an electric current seemed to close; and a spark flashed forth, the herald (as I foresaw, immediately) of many long years to come of definitely directed thought and work, by *myself* if spared, and at all events on the part of *others*, if I should ever be allowed to live long enough directly to communicate the discovery. Nor could I resist the impulse – unphilo-sophical as it may have been – to cut with a knife on the stone of Brougham Bridge, as we passed it, the fundamental formula.

His discovery of quaternions is not now likely to be recalled as of fundamental significance, except by mathematicians; but when in 1865 the National Academy of Sciences was founded in the United States, and its members balloted for the scientists from other countries whom they would invite to become associates; Rowan Hamilton came out top of their list.

In cases such as these, the tag about fortune favouring the prepared mind can be applied, supplemented by Myers's concept of the subliminal self, working to sort out the material in ways of which the conscious mind remains unaware; and it was the harder-headed scientists who were most grateful for it, as it helped to explain their insights without recourse to psychic speculations. 'Our mind is so fortunately equipped that it brings us the most important basis for our thoughts without our having the least knowledge of this work of elaboration,' Wilhelm Wundt, the physiologist and psychologist who strove to bring both disciplines together and keep them within materialist bounds, asserted. 'The unconscious mind is for us like an unknown being who creates and produces for us, and finally throws the ripe fruits into our lap.'

This hypothesis was examined by Henri Poincaré in his essay 'Mathematical Discoveries'. Poincaré was, 'by general agreement, the most eminent scientific man of his generation', Bertrand Russell wrote in the preface to the 1914 English edition of Poincaré's *Science and Method* '– more eminent, one is tempted to think, than any man of science now living'. His obituary in the *Revue de Métaphysique* in 1913 took up 130 pages in which 'four eminent men – a philo-sopher, a mathematician, an astronomer and a physicist – tell in outline the contributions which he made to their several subjects. In all we find the same characteristics – swiftness, comprehensiveness, unexampled lucidity, and the perception of recondite but fertile analogies.'

Explaining to readers in his essay that he would have to use technical expressions with 'barbarous' unfamiliar names, but 'they need not frighten you, for you are not obliged to understand them',

Poincaré described how for fifteen days, when he was a very young man, he had striven to prove that 'there could not be any functions like those since called Fuchsian functions'.

I was then very ignorant; every day I seated myself at my work table, stayed an hour or two, tried a great number of combinations, and reached no results. One evening, contrary to my custom, I drank black coffee and could not sleep. Ideas rose in crowds; I felt them collide until pairs interlocked, so to speak, making a stable combination. By the next morning I had established the existence of a class of Fuchsian functions.

He then had only to write out the results, 'which took but a few hours'.

It was not even essential, Poincaré had found, to have had his conscious mind on the problems. Embarking on an excursion, he got into a bus.

At the moment when I put my foot on the step the idea came to me, without anything in my former thoughts seeming to have paved the way for it, that the transformations I had used to define the Fuchsian functions were identical with those of non-Euclidean geometry. I did not verify the idea; I should not have had time, as, upon taking my seat in the bus, I went on with a conversation already commenced, but I felt a perfect certainty. On my return to Caen, for conscience's sake I verified the result at my leisure.

So it went on, even when he was doing his military service and his mind was on other matters. Before he was called up, he had been baffled by one particular problem.

One day, going along the street, the solution of the difficulty which had stopped me suddenly appeared to me. I did not try to go deep into it immediately, and only after my service did I again take up the question. I had all the elements and had only to arrange them and put them together. So I wrote out my final memoir at a single stroke and without difficulty.

There were many more instances and what most struck Poincaré was 'this appearance of sudden illumination', following 'long unconscious prior work'. And this had led him on to consider a hypothesis.

The subliminal ego is in no way inferior to the conscious ego; it is not purely automatic; it is capable of discernment; it has tact and lightness of touch; it can select; and it can divine. More than that, it can divine better than the conscious ego, since it succeeds where the latter fails. In a word, is not the subliminal ego superior to the conscious ego?

Unwilling to concede this superiority, however, Poincaré suggested a compromise. How, he asked, did the selection process work by which some of the products of the subliminal mind were permitted to cross the threshold? Chance could hardly be the explanation for what had happened in his own case. He preferred to believe that

the privileged unconscious phenomena, those that are capable of becoming conscious, are those which, directly or indirectly, most deeply affect our sensibility. It may appear surprising that sensibility should be introduced in connection with mathematical demonstrations which, it would seem, can only interest the intellect. But not if we bear in mind the feeling of mathematical beauty, of the harmony of numbers and forms and of geometric elegance. It is a real aesthetic feeling, that all true mathematicians recognise, and this is truly sensibility.

The material which the subliminal ego presented to consciousness might be blind, Poincaré thought, and often, for that reason, it would lack aesthetic sensibility. Consequently, only ideas which were harmonious 'and at once useful and beautiful' could appeal to a mathematician's sensibility; 'but this, once aroused, will direct our attention upon them, and will give them the opportunity of becoming conscious'.

Attractive though Poincaré's thesis was, it did not fully account for one of the features of his and some other scientists' insights. Why should the sudden illumination, following long unconscious prior work, have come to him when he was so young? It was not as if he was a mathematician, in the ordinary sense. 'I must confess,' he admitted, 'I am absolutely incapable of doing an addition sum without a mistake.'

THE PSYCHOLOGY OF INVENTION

This paradox prompted another eminent mathematician who had heard Poincaré lecture, Jacques Hadamard, to explore the evidence about scientific creativity, and present his findings in *The Psychology of Invention in the Mathematical Field*. Hadamard's interest had initially been aroused by an occasion when he solved a problem in his sleep. He had not actually had a dream, providing the solution; but 'on being very abruptly awakened by an external noise, a solution long searched for appeared to me at once without the slightest instant of reflection on my part. The fact was remarkable enough to have struck me unforgettably – and in a quite different direction from that which I had previously tried to follow.' Intrigued by Poincaré, he began to investigate to find if other mathematicians and scientists had had similar experiences.

They had – Faraday among them. Like Poincaré's, Faraday's mathematics were feeble. To von Helmholtz, it was 'to the highest degree astonishing what a large number of general theorems, the mathematical deduction of which requires the highest powers of mathematical analysis', Faraday had found 'by a kind of intuition, with the security of instinct, without the help of a single mathematical formula'. Helmholtz was a dedicated rationalist (he once told Sir William Barrett that the testimony of the entire membership of the Royal Society would not persuade him to change his mind about accepting telepathy – he would not believe in it, in fact, even if he experienced it himself). He consequently had to fall back on 'intuition' and 'instinct'. Yet Faraday's own account of the ways his mind worked went further.

He 'saw' the answers to his questions in his inner eye. It was a vision of tubes, which 'rose up before him like things', that was to guide him to his invention of the dynamo and the electric motor.

Creativity among mathematicians, Hadamard found, appeared often to depend upon their ability to exploit imagery in this way, 'most frequently visual, but they may also be of another kind, for instance kinetic. There can also be auditive ones.' The most remarkable of the visual ones are those reported by Friedrich von Kekulé, professor of chemistry at the University of Ghent. They began when, as a young man, he was returning to where he was staying in London on the last bus of the evening. He fell into a reverie, in which he saw atoms whirling before his eyes; and for the first time, they behaved in their 'giddy dance' in a way which gave him the clue he needed to form his molecular theory. Later, in 1865, another dream in the series enabled him to make what is widely regarded as the most brilliant piece of prediction to be found in the history of organic chemistry. In the dream, the atoms began twisting in a snakelike motion when, suddenly, one of the 'snakes' caught hold of its own tail. 'As if by a flash of lightning I awoke': he had realised that the molecules of certain compounds must be closed 'rings'.

Lord Kelvin, too, 'saw' solutions to problems 'as if by some process of instinctive vision denied to others', according to his biographer Sylvanus Thompson: 'the gift of the seer'. Science, Thompson lamented, 'has no specific name for this power of divination, a precious incommunicable quality of her particular genius'. Science might have no specific name for it; Kelvin himself thought divination – in its ordinary, colloquial meaning – was the product of bad observation or wilful imposture 'acting on an innocent, trusting mind'. In such matters he could be dogmatic, and often downright silly: he dismissed X-rays as a hoax, and insisted that heavier than air machines could never fly. Nevertheless, materialist though he remained, he was indeed a seer in the sense that the solutions to problems came to him in visual form, and he might then have to spend days trying to work out how and why they were correct. Whatever the source of his powers, Thompson felt, they were 'surely more akin to the innate faculty of the great artist than to the trained powers of the analyst or the logician'.

How Einstein obtained his insights remains particularly mysterious because unlike Poincaré, nothing he did in his years as an established scientist reinforced the reputation he made in his youth – rather the contrary. It was not that he rested on his laurels, but that inspiration seemed to desert him. On the principle of fortune favouring the prepared mind, it could have been expected to return to him; but no. And this has actually consoled behaviourists, enabling them to fall back on chance as the explanation of such cases. The Eureka Effect may appear to be the outcome of some undisclosed form of creative inspiration; but in reality the act of discovery, Charles Nicolle could argue in his *Biologie de l'Invention* (1932), 'is an accident'.

By Einstein's own account, in a letter to Hadamard, words played no part in the mechanics of his thinking; 'psychical entities' served his purposes, 'certain signs and more or less clear images'.

The essential feature of productive thought for him was 'combinatory play', before there was any logical construction. This helps to account for the puzzle that he had been a backward child, a slow developer, a drop-out from school; and that at the time he made his reputation with his special theory of relativity, he was working in obscurity as a clerk in a patent office. The process by which the theories were produced, according to his biographer Anton Reiser, was 'surprisingly analogous to the artist's'; he would have 'a definite vision of the possible solutions', before working on them to find if they were correct. 'The gift of fantasy has meant more to me than my talent for absorbing information,' he told his friend Janos Plesch. There were no logical paths to his discoveries; 'there is only the way of intuition.'

Is it possible, then, that there can be an extra-sensory element in the minds of scientists, enabling them to fertilise each other in some way?

Difficult though it is to decide whether inspiration can be attributed to the skills of the subliminal self in fashioning an idea and transmitting it to consciousness, or whether some outside source needs to be credited, there are cases where it is hard to avoid accepting an element of telepathy, clairvoyance or precognition. At the age of twenty Everist Galois sent a paper to the Academy of the Sciences in Paris, which was rejected. The night before he was to be the principal in a duel he revised it, adding some fresh discoveries he had made in a letter to a friend. What the paper and the letter contained, it was later realised, 'signified a total transformation of higher algebra', according to Hadamard, 'projecting a full light on what had been only glimpsed thus far by the greatest mathematicians'. Even more remarkable, in the letter to his friend Galois presented a theorem which nobody could have understood at the time, because the mathematical principles on which it was based were not known until a quarter of a century later. Galois could not have conceived the principles, as he made no allusions to them; but 'they must have been unconsciously in his mind'. In other words, Galois in some way 'knew', at the age of twenty what he could not have 'known'. His subliminal self must have supplied him with the necessary information in advance. Unluckily he did not live to comment upon his stroke of genius: he was killed in the duel.

The stage at which visualisation slips over into clairvoyance is further illustrated by Nikola Tesla, a Hungarian who emigrated to the United States in 1884, worked for a while for Edison, and became the most prolific inventor of his time. He had begun as a child to fantasise, 'seeing' new scenes initially blurred and indistinct, but 'they gained in strength and distinctness and finally assumed the concreteness of real things' – so much so that on his travels in the mind, he made friendships no less intense than those in real life. And at the age of seventeen, he found he could use these visions to experiment with inventions. When he had a workshop, and began to experiment with a turbine, he found it was 'absolutely immaterial' to him whether he tested it in his shop, or in his mind.

I even note if it is out of balance. There is no difference whatever, the results are the same. In this way I am able to rapidly develop and perfect a conception without touching anything. When I have gone so far as to embody in the invention every possible improvement I can think of and see no fault anywhere, I put into concrete form this final product of my brain.

Invariably my device works as I conceived that it should, and the experiment comes out exactly as I planned it. In twenty years there has not been a single exception. . . .

When he tried to invent a dynamo of a new type, which his professor scoffed at, his conscious efforts to visualise it failed; but one evening walking through a park a snatch of one of Goethe's poems came to him, and he began to recite.

The glow retreats, done is the day of toil.

He reached the lines about the inability of the mind's wings to lift the body.

As I uttered these inspiring words the idea came like a flash of lightning and in an instant truth was revealed. I drew with a stick on the sand the diagrams shown six years later in my address before the American Institute of Electrical Engineers, and my companion understood them perfectly. The images I saw were wonderfully sharp and clear and had the solidity of metal and stone, so much so that I told him: 'See my motor here; watch me reverse it.' I cannot begin to describe my emotions. Pygmalion seeing his statue come to life could not have been more deeply moved. A thousand secrets of nature which I might have stumbled upon accidentally I would have given for that one which I had wrested from her against all odds and at the peril of my existence.

Tesla had taken the first step towards the introduction of alternating current, though it was to take a protracted, bitter battle with the supporters of direct current before its advantages were finally admitted. He went on to produce a flood of inventions, some influential – one was important for the development of television – some eccentric, though it has often been suggested that a few of them may simply have been too far ahead of their time. The hallucinatory element, he insisted, was vital – the ability to test his gadgets in his mind as if he were testing them in his workshop, because in his mind they behaved as if they were real.

For a while I gave myself up entirely to the intense enjoyment of picturing machines and devising new forms. It was a mental state of happiness about as complete as I have ever known in life. Ideas came in an uninterrupted stream and the only difficulty I had was to hold them fast. The pieces of apparatus I conceived were to me absolutely real and tangible in every detail, even to the minutest marks and signs of wear. I delighted in imagining the motors constantly running, for in this way they presented to the mind's eye a most fascinating sight. When natural inclination develops into a passionate desire, one advances towards his goal in seven-league boots. In less than two months I evolved virtually all the types of motors and modifications of the system which are now identified with my name.

Other examples of discoveries which cannot easily be accounted for except by some form of psychic assistance include the remarkable story of the career of the Nobel laureate Barbara McClintock, described in *A Feeling for the Organism* by Evelyn Fox Keller. 'She showed a perplexing capacity to *know* that something was true,' one of the reviewers of the book, Bernard Dixon, has commented, 'typified by the occasion when half an hour's weeping and sub-conscious thinking under a eucalyptus tree on the Stanford campus led her to solve problems about the cytology of *Neurospora* which had baffled distinguished geneticists for years.' By her own account, a vision solved it: 'I was even able to see the internal parts of the chromosomes,' she recalls. 'It surprised me, because I actually felt as if I were right down there, and these were my friends.' On the strength of her experiences she is proud to call herself a mystic, which has not made her popular with many of the scientists in her field; but they have been reluctantly compelled to recognise her 'capacity to *know* that something was true', twenty years or more before the proofs have eventually shown she was right.

Ironically, the scientist who used his psychic powers to best effect, both as a theorist and as an inventor, is now rarely remembered *as* a scientist, except by devotees of the cult associated with his name. Emanuel Swedenborg's ideas and projects not merely made him outstanding in his time; some of them, like Leonardo's, so closely foreshadowed later developments that they lend support to the notion that he had precognitive as well as clairvoyant abilities.

In 1716, when he was still in his twenties, Swedenborg was appointed 'assessor extraordinary' to the Swedish Board of Mines, indicating that King Charles XII had recognised his talents and regarded him as the deputy and obvious successor to the Minister for Commerce. He had already, by that time, revealed the astonishing range of his scientific knowledge in his letters, from various places in Europe, to the Royal Society of Sciences at Upsala. 'An indefatigable curiosity, directed to various important objects, is conspicuous in all of them,' a historian of the society was to recall. 'Mathematics, astronomy and mechanics seem to have been his favourite sciences.' These were supplemented by crystallography (some authorities credit him with founding the science); by metallurgy, in which he was recognised as the foremost authority of his time; by cosmology – many of his hypotheses, in particular that the planets in the solar system originated from the sun, that the solar system is part of the Milky Way, and that there are other Milky Ways, being later confirmed by astronomers; and by anatomy and physiology – his thesis on the brain, the spine and the ductless glands proved to be a century ahead of their time. He was also a prolific inventor; his ideas included plans for a submarine, a machine gun (his patron Charles XII was involved in wars with the Danes), a flying machine, and the first mercurial air pump. In the whole history of science there is nobody with a comparable record of actual achievement coupled to inventiveness.

In the early 1740s Swedenborg decided that he must try to fuse anatomy and physiology with what he described as a rational psychology, 'consisting of certain new doctrines, through the assistance of which we may be conducted, from the material organism of the body, to a knowledge of the soul, which is immaterial'; and he expressed the hope that he might by this route 'at length contemplate the soul herself; by the divine permission'. In 1745 it seemed to him that permission was granted; he had a vision in which the Lord told him that he had been chosen to explain the nature of the soul. He decided to dedicate the rest of his life to the task, with the help of what would now be regarded as yoga-type exercises in which he became clairvoyant, so that he could converse with the spirits.

Stories of his clairvoyance were legion, the best known being of the occasion in 1759 when he 'saw' the great fire raging in Stockholm, and described its course to his fellow guests at a house in Gothenburg, 300 miles away – his description was confirmed later. And occasionally he was able to put this clairvoyance to practical use, as when in 1761 he was visited by Madame de Marteville, widow of a former Dutch ambassador in Sweden, who had received a demand for repayment of a debt her husband had incurred, but which she was sure he had repaid. A few days later she dreamed that her husband had returned to show her where he had put the receipt; and she found it in the place he had indicated. The following morning Swedenborg came to her house; he had 'seen' M. de Marteville, he told her, who had promised he would get in touch with his widow.

The fact that Swedenborg not merely insisted that his information came from spirits, but identified them as famous figures from the past, inevitably led to the suspicion that he was off his head; but accounts from people who knew him confirm that he was mad only north-north-west. A young visitor from Finland, Gabriel Porthan, heard him conducting a one-sided conversation in Latin. Swedenborg subsequently explained he had been talking with Virgil, 'a fine and pleasant fellow'. But on later visits Porthan was deeply impressed by his extraordinary range of learning in all branches of science:

Insane though he appeared to me at first, I nevertheless separated from him with the greatest gratitude, both for his highly learned conversation, and his constant and exceeding kindness both in word and deed – and above all, with the greatest admiration, although it was mingled with regret that, on a certain point, a screw in the venerable man was loose.

Although several of the most eminent scientists of the past two centuries have engaged in psychical research, and become convinced that the phenomena are genuine, few have tried to fuse the research with their own work; the tendency has been to keep the two in separate compartments. Nevertheless there have been important exceptions; one being Alfred Russel Wallace. As a schoolmaster, in his youth, he had observed that psychic phenomena could be produced in mesmeric trances – much to his surprise; and his initial rationalism had been sufficiently shaken for him to keep an open mind. Even so, he was unprepared for the consequences of a bout of malaria which he suffered in Indonesia. In his feverish state, he had been pondering the problem of evolution of species. Why did some survive, and others disappear? Malthus's idea of the checks which keep population down, disease, famine and so on, came into his mind: obviously it would be the fleetest, the strongest which would survive! 'Then it suddenly flashed upon me that the self-acting process would necessarily *improve the race*, because in every generation the inferior would inevitably be killed off and the superior would remain – that is, *the fittest would survive*.'

Wallace was in no condition at the time to write down his ideas; 'I waited anxiously for the termination of my fit so that I might at once make notes for a paper on the subject,' a paper which he sent to his friend Darwin. With characteristic magnanimity, Wallace declined to take even a half share of the credit when he found that Darwin had come to the same conclusion years earlier and had been devoting the intervening time to amassing the confirmatory evidence. Yet, as Darwin himself admitted, *The Origin of Species* might never have been published, at least in his lifetime, if Wallace's paper had not goaded him into action. He might have continued to build up the evidence, he realised, delaying completion until it was too late.

Unlike so many of his contemporaries Wallace did not forget that he owed his discovery to a flash of inspiration, rather than to working over the evidence consciously. He began to explore the phenomena of spiritualism, and what he witnessed compelled him to accept that forces are at work on the human mind which cannot be accounted for except on the assumption that we have access to information from channels other than those of the recognised senses. 'I have long since come to see that no one deserves either praise or blame for the *ideas* that come to him,' he told an audience in 1908, when he was the recipient of the first Darwin/Wallace medal. 'They come to us – we hardly know *how* or *whence* – and once they have got possession of us, we cannot reject or change them at will.' We *are*, however, responsible for the resulting acts; it is 'only by patient thought and work that new ideas, if good and true, become adapted and utilised'.

The inventor of the electroencephalogram and the discoverer of 'brain waves', Hans Berger, took a similar course. As a young man, Berger had narrowly escaped death in an accident; a few hours later he received a telegram from his father – the only time in his life that his father ever sent him one – asking to be reassured because Hans's sister had had a powerful feeling that he had been in danger. Between the wars Berger went on to conduct experiments which confirmed his opinion that thought transference at a distance was a reality. In his own case, he found he was 'a poor transmitter, but a good receiver'; working on the hypothesis that the transmission worked on a similar principle to radio, he hoped that with the help of his invention he would be able to detect an electrical process by which transmission and reception were effected. Eventually, however, he realised that this was not, and could not be, the way telepathy worked. Some form of psychic energy must be involved which could not be accounted for in conventional terms; he was convinced that its existence was of fundamental importance for science.

The experience which was to shape Sir Alister Hardy's distinguished career as a zoologist was less striking, but its consequences may yet turn out to be far-reaching. During the First World War Hardy was serving in a battalion stationed on the east coast of Britain; and near the camp there was an old lady who dispensed hospitality and would occasionally demonstrate light-heartedly her psychic powers through psychometry – holding the object given to her, and describing the owner. Occasionally she 'saw' something spontaneously; Hardy recalled that on one occasion when he had come to tea,

she suddenly said, 'Oh, I can see your brother in Germany quite clearly' (I am not reporting her exact words but as nearly as possible the gist of them). 'I can see him in his prison camp with a camp-bed, he is sitting at a table drawing what I think must be some engineering plan; on a large sheet of white paper I see him painting what seem to be squares and oblongs of red and blue.'

What she was in fact describing, Hardy realised, was what *he* had been doing that afternoon, though nobody could have known but himself. His colonel had asked him to prepare a map to illustrate one of his talks.

He didn't know how I was going to do it; it was only that afternoon that I had the idea of cutting out squares and oblongs of card, painted red and blue to represent the various units. It was an obvious thing to do, but he had only asked me to prepare a large map of the area. I spent the greater part of the afternoon – in my rather bare room in my billet with camp-bed in it – looking at the large white map and moving the red and blue cards about, following a description of the campaign.

Hardy did not then know how common this form of 'displace-ment' from one person to another is in the records of psychical research; but he found it difficult to believe that her description of what his brother was doing, and what *he* had been doing, was coincidental. A year later his conviction that Mrs Wedgwood must have been reading his mind was confirmed when she did it again. By this time he had moved to London; as a camouflage officer, he was doing experiments in dazzle effects.

I had taken a large sheet of white cardboard and then painted it all over with a most vivid pink distemper. I was then going to cut it up into all sorts of shapes for use in our experiments, but I found it took much longer to dry than I expected, so that I had it in front of me and kept looking at it to see if it was ready, for some considerable time before I cut it up. Again I am quite certain that no one could have told Mrs Wedgwood what I had been doing, for no one at the camouflage school knew her, or knew that I was going out to dinner with her. I had not sat down at the dinner table with her for more than a moment or two when she suddenly said, 'Oh, what have you been doing? I see a large pink square on the table in front of you.'

There was no need to emphasise the similarity of the two cases, Hardy felt; 'I will only add that I know I have a good visual memory and that colour and shape make a strong impression on me.' Evidently it was the strong impression which Mrs Wedgwood had picked up. Although Hardy believed that this communication was telepathic, from the point of view of the influence it had on him it would not greatly have mattered if he had preferred another interpretation, much in favour at the time: that such cases could be explained by a form of thought transference which was not extra-sensory, but transmitted by unconscious sensory processes which could be recognised and interpreted – much as Sherlock Holmes recognised, followed and interpreted what Watson was thinking in his reveries. For Hardy, the essential point in any case was that there are forces at work in the field of communication between humans, imperfectly understood, which may also be at work between animals; and if so, they may have a profound influence on the evolution of species.

Hardy was to become the leading marine biologist of his time, a Fellow of the Royal Society and, in 1946, Linacre professor of zoology at Oxford University. After his retirement he was asked to give the Giffard lectures at Aberdeen University; and choosing as his subject 'Evolution and the Spirit of Man', he presented his hypothesis that although the Darwinian theory was basically sound, it did not tell the whole story. Relating his experiences – 'anecdotal and of no scientific value, yet to me they are as important as any observation I ever made in Natural History' – Hardy surmised that if people like Mrs Wedgwood could receive impressions in the way he had described, might there not also be in the animal kingdom as a whole 'not only a telepathic spread of habit changes, but a general *subconscious* sharing of a behaviour pattern – a sort of psychic blueprint – shared between members of a species?' If so, it would add a new psychic dimension to the then strictly materialist doctrine of evolution.

Needless to say, this was not a welcome theory to most of his colleagues in biology; but none of them was able to produce a convincing rebuttal. *The Living Stream*, the published Giffard lectures, together with his earlier *The Open Sea*, point the way to a reassessment of conventional evolutionary theory, now that its limitations are being exposed not only by biologists who share Hardy's views, but also by molecular biologists approaching the subject from a very different direction.

PRODIGIES

Perhaps the strongest evidence that mathematical abilities cannot be accounted for in conventional terms has been provided not by famous scientists, but by children; in particular some child prodigies who have been able to show that they can make abstruse calculations in a flash. How? Commentators have had to fall back on 'intuition' – 'Whatever that may mean,' as Sir Oliver Lodge ruefully remarked.

Myers listed some of the more celebrated prodigies, ranging from Ampère at one end of the alphabet to Richard Whately, later to be archbishop of Dublin, at the other. Of the two, in this context, Whately is the more interesting because whereas Ampère's ability remained with him throughout his life, Whately's lasted only for three years. It began to show itself when he was five or six.

I soon got to do the most difficult sums, always in my head, for I knew nothing of figures beyond numeration. I did these sums much quicker than any one could upon paper, and I never remember committing the smallest error. *When I went to school, at which time the passion wore off, I was a perfect dunce at ciphering, and have continued so ever since.*

This coming and going of the faculty is quite common. According to Franz Gall, a 'Mr Van R' of Utica showed a similar faculty at the age of six and not merely lost it at eight, but had no idea how he had performed the calculations. Professor Safford, another mathematical prodigy, retained the faculty for long enough to establish himself as a mathematician, eventually becoming a professor of astronomy; yet by that time he could calculate no better than the next man.

Some prodigies have been highly intelligent; others have been accounted stupid in all respects, other than calculating; some have not been able to calculate in the ordinary sense at all. 'We know that Dase (perhaps the most successful of all these prodigies) was singularly devoid of mathematical grasp,' Myers observed.

On one occasion Petersen tried in vain for six weeks to get the first elements of mathematics into his head. He could not be made to have the least idea of a proposition in Euclid. Of any language but his own he could never master a word! Yet Dase received a grant from the Academy of Sciences at Hamburg on the recommendation of Gauss for mathematical work; and actually in twelve years made tables of factors and prime numbers for the seventh and nearly the whole of the eighth million – a task which probably few men could have accomplished without mechanical aid in an ordinary lifetime. He may thus be ranked as the only man who has ever done valuable service to mathematics without being able to cross the ass's bridge.

How are such feats achieved? According to Wellesley Pole, a Fellow of the Royal Society, the prodigy G. P. Bidder (who later became a QC) 'had an almost miraculous power of *seeing*, as it were, intuitively what factors would divide any larger number, not a prime'. Given the number 17,861, 'he would instantly remark it was 337×53'. He could not, he said, explain how he did this; 'it seemed a natural instinct to him.'

At the height of the positivists' domination of science, there could be only one explanation. When in 1837 the ten-year-old Vito Mangiamele, a shepherd's son with no formal training in mathematics, was tested by the French scientist Dominique Arago and his colleagues of the Academy of Sciences, the boy took only a minute to work out in his head that the cube root of 3,796,416 was 156. The committee members, unable to deny that Vito could perform such calculations, decided it could only be fraud. His instructors, they claimed, must have found a way to keep the method they had taught a secret.

This would not do for Myers. Dase and the others, he felt, were the output of 'some unseen world in which the multiplication table is, so to speak, in the air'. Oliver Lodge thought prodigies represented 'some form of possession'. Conventional psychology has no more plausible answer, nor is likely to find one until old mechanist shackles are finally thrown off.

How difficult it will be to throw them off has been illustrated by Oliver Sacks in his paper 'The Twins'. They differed from the infant prodigies in that they were adults, but from the age of seven they had been in institutions, 'variously diagnosed as autistic, psychotic or severely retarded'. At the time he meets them at the age of twenty-six, they are

a sort of grotesque Tweedledum and Tweedledee, indistinguishable mirror-images, identical in face, in body movements, in personality, in mind, identical, too, in their stigmata of brain and tissue damage. They are undersized, with disturbing disproportions in heads and hands, high-arched palates, high-arched feet, monotonous squeaky voices, a variety of peculiar tics and mannerisms, and a very high degenerative myopia.

Confronted with ordinary simple mathematical problems, the twins do 'as badly as their IQs of sixty might lead one to think'. They cannot add or subtract without making mistakes, and they cannot even understand the meaning of multiplication and division. Yet,

the twins say, 'Give us a date – any time in the last or next 40,000 years.' You give them a date, and almost instantly, they tell you what day of the week it would be. 'Another date!' they cry, and the performance is repeated. They will also tell you the date of Easter during the same period of 80,000 years.

This was in 1966. The explanation which has since found most favour among scientists who have studied the twins, put forward in Steven Smith's *The Great Mental Calculators* (1983), is that they use algorithms – a kind of mathematical shorthand. Sacks is too polite to dismiss this as the nonsense it manifestly is; if the twins could not do simple sums, algorithms would not have helped them. In any case, they could not readily be used to date past Easters, or other feats which the twins found simple. The hypothesis, Sacks suggests mildly, is 'a misapprehension'; the reality must be 'far stranger, far more complex, far less explicable'. The mistake which had been made was to regard them simply as subjects for trials and experiments; 'one must lay aside the urge to limit and test, and get to know the twins,' he decided. Then, 'one finds there is something exceedingly mysterious at work, powers and depths of a perhaps fundamental sort, which I have not been able to solve in the eighteen years that I have known them.'

How do they do their 'calculations'? 'If you ask them how they can hold so much in their minds – a 300-digit figure or the trillion events of four decades – they say, very simply, "We see it." And "seeing" – "visualising" – of extraordinary intensity, limitless range and perfect fidelity seems to be the key.' Sacks has no doubt that the twins have available to them 'a prodigious panorama, a sort of landscape', and also the ability to 'see' and retrieve anything that lies in it. Seeking to explain the process, he turns to art for an analogy: the twins, he believes, have 'not just a strange "faculty", but a sensibility, a harmonic sensibility, perhaps allied to that of music'.

But Sacks's advice has gone unheeded. Now, twenty years after first meeting the twins, he expresses exasperation – again mildly – at the fact that as soon as the 'algorithms' explanation was presented, wretchedly inadequate though it was, scientists felt there was no longer any need to bother with the twins. Eventually they were split up 'for their own good' to terminate their 'unhealthy' communication and to make them fit to lead socially acceptable lives – doing menial jobs under supervision. In the process they 'seem to have lost their strange numerical power, and with this the chief joy and sense of their lives. But this is considered a small price to pay, no doubt, for their having become quasi-independent and "socially acceptable".'

This has not been the first time, and will not be the last, when science has grasped at a straw to spare the orthodox from the embarrassment of contemplating ESP as a possible alternative. Even Sacks himself, though his descriptions of the twins point inexorably to some form of extra-sensory communication between them, does not care to contemplate that possibility. He cites the algorithm notion as if it had thrown some useful light on the problem, rather than obscured it. Yet his account, and theirs, of the way they performed as prodigies could readily be put into a textbook of parapsychology.

QUANTUM QUESTIONS

If children, and in some cases children whose IQs are abnormally low, can solve mathematical problems with ease, the implications for science are obvious: that the Eureka Effect may be there for anybody to exploit, if it can be tracked down and released. Many of the most admired achievements have been the result not of burning the midnight oil, in the accepted sense, but of the very different kind of 'midnight vigil' to which Sir Frederick Banting attributed the idea which set him on course for world fame and a Nobel Prize, with the discovery of insulin. From the nature of things, he recalled, ideas come 'when the imagination is allowed to run riot on the problem that blocks the progress of research, when the hewn stones of scientific fact are turned over and fitted in so that the mosaic figure of truth designed by mother nature long ago may be formed from the chaos'.

Why, then, do scientists still for the most part maintain that they work by induction, arguing from the particular to the general – collecting facts and assuming that eventually they will present solutions to all problems? 'Ask a scientist what he conceives the scientific method to be, and he will adopt an expression that is at once solemn and shifty-eyed,' Sir Peter Medawar has observed; 'solemn, because he feels he ought to declare an opinion; shifty-eyed, because he is wondering how to conceal the fact that he has no opinion to declare.' If taunted, the scientist

would probably mumble something about 'Induction' and 'Establishing the Laws of Nature'; but if anyone working in a laboratory professed to be trying to establish Laws of Nature by induction we should begin to think he was overdue for leave . . . It is most unlikely that more than a tiny minority of mathematical theorems were ever in fact arrived at, 'discovered', merely by the exercise of deductive reasoning. Most of them entered the mind by processes of the kind vaguely called 'intuitive', deduction or logical derivation came later, to justify or falsify what was in the first place an 'inspiration' or an intuitive belief. This is seldom apparent from mathematical writings, because mathematicians take pains to ensure that it should not be.

Biographers are often similarly determined that their heroes' reputations should not be deflated by any taint of mysticism. In his biography of Isaac Newton, published in 1855, Sir David Brewster dismissed Newton's delvings into theology and alchemy as an aberration: 'We cannot understand how a mind of such power, and nobly occupied by the abstractions of geometry and the study of the material world, could stoop to be the copyist of the most contemptible alchemical poetry, and the annotator of a work the obvious product of a fool and a knave.' A century was to pass before the unpalatable realisation began to emerge that the 2 million or so words which Newton penned on those subjects, however baffling, were a vital part of his development as a scientist. Newton had come to be regarded 'as the first and greatest of the modern age of scientists, a rationalist, one who taught us to think on the lines of cold and untinctured reason', J. M. Keynes observed. 'I do not see him in this light.' Newton, for Keynes, was 'the last of the magicians, the last of the Babylonians and Sumerians, the last great mind which looked out on the visible and intellectual world with the same eyes as those who began to build our intellectual inheritance rather less than 10,000 years ago'.

Among physicists recently there has been a startling readiness to accept such propositions, which most scientists in other fields would reject as mystical. Their findings, Ken Wilber insists in his *Quantum Questions*, giving excerpts from their writings, 'offer no positive support (let alone proof) for a mystical world view'; yet from their opinions Einstein, Planck, Pauli, Schrödinger, Heisenberg and others could all be identified as mystics. 'If they did not get their mysticism from a study of modern physics,' he asks, 'where *did* they get it?'

The excerpts provide the answer: they got it through dissatisfaction with nineteenth-century rationalism. Einstein described the form in which it had commonly been presented – that belief which did not rest on knowledge was necessarily superstition – as 'crass'. Schrödinger denounced 'the bankrupts of rationalism'. For Pauli, narrow rationalism had 'lost its persuasiveness'. And although they had different ideas about where quantum physics was taking them, they accepted that it might require the abandonment of many preconceptions. Einstein, for one, though he could not accept J. B. Rhine's evidence for telepathy, contributed a foreword to the German edition of Upton Sinclair's *Mental Radio* (1930), describing Mrs Sinclair's clairvoyant abilities, because he could not believe that Sinclair would consciously deceive his readers. Einstein accepted the fact of clairvoyance, in other words, but not the theoretical explanation.

The following year Max Planck forecast that quantum physics would lead to the discovery of new natural phenomena. 'Many surprises await us, and certain views, eclipsed at the moment, may revive and acquire a new significance.' In particular, physics was demonstrating the truth of the old doctrine 'which teaches us that there are realities existing apart from our sense-perceptions'. The following year, in *Where is Science Going?* he went further, urging that miracles deserved scrutiny. Belief in them had degenerated into fanaticism, but this should not be allowed to discredit them.

Is there, in the last analysis, some basically sound foothold for this belief in miracle, no matter how bizarre and illogical may be the outer forms it takes? Is there something in the nature of man, some inner realm, that science cannot touch? Is it so that when we approach the inner springs of human action, science cannot have the last word?

If quantum physicists had to name the most brilliant mind among them, the choice would probably fall on Wolfgang Pauli. He 'followed the road of scepticism based on rationalism right to the end', as Heisenberg put it, 'to a scepticism about scepticism', which led him to investigate the processes which precede rational under-standing, and to collaborate with Jung in the attempt to grapple with synchronicity. The laws of nature, he insisted, cannot be discovered empirically, from the given data. Intuition is required, and it needs to be fed from the store of primeval images – the collective unconscious – whose resources cannot be reached through logic. The alchemists had gone astray, Pauli argued, not because they had moved too far from material reality, but because they had relied too much on it. Quantum physics, for him, had opened up the issue again. 'I consider the ambition of overcoming opposites, including also a synthesis embracing both rational understanding and the mystical experience of unity, to be the mythos, spoken or unspoken, of our present age.'

Although reductionism, rationalism's *reductio ad absurdum*, still dominates the biological sciences, some of the most eminent researchers in neurophysiology have felt compelled to follow the same course as Pauli, becoming disillusioned with their past faiths. All Wilder Penfield's experiments on the human brain – half a century's work, which had won him an international reputation – had been based, he recalled at the end of his life, on the assumption that the mind is completely dependent upon the brain, and had in fact been designed to confirm that proposition; but 'all of them had proved the exact opposite'. A Nobel Prize winner, Roger Sperry, agreed in 1981 that neurological research on the relationship of mind and brain had compelled 'a direct break with the long-established materialist and behaviourist doctrine', necessitating the acceptance of intuition as the key reality. Yet another Nobel laureate, Sir John Eccles, has since derided the reductionist concept of mind as 'a superstition without rational foundation'.

If mind exists independently of brain, using the brain for its own purposes, the rationalist case – at least in the form it has traditionally been presented – collapses. 'Mind' need no longer be confined, or indeed even localised in space, or in time. Communication between minds becomes easier to accept, with all that this implies about the genesis of the Eureka Effect. And although the activities of the Unknown Guest are not thereby explained, they become easier to fit into the picture of life on which science, tempered by mysticism, needs to get to work.

The Superconscious Self

The evidence relating to daemon, muse and the Eureka Effect lends massive support to Myers's concept of the subliminal self: a part of our total self, but an extremely important one, capable of behaving as if it is an independent entity. Its powers are such as to justify Dame Edith Lyttelton's contention, half a century ago, that it deserves to be thought of as our superconscious self, capable of gathering information through extra-sensory sources, feeding us with intuitions, and on occasion providing us with 'the kind of vision which is either called prophecy or inspiration'.

Dame Edith – a member of the Balfour family, the widow of a former colonial secretary, and a British delegate at the United Nations – had become interested in the subject when she found that she could produce flashes of ESP in automatic writing; but she was under no illusions about the quality of the material it presented. In *Our Superconscious Mind* she argued that it was essentially unreliable because of the problems the superconscious self faces, in getting its information through to us, compelling it to resort to ruses such as automatism and hallucination, 'some clumsy, some obscure'. Nevertheless the information could be valuable, sometimes prompting action which provided protection from danger or death. The important point, she felt, was not where the information came from, but whether, when it was critically examined, it was meaningful and helpful.

The case histories with which Dame Edith backed her thesis indicated that although certain gifted or fortunate individuals could be described as having superconscious personalities, anybody and everybody enjoys access to a superconscious self. This was a view which had been put forward by Oliver Wendell Holmes in his onslaught against mechanistic materialism. 'The lout who lies stretched on the tavern bench, with just mental activity enough to keep his pipe from going out,' he had asserted, 'is the unconscious tenant of a laboratory where such combinations are being constantly made as never Woehler or Bertholet [leading scientists of Holmes's student days] could put together'; a laboratory 'where such fabrics are woven, such colours dyed, such a commerce carried on with the elements and forces of the outer universe, that the industries of all the factories and trading establishments in the world are mere indolence and awkwardness and unproductiveness compared to the miraculous activities of which his lazy bulk is the unheeding centre'.

Holmes cited the common experience – common among people who have no intellectual pretensions – of using guile to persuade the unconscious to revive a memory.

No effort of the will can reach it; but we say, 'Wait a minute, and it will come to me', and go on talking. Presently, perhaps some minutes later, the idea we are in search of comes all at once into the mind, delivered like a prepaid bundle, laid at the door of consciousness like a foundling in a basket. How came it there, we know not.

The other well-worn way of tapping the superconscious is to use it as an alarm clock. Many people have only to say 'seven o'clock' to themselves, firmly, last thing at night, and they will wake up precisely at that time.

Spontaneous promptings by the superconscious self, in the form of casual intuitions, are also familiar. Nobody would be likely to be dispute that they can provide us with timely warnings of a kind which we cannot consciously account for. The controversial issue that remains is whether they can be extra-sensory communications. And there is abundant testimony that they can: that the superconscious self is capable of picking up transmissions of the kind which, when they reach consciousness, we call premonitions.

On 10 February 1847 Samuel Wilberforce, newly appointed bishop of Oxford, was conferring with some of his clergy when he suddenly exclaimed, 'I am certain that something has happened to one of my sons.' His son Herbert, it later transpired, had been injured in an accident on board a ship at the time. 'I was so possessed with the depressing consequence of some evil befalling him,' Wilberforce wrote to tell his sister, 'that I was unable to shake off the impression.'

In this case there was nothing that the bishop could have done; but it is one of many cases in which the recipient of a distress signal of this kind would have reacted promptly, had it been possible to help. Sometimes a recipient has reacted promptly and, as it turns out, unnecessarily.

While Alan Whitehorn, father of the journalist Katharine Whitehorn, was a master at Mill Hill, one of the boys in his house was Gopal, son of Sarvepalli Radhakrishnan, at that time professor of oriental religion at Oxford University, and later president of India.

One afternoon he came to say goodbye to his son and to me, before setting off for India, stopping in Paris on the way to Marseilles. The next evening Gopal got leave from the matron to climb out on to a flat roof to retrieve a ball; he put his foot on to a glass skylight and came through, a drop of perhaps 12 feet. We put him in the sickroom, because although not seriously hurt, he had twisted an ankle and been slightly cut by glass. We informed his temporary guardian, in Swiss Cottage, and next day he came out to see the boy and myself. He suggested that he and I should give the father the same reassuring account of the matter, because otherwise we should have Radhakrishnan, a rather anxious father, coming back from France. That being agreed, the guardian went home to Swiss Cottage, where he found Radhakrishnan on his doorstep, demanding to know what had happened to Gopal the evening before. Next day Radhakrishnan came out to Mill Hill, and he told me that, as he was sitting reading the paper in his Paris hotel, he suddenly felt that something had happened to Gopal: this was the time of Gopal's descent through the ceiling. He tried to get me on the telephone; but as there was a good deal of delay, he took the next train to England, to find out for himself. He told me that similar instances of telepathy had happened to him once or twice before.

Cases like these strongly suggest that there is a mechanism by which alarm can be transmitted and picked up by somebody 'tuned in'. There are plenty of examples of effective action being taken as a result. In a few cases, it is as if a distress signal has been directed successfully at the person who is best placed to come to the rescue, as in an experience related by Cromwell Varley, FRS (he was the engineer directly responsible for the laying of the first Atlantic cable). On one occasion, experimenting with pottery, Varley unwittingly inhaled some fumes which left him subject to nightly glottal spasms; and his doctor advised him to keep a bottle of ether beside his bed. Detesting the smell of ether, Varley decided to experiment with chloroform instead.

When it was necessary for me to use it I leaned over in such a position that as soon as it produced insensibility I would fall backward and let the sponge drop. One night, however, I fell back on my bed, still holding the sponge, which remained applied to my mouth.

Mrs Varley, who was nursing a sick child, was in the room above mine. At the end of some seconds I became conscious again. I saw my wife above, and myself lying on my back with the sponge over my mouth, with an absolute inability to make any movement whatever. By force of my will I conveyed into her mind the vivid idea that I was in danger. She rose under the impulse of a sudden alarm, and came down.

Another such case was reported in the summer of 1955. In Boston, Massachusetts, a welder was working in a trench when the sides came in, burying him. According to Guy Playfair.

Several miles away one of his workmates, Tommy Whitaker, was welding on another job when he spontaneously had the idea that he should go over to Washington Street, just to see if all was well. He had no idea that Jack was there; he just felt that he ought to go there, and the feeling became so persistent that he left work early, explaining to a colleague that 'there might be something wrong'.

When he got to Washington Street, he found a company truck with its generator running, but no sign of anybody around. Then he noticed that part of the water-pipe trench had caved in, and looking closer he saw a hand sticking out of the earth. Half an hour later, Jack Sullivan was brought out alive.

Later, Sullivan said that when he realised what had happened, a vivid picture of Whitaker had come into his mind. Whitaker, on the other hand, had no idea that his workmate was in danger. He did not even feel any great sense of urgency, merely – according to the investigators – a nagging feeling that he ought to go to the place. 'He didn't know why, but he knew he wouldn't be comfortable until he had.'

In his *Mental Radio* Upton Sinclair, then at the height of his fame following his denunciations of tooth-and-claw capitalism in *The Jungle*, *Oil* and other works, amazed his rationalist followers with his admission of his belief in clairvoyance, mainly on account of his wife's prowess; and one of his examples had been given to him by Bruno Walter. At a luncheon to which Walter had been invited on a tour of the United States, he suddenly felt extremely ill, and his host called a taxi for him. When it did not arrive, Walter felt he must find one for himself, and went out into the street. At the corner, he saw his manager driving a car – 'a most fortunate accident,' he thought. It was no accident, his manager insisted; half an hour earlier, 'he had been seized by an intense feeling that Mr Walter was in trouble, and had been moved to get into his car and drive. He did not know where Mr Walter had gone, but simply followed his impulse to drive in a certain direction.'

PRECOGNITION

In such cases the link appears to be telepathic. But there are others where the premonition has been about some future event; sometimes producing a feeling so powerful that there has been an almost physical compulsion to act on it – as in a case which attracted attention because of the esteem in which the rescued man was held. Americans familiar with their country's history, Robert Dale Owen claimed, 'would remember well Dr Linn, of Missouri. Distinguished for talents and professional ability, but yet more for the excellence of his heart, he received, by a distinction as rare as it was honourable, the unanimous vote of the Legislature for the office of Senator of the United States'; and in 1840 he went to Washington to perform his professional duties. Invited to a formal banquet, he was prevented from attending by an attack of indigestion; and his wife went in his stead, leaving him in the company of a friend, General Jones.

During the course of the dinner Mrs Linn began to feel uneasy about her husband; and although fellow diners pooh-poohed her alarm, she eventually decided she must return. The general, she was told when she arrived, had left half an hour earlier. She went up to the bedroom, the door of which was closed. As she opened it, a dense smoke burst upon her, in such stifling quantity that she staggered and fell on the threshold. Recovering herself after a few seconds, she rushed into the room. The bolster was on fire, and the feathers burned with a bright flow and a suffocating odour.

Her dress caught alight when she tried to beat out the flames, but fortunately there was a full bathtub in the room and she was able to extinguish them. 'Finally, exerting her utmost strength, she drew from her bed her insensible husband.' Half an hour passed before he showed any signs of life, and it was months before he fully recovered. Had she returned even a few minutes later, he could not have survived.

Always careful to obtain attestation for such stories, Owen – himself formerly a congressman – wondered whether Mrs Linn's alarm should be attributed to precognition. From the attestations, he worked out that her decision to leave the banquet must have been taken more than an hour before she reached her husband; but as General Jones had been with him until half an hour before her arrival, presumably the fire could not have started before he left. 'If, at the moment Mrs Linn was first impressed, no condition of things existed which, to human perceptions, could indicate danger,' Owen felt entitled to assert, 'then, unless we refer the whole to chance coincidence, the case is one involving not only a warning presentiment, but a prophetic instinct.'

Four years later there was a case which caused an even greater sensation. The United States' newest warship, the *Princeton*, was being put into commission; and the President, John Tyler, was invited to go on a cruise, along with members of his cabinet, their wives, and other dignitaries. There was also to be a demonstration of the *Princeton*'s largest cannon, facetiously named 'the Peacemaker'. Among the guests was Nathaniel Tallmadge, governor of Wisconsin. When the time came to fire 'the Peacemaker', he took up his position beside the breech.

He felt no apprehension of danger; and the first, second and third discharges were unaccompanied by any unpleasant results. The party then went below for refreshments. After dinner the Governor returned to the deck, where he observed that the great gun was about to be discharged for the fourth and last time. He at once assumed his former position. But the Commodore, President, and heads of the Executive Departments, were still below, and the firing was delayed for a few moments on their account. It was then that a mysterious feeling of apprehension and dread suddenly seized the Governor, and under an irresistible impulse he turned away and followed the ladies into the cabin.

He had hardly reached the cabin when there was a loud explosion,

and the next moment came the startling and terrible intelligence that five distinguished gentlemen, including two members of the Cabinet, had been instantly killed by the last discharge. In his description of that frightful accident, Governor Tallmadge says: 'I rushed on deck, saw the lifeless and mangled bodies, and found that the gun had burst at the very spot where I had stood at the three former fires, and where – if I had remained at the fourth fire – I should have been perfectly demolished.'

One of many accounts of premonitions of this kind was investigated by Richard Hodgson while he was running the American Society for Psychical Research. His informant, Marshall Wait (whose respectability Hodgson vouched for), described how he had landed off a boat in Stillwater, Minnesota, and found that he would have to make his way alone to his hotel. It was dark, but he could see the lights of a bridge in the distance, and knowing that the hotel was near it, he started to walk along the dock towards it.

I had gone but a very short distance when I suddenly felt so strong an impulse to turn and go the other way that I instantly obeyed. I saw nothing, heard nothing; I did not even have an impression of danger, though I did have a feeling that it must be in some way better to turn.

It was. Had he not turned, he found the next day, he would certainly have gone off the edge of the dock into the river; 'and as I am but a feeble swimmer under the most favourable circumstances, and was encumbered with a fall overcoat and a heavy satchel, I would just as certainly have been drowned.'

Myers, recording the episode, pointed out that 'tactile sensibility' must be allowed for; there might have been something in the air – perhaps a slight change in pressure. Yet it would still have required Wait's subliminal self to intervene, making sure that the message got through to him. Whether it came from 'tactile sensibility' – a distinctly far-fetched proposition, but Myers had to defend himself from the accusation that he had not allowed for that possibility, still being advanced by physiologists and meekly accepted by psychologists – or from ESP, was of little importance to Wait.

Predictably, many similar premonitions have been reported by people in the forces in time of war. The temptation is to set them aside since they must have often proved groundless; but occasionally the outcome strongly suggests precognition, as in a case sent in to the Koestler Foundation. In 1917 W. E. Cotterell, a junior officer in a Labour Company, was having dinner in the mess – a corrugated lean-to beside a farm building, well behind the lines, but occasionally strafed – when a howitzer shell landed beside it. As the explosion spent itself upwards, no damage was done to the mess, and the officers were able to get on with their meal.

About a fortnight later they were going about their work calmly.

All, that is, except myself, who had developed during the shelling a strange feeling of exaltation. I had a strong feeling that if we stayed on that side of the camp something tragic would happen. So strong was the feeling, a communication without words, that I met my fellow officers and begged them to shift the mess to the other side of the camp. They laughed at first but there must have been some sense of urgency about my appeal that decided them to humour my whim (I was the junior company officer).

The next meal was served to the officers in a bell tent on the far side of the camp. While they were having it howitzer fire began again, and they realised that the first shell must have fallen near the old mess. When they went over to see what had happened they found to their astonishment that it had fallen into the same hole as its predecessor – but with very different results.

The walls of the mess looked like a colander. We went inside and sat in our usual seats. Someone had left a packet of Gold Flake cigarettes on the edge of the table, as if for the purpose. Half an inch had been shorn off from the ends as if by a razor. We noted where the splinters had entered one side and gone through the other. We should all have been fatally wounded, several splinters passing through each of us.

Tales of this kind would be harder to credit were it not for the fact that there have been several reports of precognitive information being related to radio or television – or so it has seemed. A recent example has been given by Keith Hearne of the Department of Psychology at Hull University. A young woman living in Cleethorpes, in south Humberside, described how she had been watching television at early lunchtime on 1 June 1974,

when I saw the word 'Newsflash' appear on the screen. A voice said that a serious accident, involving several deaths, had occurred at Flixborough. I was alone at the time. Two friends who were living with me came in a little later (between noon and 2 p.m.) and I mentioned the news to them.

A huge explosion wrecked a chemical plant at Flixborough, in south Humberside, at 4.53 p.m. that day, killing twenty-eight people and injuring hundreds. As her two friends confirmed the story, Hearne feels that it 'strongly supports the precognitive hypothesis'. It also suggests that there may be occasions when an experience of this kind – though not this one: the woman who 'saw' the newsflash naturally assumed at the time that it referred to something that had already happened – could be used to give a warning.

Often it has not been easy for people who have had premonitions to act on them, when they know that to do so will cause inconvenience and irritation, and leave them looking foolish if the worst does *not* happen. Louisa Rhine has recounted the experience of a woman who had saved up to go on an excursion boat with her husband and their baby, but after the gangplank had been lifted, got 'butterflies' and insisted it should be lowered again, so that they could get off – much to her husband's annoyance; he would not speak to her all the way home. When they got back, they heard on a news bulletin that a freighter had hit the excursion boat, and it had sunk in fifteen minutes. 'There was no panic; that was why everyone was rescued,' she told Mrs Rhine. 'I might have caused a panic had I stayed on board with a baby. I don't know.'

Mrs Phyllis Morris had an even more difficult decision to take, in that the premonition was not her own, but her small daughter's. In *Out of the Mouths of Babes*, among other cases where children have displayed psychic powers, Alison H. Cooke relates how Mrs Morris had been ordered to leave Singapore when the Japanese were approaching in 1942, and was about to board an aeroplane with her small children when her daughter cried, 'No! Alleoplane go bomb, bomb, and fall in the water.' Mrs Morris surrendered their places, and prepared the next day to board a ship; but again her daughter begged her not to, in similar terms – 'This boat go down in water, go bomb, bomb.' When her small son backed his sister, Mrs Morris gave way again. The next boat was welcomed by the children, and they got away safely to Australia. On arrival they were told that the plane they would have gone by had crashed, with no survivors; and the ship had been sunk, with heavy loss of life. 'Are we alive today because I heeded a child's cry?' Mrs Morris wondered. 'Who can tell?'

Cases where premonitions have been ignored, with fatal consequences, often remain unreported because the victims are not alive to tell their tales. But in one, there was a lucky escape. Betty MacQuitty, author of *The Battle for Oblivion* – the first comprehensive study of the discovery of anaesthetics – had arranged to fly out to Malta, and then on to join her husband in Tripoli where he was producing a film, when

I had a premonition that the plane was going to crash. I do not know how the idea came into my mind. It was not a dream, I just suddenly *knew*. I thought of cancelling the flight, but I am somewhat of a fatalist and was very anxious to go. Also I believed that it would be possible to get out of the plane safely, providing I got out very quickly. So I put on shoes that could be kicked off to make climbing out of the plane easier, and – surprisingly, considering it was August – decided that if the plane crashed in the sea I might find myself afloat on a life raft in the Mediterranean at night when it would be very cold – so I put on a vest. A friend, Sydney Box, took me to the airport but somehow we got caught up in the early morning traffic and arrived just three minutes later than the proper reporting time, and, although it was still forty-two minutes before the plane was due to leave, BOAC refused to allow me on board. In spite of my tears and Sydney's remonstrations, nothing would melt the heart of the girl at the ticket counter.

As they drove disconsolately home, she told Box of her premonition, and they laughed at the precautions she had taken to ensure when the crash came that she would be able to escape quickly and safely. From her point of view, she remarked, the disaster was not that the plane would crash, but that there was a six-week waiting list at the time for seats to Tripoli. As it happened, however, a seat fell vacant on a direct flight the same day, so that she actually reached Tripoli before the plane she would have been on – the connecting flight from Malta.

And *this* plane did crash. It came in to land at Tripoli airport in a sandstorm. The pilot might have been talked down at the nearby US airbase at Wheelers Field, but instead attempted a landing, clipping the trees at the approach to the airport, and belly-landing.

What followed was macabre. The aircraft which crash-landed was an old Argonaut; it had four escape hatches, but two of them on one side of the cabin were damaged on impact, leaving only two by which the passengers could escape. Sitting in the seat next to the front one was a Nigerian chieftain, who had been due to fly on with the plane to Kano. He was very fat and was wearing his ceremonial tribal robes and when he put his head out of the escape hatch he got stuck and burned to death.

Only one escape hatch, therefore, could be used.

Sitting next to this was an elderly lady. It was the first time she had flown and she thought it was just a normal landing, a little bumpy. The first thing that happened, she said, was that the steward came down the gangway, pushed open the escape hatch and jumped out (the crew had got out through the cockpit). All the passengers who escaped from that plane (and about half of the forty-odd passengers who were on it did) stood on her lap to get out of the escape hatch – later in the hotel she pulled up her skirt and showed the bruises on her thighs. Every time she tried to get up to get out, she found herself trapped by her safety belt, and someone else stood on her. Eventually she managed to release the catch and climb out – the last one.

Betty MacQuitty still ponders the episode, uncertain about what it reveals. Certainly her premonition was justified: the Argonaut did crash; people did try to escape quickly. 'Only one thing seems certain to me, the crash was pre-ordained.'

Perhaps the most frequently encountered of all the forms of guidance, of this kind, is the sudden feeling of absolute certainty that something is going to happen, ranging from knowing exactly what somebody is about to say, to seeing a name of a horse in a list of runners and feeling sure – not just confident – it will win. A few people have this frequently, and can even exploit it judiciously, to win bets.

Charlie Chaplin had this feeling of total conviction from time to time, as he recalled in his autobiography. With a couple of friends – the tennis champion Henri Cochet was one of them – he went into a cocktail bar in Biarritz where there were gambling machines – three wheels, with numbers on them from one to ten.

Dramatically I announced, half in fun, that I felt possessed with psychic power, that I would spin the three wheels, and that the first wheel would stop at nine, the second at four, the third at seven. And, lo, the first wheel stopped at nine, the second at four and the third at seven – a million-to-one chance.

H. G. Wells, when told the story, predictably said it must have been coincidence. Chaplin, who had often had such hunches during his life, and who was sure he had extra-sensory perception, disagreed.

RETROCOGNITION

The superconscious appears to be capable of summoning up the past, as well as giving intimations of the future. The best-known account is in *An Adventure*, by the two Oxford dons Charlotte Moberly and Eleanor Jourdain, published in 1911, ten years after their 'time slip' at Versailles in which they had come to believe they must have been transported back into the eighteenth century. Vigorous attempts by sceptics since to explain their experience away have failed to shake their – originally pseudonymous – case.

Except as further proof that the superconscious self can travel in time as well as space, retrocognition seems rarely to provide any benefit; but one of the most assiduous of researchers into the subject, the psychiatrist Dr Arthur Guirdham, has come to believe that it can have important implications for health. When he found that a neighbour had had visions as a child of what he was able to identify as a Cathar community in the south of France, he had her information checked by a leading French expert, who not merely confirmed that they were accurate, but on one occasion even had to admit, on the strength of fresh evidence, that she had been right and orthodox historians wrong. Later, Guirdham began to track down links which convinced him that the retrocognition was in reality reincarnation, and that the traumas of past lives could result in symptoms recurring in present lives: important to realise, he feels, even if there may be no way of preventing them.

Proving the existence of retrocognition presents difficulties, because when proof is found – say, in some old book – it can be claimed that the individual who had the experience might have read the book, and forgotten it. For people who *have* the experience, though, it can be satisfying in its own right, as one was for William Rees-Mogg, editor of *The Times* from 1967 to 1979 and, since then, chairman of the Arts Council. 'All my life – or at least since the age of eleven,' he has written in *An Humbler Heaven*, 'I have had premonitory dreams. The great majority of them have been like flashes of trivial foreknowledge, absolutely convincing to anyone who has experienced them, absolutely unconvincing to anyone who has not.' He also describes a single experience which occurred when he was just about to take an afternoon nap in the room where his father had died not long before.

Momentarily I was walking on the left-hand side behind a coffin in Camley Church, the church where my father was buried. The man in front of me was wearing a green greatcoat in a coarse heavy material I had never seen before; under my feet there was the crunch of straw or rushes as though I had been walking in a barn. I did not then know, but have since established, that in the eighteenth century it was still customary to spread rushes on the church floor.

These experiences, Rees-Mogg admits, have little evidential value for anybody else; nor does he present them *as* evidence. Nevertheless,

they do have great evidential value for me. If someone who has complete confidence in his senses, and knows himself to be in his right mind, finds that he has premonitory dreams which do in fact foretell, has a sudden glimpse into the past which is as real in physical detail as an experience of the present, and, above all, has sudden intimations of the spiritual harmony of life, he has no right to call on anyone else to be convinced, but he is very likely to be convinced himself. And of what will he be convinced? He will feel that the materialist explanation, which depends on the absolute character of time, cannot be true. He will tend to believe that the explanation of the universe is spiritual rather than material, and that is a large beginning.

SECOND SIGHT

In those parts of the world where acceptance of extra-sensory perception has resisted the intrusion of rationalism, such as the Highlands and Western Isles of Scotland, 'second sight' has been taken for granted. Some individuals, it has been assumed, enjoy it — though, as Samuel Johnson noted during his tour with Boswell, 'those who profess to feel it do not boast of it as a privilege, nor are considered by others as advantageously distinguished.' 'Feel' was sometimes the appropriate expression: it would come in the form of a presentiment. But some people are literally clairvoyant, in the narrow sense of the term. They 'see', in the mind's eye, 'stills' or sometimes the equivalent of film, relating to whoever they are with at the time.

In the early years of the nineteenth century Johann Zschokke, an internationally celebrated author and historian and, paradoxically, one of the leading figures in the rationalist movement, felt compelled to admit that he possessed 'a singular gift of visions'. Meeting people for the first time, he might suddenly 'see', in his mind's eye, their life stories — much as if he had known them all their lives, and was simply recalling episodes to memory. As an example, he recalled an occasion when he was irritated by the arrogance of a young merchant he had encountered at an inn. He offered to relate the merchant's past to him, and the rest of the company. The merchant for his part agreed that he would confirm whether Zschokke's account was accurate.

I then related what my vision had shown me, and the whole company were made acquainted with the private history of the young merchant: his school years, his youthful errors, and lastly with a fault committed in reference to the strong box of his principal. I described to him the uninhabited room with whitened walls where to the right of the brown door, on a table, stood a black money box, etc. A dead silence prevailed during the whole narrative, which I alone occasionally interrupted by enquiring whether I spoke the truth. The startled young man confirmed every particular and even, what I had scarcely expected, the last mentioned. Touched by his candour, I shook hands with him over the table and said no more.

As a rationalist, Zschokke found his clairvoyance embarrassing. He could not induce it, even if he had wanted to, as he might well have done if he had needed to find out more about somebody. 'I cannot say that it was ever the slightest service,' he complained. 'It manifested itself rarely, quite independently of my will, and several times of persons whom I cared little to look through.' And clairvoyance can be even more disturbing if it gives insight into the future, as Michael Bentine found when he was in the RAF.

When Michael was ten years old his father, who had been persuaded to attend a spiritualist meeting, came back deeply impressed because the medium had given him information which she could not have known except through some psychic channel; he had forgotten it himself. As a result, he began to engage in psychical research, and young Michael was often present when mediums, some brilliant, some patently bogus, went through their routine, from automatic writing to ectoplasmic materialisations. In the process, Michael himself developed psychic powers, and they were not always welcome, notably during the war. Denied the opportunity to train as aircrew – a faulty injection, which nearly killed him, damaged his eyesight – he became an intelligence officer instead, and in the winter of 1943 found himself briefing crews before they took off from Wickenby to bomb Germany. In this job,

I found my clairvoyance channelling itself into an appalling rut. Now that I was accepted as a briefing officer and got to know my crews better the rapport between us grew much stronger. This was a good thing for the work in hand, but it had a loathsome side-effect.

Every night that the Wickenby wing was operating I would make it my business to drop in to the mess – just to check that everyone had their escape kits and to chat to anyone who felt like it, about anything but the operation. Again and again, I would see the faces of one or other of these friends turn into a skull in front of my eyes, and I knew he would die that night.

This was *objective* clairvoyance of a hideous sort, and although I had become used to *subjective* clairvoyance and could control its manifestations

– at least to the extent of stopping it if it became dominant – in this case the whole process was involuntary and I could *not* get rid of it.

Eventually he did, with the help of prayer. The worst part about it, he recalls, was that there was no way in which he could save them.

Yet clairvoyance has often, for Bentine, appeared in the role of daemon rather than of the Unknown Guest. After demobilisation his career took the form of 'an erratic hotch-potch of "extra" work in films, the odd cabaret engagement and bits and pieces of television'. He needed something to make his name. Staying with his brother, he was fooling around with a chair when the back came off in his hands; his brother took it, in mock solemnity, and pointed it at the culprit, as if it were a submachine gun. After some more fooling with it, Bentine was walking home holding the remains when 'I suddenly realised what I *really* held my hands – a comedy routine of complete originality'.

It actually took three months of rehearsal before I got it right. Sounds ridiculous, doesn't it – but that is how long it took me to turn a rough, halting series of visual pictures into a smooth, rapidly flowing, fast-moving and totally natural sequence of visual 'gags' that fitted the high standard required by a music-hall performance.

I don't believe that the 'accidental' breaking of that chairback when three visual minds were present was purely by chance. Certainly the flash of realisation on that long walk home was pure, subjective clairvoyance. Of that I am sure. Someone told me, and showed me, what to do with the broken remains of a Victorian wooden dining-room chair.

In addition to his successes on the stage, on radio (as one of the original 'Goons') and on television, Bentine has had a parallel career as a writer; and in *The Door Marked Summer* he gives the credit for his success in this field to his early initiation by his parents into the psychic world. They were careful to keep a critical eye out for both emotional overstimulation and deception, and the chance they gave him and his brother

to develop our awareness of other planes of consciousness was well beyond the scope of conventional education or normal religious teaching. This early training gave me a survival mechanism far superior to the much vaunted pragmatism of today's youth, because it opened the doors for creative thought, and has been the main reason why I can earn my living as a writer. The subjective clairvoyance that developed from my father's researches has become so integral a part of my life that I can switch it on and off like a computer. Should I over-use it the price is asthma or migraine, but sensible employment of sensitive awareness enables me to earn a living without hurting other people, and to be given the opportunity to see a little further and a little clearer into the future.

There have been occasions when helpful second sight has occurred out of the blue. When Dame Edith Lyttelton appealed for cases of premonition in a broadcast in 1937, one of the accounts sent in to her came from Patti Alberigh-Mackay, recalling an experience she had had while attending the Bloomsbury School of Art. To pay her way she was teaching at the same time; and she was worried because she had to prepare a class for a geometry examination, and geometry was not one of her subjects. 'On the morning of the examination, when I awoke I saw to my astonishment on the wall opposite my bed an elaborate problem, minutely lettered, and I grasped at once the fact that I knew how to solve it.' An hour before the examination was due to begin she collected her students, wrote the problem on a blackboard, and showed them how to solve it. After the exam was over the students rushed to tell her she had saved them. Not only had the problem been in the paper: it had been the question with the highest marks. Comparison with the question and what was still on the blackboard showed that they were identical. Patti was no longer in touch with those pupils, she had to admit when Dame Edith checked, but her sister corroborated her story.

Occasionally second sight picks up a cry for help. 'One evening some years ago,' the author and naturalist W. H. Hudson recalled in *A Hind in Richmond Park*,

I was walking home in a London street thinking of nothing except that I was thirsty for my tea and that the wind was very delightful, when something extraordinary occurred, something never hitherto experienced. This was the appearance of a face – the face of a girl well known and very dear to me, who lived at the time with her people at a distance of 80 miles from where I was. It was the face only, the vivid image of the face, so vividly seen that it could not have appeared a more real human face if the girl had actually come before me.

As nothing of the kind had ever happened to him before, he surmised that it might be some kind of telepathic communication from a fourteen-year-old girl he loved 'as if she were his daughter', and whom he wanted to adopt. That was something she would have liked, too, but there had been problems, and the project had been abandoned. Cautiously, he wrote to the girl's mother in general terms and was reassured that nothing was the matter. The next time he visited them, too, he was told that all was well. But then, the mother admitted that a day or two before she had received his letter, there had been a painful scene with the girl, who had suddenly, to their amazement, broken out in passionate revolt against them.

She told them that she had prayed to Heaven to send me to her assistance – to protect and deliver her from them. She had also, she said, made up her mind to leave them, and if she had no money to pay the railway fare, she would walk and live on charity until she came to where I was or she found me.

On one occasion, at least, second sight may have saved a life. In one of the cases which Edmund Gurney investigated in the early years of the Society for Psychical Research, Mrs Bettany recalled how while she was out for a walk, when she was ten years old,

I saw a bedroom known as the White Room in my home, and upon the floor lay my mother, to all appearances dead . . . I could not doubt that what I had seen was real, so instead of going home, I went at once to the house of our medical man and found him at home. He at once set out with me for my home, on the way putting questions I could not answer, as my mother was to all appearances well when I left home. I led the doctor straight to the White Room, where we found my mother lying as in my vision.

Her mother had had a heart attack. 'I distinctly remember being surprised at seeing my daughter in company with the family doctor outside the door of my residence,' her father told Gurney. Only on being asked *when* his wife had been taken ill did he realise that it must have been after his daughter had left the house to take her walk.

THE IMPLICATE ORDER

What is now loosely described as extra-sensory perception, embracing telepathy, clairvoyance, precognition and retrocognition, fell into disrepute as a superstition in the eighteenth century because of its links with the miraculous and the supernatural; and in the nineteenth, positivists danced on its grave, arguing that physics had shown such communication to be contrary to the laws of nature. It has been left to the quantum physicists to show that those laws were based on faulty premises; photons communicate with each other in ways which Einstein argued would constitute a telepathic component (parapsychologists would prefer psychokinetic). Conventional physicists, worried, have presented a variety of excuses for the way the photons behave, which do not involve acceptance of ESP; but they have been unable to prevent the collapse of the case against ESP in its earlier form.

In an article 'On the intuitive understanding of non-locality as implied by quantum theory' in 1974, Professor David Bohm introduced the idea of 'the intimate interconnection of different systems that are not in spatial contact', which for him represented 'the most fundamentally different new feature of all', leading as it did to 'a new notion of *unbroken wholeness* which denies the classical idea of analysability of the world into separately and independently existing parts'. In his *Wholeness and the Implicate Order* (1980) he has since elaborated the theory, providing a framework into which ESP can readily be slotted.

The role of ESP has been even more clearly identified in Rupert Sheldrake's *A New Science of Life*, in which he puts forward the hypothesis of 'formative causation'. Crystals, plants, animals and people develop, Sheldrake argues, along lines dictated by a nonmaterial field of force, which in general follows established patterns, but is capable of evolutionary adaptations of behaviour as well as of form. The changes are effected by 'resonance', of a kind which cannot be detected by any of the established scientific tests; in other words, through some form of extra-sensory communication.

Although the editor of *Nature* denounced the theory in a leading article, 'A Book for Burning?', correspondents pointed out that, as Sheldrake had insisted, it could be tested. It had in fact been tested earlier with experiments on rats, which had supported it. Further tests, though their results have not been consistent, have since lent additional confirmation. Considering the combined weight of the implications of Sheldrake's and Bohm's ideas, the accumulated results of psychical research over the years, and the mass of historical backing for ESP, blindly to reject it in its role of one of our invisible assets is surely childish.

Hallucinations

In one respect, experiences like those of Zschokke and Bentine fall outside the standard pattern of hallucination, in that they are recognised for what they are by the percipients. Ordinarily what is experienced is assumed, at the time, to be real. 'Every hallucination is a perception, as good and true a sensation as if there were a real object there,' William James claimed in his *Principles of Psychology* (1890). 'The object happens *not* to be there; that is all.'

Hallucinations or visions are still widely regarded as a form of mental disorder, as they often are. Yet the evidence that they can be experienced by people in full possession of their faculties is overwhelming. When in the 1880s Edmund Gurney conducted his investigation of cases reported to the Society for Psychical Research, with the help of correspondence and interviews, he found that the great majority of accounts had been provided by contributors who were manifestly sane, and had been in good health at the time. The follow-up by the Society in 1894 confirmed this impression. As American agent for the inquiry, William James wrote, he had collected hundreds of cases of hallucinations in healthy people. And to Francis Galton's astonishment, when he conducted an investigation of his own in the early 1900s among acquaintances, including many scientists, he found that hallucinations of sight, sound and the other senses occurred 'far more frequently than is commonly supposed among people moving in society, and in good working health'.

In France, Camille Flammarion came to the same conclusion from the thousands of cases sent in to him. Whenever similar inquiries have been conducted since – as by Celia Green and Charles McCreery in Britain, and Aniela Jaffé in Switzerland – there has been confirmation that hallucinations of the senses, though rare in the lives of most of us, are not necessarily pathological, and can be productive.

Jaffé's *Apparitions* (1957) is instructive because, as Jung (with whom she worked) observed in a foreword, its contents were so unexpected, revealing as they did that among the Swiss, 'commonly regarded as stolid, unimaginative, realistic and materialistic, there are just as many ghost stories and suchlike as, say, in England and Ireland' – and the same kind of experiences, related by people who are neither gullible nor superstitious. 'Naturally enough our scientific age wants to know whether such things are "true",' Jung complained. 'Nobody thinks of asking the fundamental question: what is the real reason why the same old stories are experienced and repeated over and over again?'

The only plausible reason is that the 'same old stories' *are* experienced: that hallucinations can occur in the lives of people who are neither insane nor 'psychic'. And sometimes they appear to be performing a potentially useful function – as if to show us just how ingenious the ruses of the superconscious mind can be, to get information across to us.

In 1935 a young RAF officer, Victor Goddard, was flying south from Scotland when he ran into bad weather, after takeoff, and decided to check his position at Drem, a World War One airfield which, as he had just visited it, he knew had reverted to farmland.

Yes, this was Drem airfield, right enough – I recognised the hangars as I crossed the boundary fence at less than 30 feet in driving rain. Then suddenly the scene was lit with brilliant light which I supposed was sunshine. The airfield was clear, new-mown and clean, the nearest hangar doors were open and on the tarmac apron, wet from recent rain, stood parked, four aeroplanes – three biplanes (Avro 504s) and then a monoplane of unknown type. Emerging through the hangar doors there was a second monoplane being pushed by two mechanics, one on the tail, one on the starboard wing. The mechanics who were there attending them, were all in dungarees of blue.

It was, Goddard realised, a hallucination – perhaps brought on by a narrow escape from a crash. When he landed he told his wing commander, who advised him to lay off the Scotch whisky. Although he had not taken any whisky, he realised he might get the reputation of being 'mental', and decided to say no more about it.

There, the story might have ended, had it not been for the fact that in 1939,

Drem airfield, already then rebuilt, reopened as a flying training school with yellow Avro 504s and Magisters. The Magister was new; it was a trainer monoplane; it was the spitting image of the monoplane I saw, that stormy day, four years before at Drem. None of that type existed back in 1935 – not in our normal consciousness. Meanwhile, our airmen's dungarees had also been transformed; no longer were they brown, but blue.

I realised, or recognised, this happening quite suddenly. It took me by surprise and shook me more alarmingly than had that vision shaken me when I experienced it in 1935. For I had then to rationalise the fact that time and happenings are not as I supposed. The training school at Drem and many features of its novelty were there as I had actually seen them, several years before that school became a complex, active entity in space-time consciousness for everybody else.

The experience, Air Marshal Goddard (as he eventually became) has recalled in *Flight Towards Reality*, changed his life in a number of ways, but particularly by opening up 'a great new vista in my understanding'. First as the officer in charge of the RAF's European Intelligence and later as Chief of the Air Staff in the Far East, he realised that it had been of decisive importance in freeing his imagination from convention's rigid conditioning.

Visual hallucinations of this kind, admittedly, are rarely reported. A more common variety are apparitions of people, thought of as ghosts, if they are dead, and doppelgängers, or doubles, if they are living.

DOUBLES

Stories of doubles range from episodes in which men or women have been seen in two places at once – while Alfonso Liguori, founder of the Redemptorist Order, was celebrating mass in a church in southern Italy he was also seen leading the prayers for the dying Pope Clement XIV in Rome – to Goethe's account of leaving Sesenheim (and his beloved Frederica) and seeing himself, 'not with the eye of the body but with that of the mind', riding back – as he did ten years later, in the very clothes he had 'seen'.

Tradition has it that such 'doubles' led Goethe to believe in the reality of a future life – one of the most commonly recorded results of seeing hallucinations of people, living or dead. But on occasions doubles have seemed merely to be providing evidence of the ability of the human mind to project an image of the person; not necessarily consciously, as Yeats once found when he was staying with friends in Paris.

I had got up before breakfast and gone out to buy a newspaper. I had noticed the servant, a girl who had come from the country some years before, laying the table for breakfast. As I had passed her I had been telling myself one of those long foolish tales which one tells only to oneself. If something had happened that had not happened, I would have hurt my arm, I thought. I saw myself with my arm in a sling in the middle of some childish adventures. I returned with the newspaper and met my host and hostess in the door. The moment they saw me they cried out, 'Why, the *bonne* has just told us you had your arm in a sling. We thought something must have happened to you last night, that you had been run over maybe' – or some such words. I had been dining out at the other end of Paris, and had come in after everybody had gone to bed. I had cast my imagination so strongly upon the servant that she had seen it, and with what had appeared to be more than the mind's eye.

On another occasion Yeats's double actually transmitted information which he had in his mind to send a fellow student. He had been thinking intently about it, but had hesitated to write.

In a couple of days I got a letter from a place some hundreds of miles away where that student was. On the afternoon when I had been thinking so intently I had suddenly appeared there amid a crowd of people in a hotel and as seeming solid as if in the flesh. My fellow student had seen me, but no one else, and had asked me to come again when the people had gone. I had vanished, but had come again in the middle of the night and given the message. I myself had no knowledge of either apparition.

Goethe's longing to return to Sesenheim, and to his beloved Frederika, led to an encounter with his own double.

One of the strangest of presentiments surprised me. I saw myself coming to meet myself, on the same way, on horseback, but in a garment such as I had never worn. It was of light grey, mingled with gold. As soon as I had aroused myself from the dream, the hallucination entirely disappeared. Remarkably, nevertheless, eight years afterwards, I found myself on the same road, intending to visit Frederika once more, and in the same garment which I had dreamed about and which I now wore, not out of choice but by accident.

By providing him with the assurance he would see Frederika again, 'this wonderful hallucination had a quieting effect.'

Examples of even more helpful doubles have occasionally been reported to the Psychophysical Research Institute. An engineer has described how, while working for a Dutch company, he found himself faced with a baffling repair job. One night

I was awakened in my sleep and saw (in colour) on the table of our bedroom that book-keeping machine, while a brilliant electric lamp was lighting, and saw myself, fully dressed, take out with the fingers of my left hand a little triangle formed from the machine and give it with a pincher or pinner at one end a pinch, making it somewhat longer, and placed that part back in the machine.

At the day following on that nightly experiment I did the same manipulation done in the preceding night and see, the machine was working in the hundreds all correct.

The hallucination, he emphasised, was both of the machine, and of himself at work on it. At the time, it was at the Dutch company's repair shop, and it was there that he mended it.

The most curious, and surely the most engaging, account of a double was provided for the American Society for Psychical Research in 1889, and checked by its indefatigable representative Hodgson. Crossing the Atlantic, the *City of Limerick* ran into a fierce and protracted storm; and it was not until eight days later that S. R. Wilmot, one of the passengers, was able to sleep comfortably. Towards morning he dreamed that he saw his wife, who was at their home in Connecticut, come to the door of his stateroom in her nightdress; seeing that he was not not the only occupant she seemed to hesitate, but then came over to him, kissed him and caressed him for a few moments before leaving.

Upon waking I was surprised to see my fellow passenger whose berth was above mine, but not directly over it – owing to the fact that our room was at the stern of the vessel – leaning upon his elbow, and looking fixedly at me. 'You're a pretty fellow,' he said at length, 'to have a lady come and visit you in this way!' I pressed him for an explanation, which he at first declined to give, but at length related what he had seen while wide awake, lying in his berth. It exactly corresponded with my dream.

Almost the first question Wilmot's wife asked him when he arrived was whether he had received a visit from her. She had been alarmed because of a report that a ship which had left Boston had been wrecked in the storm, and she had lain awake worrying about him.

About four o'clock in the morning it seemed to her that she went out to seek me. Crossing the wide and stormy sea, she came at length to a low black steamship, whose side she went up, and then descending into the cabin, passed through it to the stern until she came to my stateroom. 'Tell me,' she said, 'do they ever have staterooms like the one I saw, where the upper berth extends further back than the under one? A man was in the upper berth, looking right at me, and for a moment I was afraid to go in; but soon I went up to the side of your berth, bent down and kissed you, and embraced you, and then went away.

Wilmot's tale was confirmed by his sister, who had been with him on the voyage. His fellow passenger had asked her whether she had come to the stateroom, which had astonished her; and her brother had told her of his dream at the time.

One double, encountered recently, suggests that the super-conscious mind has a sense of humour. Frank Smyth has written extensively on ghosts, among other subjects; and on one occasion he invented one, a 'phantom vicar', haunting a stretch of the Thames. To his surprise and amusement, people began to see and report the ghost, until he was unable to maintain the pretence any longer, and admitted the hoax. Inevitably this 'blew his credibility', as he puts it, as an investigator and chronicler.

In the winter of 1985 he was staying in a country inn, and around one o'clock in the morning was sitting over a nightcap with the landlord's son, a Marxist, who was lecturing him on dialectical materialism when a young woman, whom they took to be the barmaid who had been serving them, walked past them, through the bar; then, a little later, she came back through the door at the end of the bar. It was at this point that they realised, first, that there was no barmaid in the pub – she had gone home for the night – and second, that even if she had returned for something, she could not have used the 'door' at the end of the bar as it did not open – it was sealed into the panelling.

So for once, Smyth had actually seen a double and not only had a witness, but a witness who was resolutely sceptical – prepared to testify that he had seen the girl walking across the bar, but not that she was a ghost (though he was later unwilling to stay in the bar on his own – 'so much for dialectical materialism!'). Smyth could reassure himself that he was 'neither drunk nor daft'. But after the phantom vicar, who would believe him?

APPARITIONS

The most striking form hallucinations of people take, however, is the crisis apparition – the term 'apparition' being used to leave the issue open whether the individual who 'appears' is alive or dead. It is commonly linked with danger or death – threatened, impending or actual; because, Schopenhauer suggested, it was enough

for a person to think of us with strength and intensity to conjure up in our brains a vision of his form, not only through imagination, simply, but in such wise that this vision presents itself to us as a corporeal image, that we should not know how to distinguish from reality. The dying, in particular, manifest this power, and appear in consequence, at the hour of death, to their absent friends, – to several at once, and in different places. The cases have been so often affirmed and attested in various quarters that I consider them certain beyond a doubt.

Angus Smith, one of the most respected scientists of his time, echoed Schopenhauer in a letter to William Barrett in 1876: 'I am not aware of any law of nature,' he observed, 'which is sustained by so many assertions, so well attested so far as respectability goes.' This has remained true, doubtless because such an indelible imprint is left on the mind of anybody who has the experience.

In crisis-apparition cases, C. D. Broad, professor of philosophy at Cambridge University, suggested in his introduction to Tyrrell's *Apparitions* that 'it does seem pretty clear that the phenomenon is telepathic in origin'. The telepathic message is received by the subliminal mind, which 'makes use of the psychophysical machinery of hallucination to "get itself across" – to make itself consciously known to the percipient and thereby to influence his emotions and his actions'.

Inevitably, chance coincidence is the excuse used by rationalists to explain away any apparent telepathic link, and overheated imagination to account for the hallucination; but here, Samuel Johnson offered a common-sense guide. 'Sir,' he told Boswell,

I make a distinction between what a man may experience by the mere strength of his imagination, and what imagination cannot possibly produce. Thus, suppose I should think that I saw a form, and heard a voice cry, 'Johnson, you are a very wicked fellow, and unless you repent you will certainly be punished'; my own unworthiness is so deeply impressed upon my mind that I might *imagine* I thus saw and heard, and therefore I should not believe that an external communication had been made to me. But if a form should appear, and a voice should tell me that a particular man had died at a particular place, and a particular hour, a fact which I had no apprehension of, nor any means of knowing, and this fact, with all its circumstances, should afterwards be unquestionably proved, I should, in that case, be persuaded that I had supernatural intelligence imparted to me.

Psychical researchers have since shied away from the term 'supernatural' on the reasonable argument, put forward by Alfred Russel Wallace, that if such experiences happen they are *facts*, and must be natural. But they would agree with Johnson that one test is whether the manifestation is veridical – as in Johnson's example.

The impression left by a survey of crisis apparitions of the dead or dying is that they are trying to impart a message, before it is too late. Often it appears to be consolatory; saying, in effect, 'Do not grieve!' – as in one of the cases reported by Sir Ernest Bennett in his carefully documented *Apparitions and Haunted Houses*. The chairman of Arundel bench of magistrates, Dr Eustace, had felt confident when his wife died that she would enter another life; but gradually pessimism took over. Then, one evening while he was walking in his garden and thinking of other things,

I came instinctively to an immediate halt, for standing on the lawn beyond the rose garden and less than thirty yards from me was my wife. She stood looking straight at me as though she had been expecting me. Her face and figure were as distinct and as clear-cut as in life. She wore no hat and the slight evening breeze did not ruffle her hair or disturb the folds of her dress.

> She looked in perfect health, but

what struck me most was the expression with which she regarded me. Steadily, without change of aspect, she gazed intently at me without suggestion of either joy or sorrow, but with a puzzled look of remonstrance as though she were surprised and disappointed with me over something I was doing and from which she wished me to desist. Translated into words her expression would well have been rendered by: 'How stupid of you!' 'Why so foolish?' The vision lasted a full minute at least. I was fully aware throughout that it was a vision, for, although I believe that I smiled and that my face reflected my joy at seeing her, I made no attempt to speak or to approach her. With her eyes still meeting mine, she faded from my sight – not suddenly but quite gradually.

It would be easy to dismiss Dr Eustace's experience as a pathological symptom. He thought it was, himself; 'presently I would begin to hear voices,' he feared, 'and would finally succumb to an attack of delusional insanity.' But when he confided this fear to his sister-in-law,

she at once replied: 'I quite forgot to tell you that yesterday as I came from church' (she belongs to the Church of England and attends St Nicholas Parish Church, Arundel) 'Mrs Welch, coming from mass at St Philip's, stopped me, and said she wanted to say something to me.' (Mrs Welch is an elderly lady and much crippled, but a very well-read and matter-of-fact person. My wife had made her acquaintance through attending St Philip's, and had often assisted Mrs Welch to her pew. My sister-in-law, however, knew her only very slightly.)

Mrs Welch described how she had gone to the midnight service on Christmas Eve, Mrs Eustace had helped her to her seat and later 'when I went up to the chancel steps, she came with me and helped me down and up from my knees and then assisted me back to my seat.' She was surprised not to see Mrs Eustace at the end of the service, as she wanted to thank her; but when she attended mass on Christmas morning, the priest announced that Mrs Eustace was dead; 'thus I knew that it was her spirit which was in the church at the service on Christmas Eve, and that it had come to help me.' At the time of the service, Dr Eustace recalled, he was by his wife's bedside in the nursing home. It was then that she became unconscious, dying three hours later.

A West Country general practitioner has recently reported a case of this kind. The husband of a patient of his had been killed in a road accident, and she could not get over her grief. He warned her that it would take time, and that her mind might play tricks on her. It did. The next time she came, it was to say, 'You were quite right, doctor, I've seen him.' He had appeared to her, sitting in a chair; and her depression was banished.

In one of Aniela Jaffé's examples, the dying person was able to convince his daughters that their 'seeing' him was genuine by appearing to both.

It was in Zurich, 18 October 1940. I took my usual way back to work after lunch; it was 1.45 p.m. As I walked along towards the Obere Zaeune, I suddenly saw my father. Strange, I thought, he's been away for the last fortnight, why has he come back so unexpectedly? I hastened my steps and called out: 'Hello, Father!' The words were hardly out of my mouth when he disappeared. I looked around on all sides, wondering whether I had been dreaming. My father was nowhere to be seen. Deeply perplexed and absorbed in thought, I went on to my work. No sooner had I arrived than I had a phone call from a relative, telling me that my father had died of a stroke in the night. I immediately rang up my sister to give her the bad news, and told her about my eerie experience. What did she tell me? I could hardly believe my ears. At that very time Father had appeared to her in the Bahnhofstrasse, and had suddenly disappeared again. Then I understood. Our father, who loved us so much, had wanted to show himself to us once more as he was when still alive. It was his farewell.

There have also been a number of cases where the dying have returned as hallucinations to remind the living of some past promise. In his youth Henry Brougham, Lord Chancellor in the Whig government which passed the Reform Bill of 1832, had made a compact with a friend, 'G . . .', '*written with our blood*, to the effect that, whichever of us died first should appear to the other, and thus solve any doubts we had entertained about "life after death" '. Later his friend went to India, and they lost touch. On a visit to Scandinavia many years later, Brougham was enjoying a hot bath.

I turned my head round, looking towards the chair on which I had deposited my clothes, as I was about to get up out of the bath. On the chair sat G . . ., looking calmly at me. How I got out of the bath I know not, but on recovering my senses I found myself sprawling on the floor. The apparition, or whatever it was, that had taken the likeness of G . . ., had disappeared.

'So painfully vivid, and so unfading was the impression,' Brougham wrote, 'that I could not bring myself to talk of it.' And when, after he returned to Edinburgh, a letter from India arrived telling him that G . . . had died on the same day that Brougham had seen his apparition, Brougham still insisted it was 'coincidence'.

Requests by apparitions of the dead for the living to perform some service have also often been reported; the best-known example being the sudden appearance to Achilles of Patroclus' mournful shade –

> His very self; his height, and beauteous eyes
> And voice; the very garb he wont to wear

– to rebuke Achilles for failing to have the appropriate funeral rites carried out so that Patroclus could cross the Styx; a request which not merely goaded Achilles into performing that task, but also into pledging himself to feed Hector to the dogs.

'I must not forget an apparition in my country,' John Aubrey recalled in his *Miscellanies*,

which appeared several times to Doctor Turberville's sister, at Salisbury; which is much talked of. One married a second wife, and contrary to the agreement and settlement at the first wife's marriage, did wrong the children by the first ventor. The settlement was hid behind a wainscot in the chamber where the Doctor's sister did lie; and the apparition of the first wife did discover it to her. By which means right was done to the first wife's childen.

Sometimes apparitions of the dead appear to be moved by remorse. In the 1820s Justinus Kerner made a careful study of a psychic woman, Frederica Hauffe, 'the Seeress of Prevorst'; and in the course of it she described an apparition, a man with a squint, who was plaguing her about a document which had not been found after his death. Kerner recognised the man. He had had a dubious reputation, and a colleague had been blamed for a financial transaction in which he had been involved, and for which he might have been responsible. The apparition, according to Madame Hauffe, told her that the document was in the files of an office where a man was working; and from her description, Kerner recognised that it was Judge Heyd. Told what had occurred, Heyd found the document. As he commented to Kerner, 'even if incredulity must attribute everything to suggestion or a plot' some things remained inexplicable.

The fact that only I knew that I was sitting at work in an unusual position on the last day of the Christmas holidays.

The fact that quite accidentally and contrary to regulations, a chest was open in the room.

The accurate determination of the position of the document, which was not found in its correct numerical order.

The indication of the small and long-standing bending of the corner of the paper of the document.

The contents enabled the widow of the wronged man to clear his name; and the man with the squint ceased to plague Madame Hauffe.

Another example was provided for the Society for Psychical Research by Count Perovsky Petrovo-Solovovo, a Russian whose interest in psychic phenomena was tempered by a lifelong fear of letting himself be deceived, and who was meticulously careful to check his case histories. It consisted of a letter written by Baron F. von Driesen describing what had happened after the death of his father-in-law, N. I. Ponomareff, with whom he had been on bad terms. On the eve of a liturgy which was to be said for the repose of Ponomareff's soul, Driesen had gone to bed and had just snuffed out the candle when he thought he heard somebody moving in the next room, and went to investigate. There

I saw M. Ponomareff standing before the closed door. Yes, it was he, in his blue dressing gown, lined with squirrel furs and only half-buttoned, so that I could see his white waistcoat and his black trousers. It was he undoubtedly. I was not frightened. They say that, as a rule, one is *not* frightened when seeing a ghost, as ghosts possess the quality of paralysing fear.

'What do you want?' I asked my father-in-law. M. Ponomareff made two steps forward, stopped before my bed, and said, 'Basil Feodorovitch, I have acted wrongly towards you. Forgive me! Without this I do not feel at rest there.' He was pointing to the ceiling with his left hand whilst holding out his right to me. I seized this hand, which was long and cold, shook it and answered, 'Nicholas Ivanovitch, God is my witness that I have never had anything against you.'

The apparition then vanished and Driesen, crossing himself, returned to his bed. The next morning

my wife's brothers, as well as our neighbours and the peasants, assembled, and the liturgy was celebrated by our confessor, the Reverend Father Basil. But when all was over, the same Father Basil led me aside, and said to me mysteriously, 'Basil Feodorovitch, I have got something to say to you in private.' My wife having come near us at this moment, the clergyman repeated his wish. I answered, 'Father Basil, I have no secrets from my wife; please tell us what you wished to tell me alone.'

Then Father Basil, who is living till now in the Koi parish of the district of Kashin (Gov. of Tver), said to me in a rather solemn voice, 'This night at three o'clock Nicholas Ivanovitch (Ponomareff) appeared to me and begged of me to reconcile him to you.'

Still not quite satisfied, Count Perovsky called on Driesen, who, though he maintained he did not believe in such things, stated 'that if he were going to die tomorrow, he should still be ready to swear to the fact of his having seen the apparition'. There still remained Father Basil, who had not answered Perovsky's request for his version of the story – understandably, Perovsky realised. Driesen promised to obtain Father Basil's account of the episode. When it arrived, it confirmed that Driesen had told him that Nicholas Ponomareff appeared 'on the night of November 29–30th, having died nine days before', and that it had begged of the Baron to be reconciled to him. 'I may add that to me did he also appear at the same time and with the same request, which fact, before hearing the Baron's narrative, I communicated to all those present at the liturgy.'

In any discussion of eminent advocates, Sir Thomas Erskine is likely to be named among the greatest in the history of the English Bar. As a young man, he had been away from his native Scotland for a while; but on the morning of his return to Edinburgh,

as I was descending the steps of a close, coming out of a bookseller's shop, I met our old family butler. He looked greatly changed, pale, wan and shadowy, as a ghost. 'Eh! old boy,' I said, 'what brings you here?' He replied, 'To meet your honour, and solicit your interference with my lord to recover a sum, due to me, which the steward at our last settlement did not pay.' Struck by his looks and manner, I bade him follow me to the bookseller's into whose shop I stepped back; but when I turned around to speak to him, he had vanished.

Recalling that the butler's wife carried on a job in Edinburgh, Erskine went to visit her.

I found the old woman in widow's mourning. Her husband had been dead for some months; and had told her, on his death-bed, that my father's steward had wronged him of some money, but that when Master Tom returned, he would see her righted. This I promised to do, and shortly after fulfilled my promise.

The impression the episode had left on him, he told Lady Morgan, was indelible; he was consequently extremely cautious about rejecting such 'supernatural visitings'. Sceptical though she was, Lady Morgan greatly admired Lord Erskine – as he had become; and she was convinced that he *believed* he was telling the truth.

An apparition on this model has been reported recently to the Society for Psychical Research. While Miss D. E. Warren was working in a London hospital, she heard a colleague had died from burns she had sustained in an accident.

On the Sunday morning after Alice's death I was emerging from sleep into full consciousness, and was aware that a young girl had entered the room. My bed faced the door, and I raised myself on my elbow to see more clearly.

With astonishment I saw the apparition of this young nurse. 'Alice,' I said. She smiled and said in her typical lilting voice, 'Return the books. You will return the books?' Her request seemed urgent, and although I had no idea what she was talking about, I replied, 'Yes, Alice, I'll return the books.' She then retreated a few steps and vanished.

Miss Warren went to the hospital, and reported what she had heard. Alice's books, it was found, had been packed by her mother; when they were taken out and examined, two were found to belong to people working in the hospital.

Occasionally the dead have returned as hallucinations as if to look after somebody they have loved. One winter evening Silas Weir

Mitchell, the leading American neuropsychiatrist at the turn of the century, was aroused by a ring at his front-door bell, and went down to find a shabbily dressed girl on the step, who begged him to come with her to treat her seriously ill mother. Impressed, in spite of his irritation at being called out by somebody he did not know, Mitchell followed the child through the snow, and found that her mother was in fact a former servant of his, suffering from pneumonia. He did what he could for her, telling her of his admiration for her daughter. 'My daughter died a month ago,' the woman replied, and showed him where her clothes had been kept. Examining them, he found they were the same clothes and shawl in which he had seen the girl, neatly folded and dry; they could not have been worn that night.

VOICES

Hallucinations of hearing have been reported from earliest times; but people who have never experienced them still find it difficult 'even to imagine that there can be mental voices that are heard with the same experiential quality as externally produced voices', Julian Jaynes of Princeton University has observed in his remarkable work, *The Origins of Consciousness*. 'After all, there is no voice or larynx in the brain!' Yet 'it is absolutely certain that such voices do exist, and that experiencing them is just like hearing actual sound.'

For Jaynes, 'voices' have had an important evolutionary role, marking as they did the transition to consciousness. The central nervous system was supplying information audibly, which people interpreted and obeyed as coming from the gods – as in the *Iliad*. We can now realise, Jaynes claims, that this was a device; that the gods were myths. Nevertheless they were 'the absolute prerequisite to the conscious stage of mind in which it is the self that is responsible'.

Jaynes appears to rule out the possibility that the voices may be carrying information from some external source. Yeats would have disagreed. True, his voice – like Socrates' – was a form of conscience: 'it does not tell me what to do, but often reproves me.' It would rebuke him – 'That is unjust!' – but he knew too much about the mechanisms of hallucination to assume that they can all be explained as emanations from the central nervous system. In any case, whatever the source, they appear to be one of the methods the subliminal self uses to penetrate consciousness – easier, doubtless, on some occasions than visions, as our eyes are kept so constantly busy with the outside world, except in sleep. For Socrates and Joan of Arc, clairaudience was the subliminal self's normal route. In other cases it has had to burst through; as it did for Saul when, 'breathing out threatenings and slaughter against the disciples of the Lord', he took the road to Damascus. 'Saul, Saul, why persecutest thou me?' the voice of the Lord asked him, and told him what he must do. In Damascus he was baptised with his new name, Paul, and began the career which, more than any other man's, set the course which the Church was to take.

Because the link with heresy and witchcraft made it unwise for people to admit to hearing voices, and because, later, such an admission could have led to their being put into a lunatic asylum, it was not until a century ago that Gurney's careful researches revealed how common clairaudience still was, among eminently sane people. And although the voices which were heard might have nothing significant to say, in many cases they were useful. 'I have on many occasions, throughout the last thirty-five years at least, experienced the sensation of a soundless voice speaking words directly into my ear from outside of me,' the Reverend P. H. Newman wrote to tell Myers. 'Whenever this has been the case, the information and advice given has been correct.' This was quite different, he insisted, from presentiments, which for him could be false. Presentiments came from within; 'this voice is distinctly *ab extra*.'

I was visiting friends at Tunbridge Wells, and went out one evening, entomologising. As I crossed a stile into a field, on my way to a neighbouring wood, the voice distinctly said in my right ear, 'You'll find "Chaonia" on that oak.' (This was a very scarce moth which I had never seen before, and which most assuredly I had never thought of seeing.) There were several oaks in the field, but I intuitively walked up to one, straight to the off side of it, and there was the moth indicated.

From the United States, Hodgson reported a story which had impressed him, and which he had investigated. Anxious to qualify as a doctor at a time when it was not easy for women to do so, Mary

Graham had learned book-keeping and worked for eight years as a clerk, accumulating her savings in a bank which had been founded on philanthropic principles and which purportedly had the backing of the guarantees of well-known citizens.

One morning Miss Graham woke hearing a voice say, 'Miss Graham, take your money out of the bank.' Going to sleep again, she woke in the morning inclined to treat it as a dream. She quite believed in these voices, from frequent experience, but came within a recent legal definition of sanity by not obeying their suggestions unless otherwise commending themselves to her judgement. Accordingly, instead of going to the bank, she fulfilled an engagement in another part of the town with her dress-maker. Here she was obliged to wait, finding herself in the same room with another lady who seemed determined to talk to her. Rather impatient at being delayed, Miss Graham was not socially inclined till the stranger suddenly asked, 'Do you know anything of Howe's Bank?' She replied with interest, 'Only that I have an account there.' Her interest deepened as the lady proceeded to give details about the unsafe situation of the bank, with which her husband was connected, winding up with saying, 'I felt compelled almost against my will, to tell you all this, and must beg you to say nothing about it for a few weeks.'

Miss Graham decided that she would lose no time in making herself safe and only just succeeded in going home for her bank-book, and drawing out her deposit, before the hour for closing. *The bank stopped on the following day.*

The story was confirmed, sadly, by a friend of Dr Graham's, Dr Caroline Hastings, professor of anatomy at a Boston medical college: 'I went with Dr Graham when she drew her money, and might have taken mine, but did not.'

Examining the reports of nearly 300 'call' cases, as she described them, which had been submitted to her, Louisa Rhine divided them into three categories: those where the voice was impersonal; those where it sounded like somebody living; and those where it sounded like somebody dead. The most striking difference between the categories, she noted in *The Invisible Picture* (1981), was that out of the 188 cases where the 'voice' seemed to be of some living person, only one was a warning.

A man was driving a truckload of timber down a highway from upstate New York to Long Island one morning about three. He had fallen asleep at the wheel when very clearly and shrilly he heard his mother's voice calling him just as she used to do when he was a child at home. He awakened with a start to find that he was only about two feet from the wall of an overpass. No doubt it would have meant instant death if he had not awakened just in time to swerve the truck away from the wall.

Dr E. West Symes told Myers how one Christmas Eve, just after midnight, he heard a ring at his front-door bell. Picking up the receiver of the speaking tube which he had had installed next to his bed, he was told by a man,

whose voice I well knew and recognised, that I was to go at once to see his wife, who was in labour and urgently needed my assistance. I got up, dressed, and went to the house, knocked with my stick several times on the back door, but failing to get an answer returned home to bed. I went to church the next morning, Christmas Day, at 7 a.m., and shortly after nine the same gentleman called again and said I was to go at once to his wife. I asked him whether he came in the night and he said, 'No, but I *nearly* did at 12.30 this morning.' I said nothing, but went and attended the lady, and then asked for particulars, *without putting any leading questions*. They told me she had been much worse at 12.30 a.m. and had wanted me to be sent for, but that the nurse didn't think it necessary. They also said they heard my knocks on the back door, but being Christmas morning they thought it was 'the waits', and so did not answer . . .

Mrs Symes testified that although she had not actually heard the voice of the caller (as she usually could), she *had* heard her husband answering, as if questioned.

The 'voice' is not, as a rule, recognised by the hearer. Many cases have been reported of anonymous clairaudient warnings which have turned out to be justified. 'When I was about sixteen,' Lady Eardley told Myers,

I had a mild attack of the measles. I was staying with my godfather and godmother. After two or three days in my room I was told that I might have a warm bath; greatly pleased, and feeling well again, I went to the bathroom, locked the door, undressed and was just about to get into the bath, when I heard a voice say 'Unlock the door.' The voice was quite distinct and apart from myself and yet seemed to come somehow from inside myself. I could not say whether it was a man's or a woman's voice. I was startled and looked round, but of course no one was there. Again I heard the voice, 'Unlock the door.' I began to get frightened, thinking that I must be ill and delirious – but I did not feel ill. I resolved not to think of the voice, and had stepped into the bath, when I heard it a third time – and I think a fourth time – still saying 'Unlock the door.' On this I jumped out and I *did* unlock the door; and then stepped into the bath again. As I got in, I fainted away and fell flat down in the water. Fortunately as I fell I was just able to catch at a bell-handle, which was attached to the wall just above the bath. My pull brought the maid, who found me (she said) lying with my head under the water. She picked me up and carried me out of the bathroom – knocked my head against the doorpost as she did so, which brought me partly round for a moment. If the door had been locked I should certainly have been drowned, as far as I can tell.

This was the only occasion, she insisted, upon which she had had a hallucination of any kind. As usual, Myers cautiously made the point that this had not necessarily been a psychic experience: 'Lady Eardley's subliminal self may have foreseen the impending fit,' and generated the auditory hallucination to avert what might have been a fatal result. In similar cases, hyperacuity of one or other of the senses, the theory was, might be sharp enough to pick up certain indications in time to present a warning when one was needed. It tended to be advanced in cases such as one reported in the *Boston Transcript*, investigated by Richard Hodgson for the Society for Psychical Research. The individual concerned had gone to his dentist:

A few weeks ago I had occasion to require the services of a dentist and when I went to his office at the time appointed I found him in a very excited state of mind, caused, he told me, by a very strange occurrence. The office is a pleasant room facing the Common on Tremont Street, and in one corner, the farthest from the window, the dentist had a small work-bench, partitioned off from the rest of the room, and there he had his copper vessel which he used when vulcanising the rubber for the setting of false teeth. He had been working at a set of teeth, and was bending over the bench on which was the copper containing the rubber when he heard a voice calling in a quick and imperative manner these words: 'Run to the window, quick! Run to the window, quick!' twice repeated. Without thinking from whom the voice could have come, he at once ran to the window and looked out to the street below, when suddenly he heard a tremendous report in his workroom, and looking round he saw the copper vessel had exploded, and had been blown up through the plastering of the room. He went into the workshop and found things in a most confused condition, the bench of two inches thickness was broken downwards by the concussion and everything in the room showed marks of the violence of the explosion.

Inclined though Hodgson was to accept a rationalist explanation if one were possible, he felt it was not easy in this case; nor was it easy in some of the examples Flammarion collected – including one from the celebrated playwright Victorien Sardou. 'To give one example in a hundred,' Flammarion wrote, Sardou had told him that when he was crossing the Rue de la Banque one day a voice in him cried, 'Cross over!' He did 'and immediately afterwards a stone, loosened from a cornice, fell upon the sidewalk over which he had been about to pass'.

From the numerous cases in the files of what was then the Religious Experience Research Unit, now the Alister Hardy Centre, Koestler selected one for *The Challenge of Chance* from a former coal miner, recalling the time when as a young man he had been working down a pit in Kansas.

One day before noon I pushed out to the entry a loaded car (1800 to 2000 pounds). A man driving a mule would hook the mule to the car and drive it away. As I had crawled back to work the driver yelled, 'Kid – here's an empty for you.' As I started out for the car I heard a voice, 'Stop.' I sat there, I did not move, then I heard, 'Quick, go, go.' I was scared. I crawled as fast as I could to the face of the room (the passage was three feet high) then through the cross cut (this is an opening between the rooms allowing air to circulate). I cannot describe the noise the falling rock made. The falling roof pushed the air with great force – my miner's lamp was put out, I could see nothing. The room next to mine being worked out, the rails had been removed so I had no way of knowing which way to go. The men who had heard this rockfall came then, and I could see by the light of their lamps the way out.

. . . My father who worked in the mine said later that hundreds of tons of rock had fallen. He had never seen so much rock come down. I never went back to that mine, nor did my father.

If it had not been for that voice 'Stop' and a few seconds later 'Quick, go go,' I would have been covered with that rockfall.

Similar examples continue to appear from time to time in autobiographies. In *Some Unseen Power* (1985) Philip Paul, press officer to the Pharmaceutical Society of Great Britain, has recalled an episode from the Second World War, when he was walking to work during the Blitz.

Many places had been blasted and burnt; debris lay everywhere. Fire engines, pumps and rescue squads were hard at work. The alleyway narrowed and, through smashed windows, I saw that a building had been gutted to a smouldering ruin, leaving a three- or four-storey-high wall flanking the alley standing in isolation.

Suddenly a voice within me told me to stop. For a few paces I ignored it. There were many people around me, almost all walking briskly in the same direction. But the warning persisted. So, putting a foot on a pile of rubble, I pretended to tie a shoelace. At that moment, the high wall ahead collapsed into the alleyway, filling it 10 feet high and burying the walkers a few yards ahead of me. Gasping in the choking dust, I helped extricate two or three people who were visible at the edge of the pile. Others could not be reached.

Recently such accounts, common enough in time of war, have tended to be related to the chief source of danger in time of peace: traffic. One such case sent to the Foundation has come from Mrs Glenda Hawley, a stress-management consultant who practises in Moscow, Idaho.

I was driving my car alone at night in a residential section, and decided to make a left turn. The street light at the intersection was not very effective, because of the heavy foliage on the large old trees lining the street. Consequently the intersection was heavily dappled with shadows. As I entered the intersection, I prepared to make a left turn. Suddenly an urgent feeling that was more like an urgent voice in my head said 'Don't turn!' It was so unexpected and decisive that I went straight ahead and just as I was in the middle of the intersection, two boys riding one bicycle came out of the shadows towards me (no lights). If I had made the left turn as I had originally intended to do, I would have hit them broadside and likely killed or badly injured them.

Green and McCreery have a report of a 'double' giving a similar clairaudient warning, in an episode which will give any motorist who reads it a 'there, but for the grace of God' shiver down the spine.

About five years ago I was driving a car in the Isle of Wight along a road without a footpath. Two small children were walking steadily hand in hand along the left hand side of the road with their backs to me. I sounded my horn but they did not turn their heads so I could not tell if they knew that I was there or not. However they were walking calmly and steadily along the side of the road, and I decided that it was safe for me to proceed. At that instant I heard the sound of my own voice as I explained to the coroner how I had come to kill the children. It gave me such a shock that I stopped the car sharply about a yard short of the children, and at that instant, without any warning at all and without looking round, both children dashed straight across the road in front of me.

In most cases of clairaudience, the warning is directed at the hearer; but in some, it has been transmitted to another person. In the Society for Psychic Research's collection there is an account of the experience of a clergyman's wife, living near Edinburgh. She had told her daughter to go for an afternoon's walk,

and as she was quite alone I advised her to go into the railway garden (a name she gave to a narrow strip of ground between the sea-wall and the railway embankment, which was closed by a gate at either end). A few minutes after her departure I distinctly heard a voice, as it were, within me say, 'Send for her back or something dreadful will happen to her.'

Sure that nothing could happen to her daughter in the railway garden, the mother paid no attention to the 'voice', even when she heard it again.

But soon the voice renewed the warning, in nearly the same words as before, 'Send for her back, or something terrible will happen to her.' At the same moment I was seized with a violent trembling, and a feeling of great terror took possession of me. I rose hastily, rang the bell, and ordered the servant to go immediately and bring Miss A. home, repeating at the same time the words of the warning, 'or something dreadful will happen to her'. The servant, in order to quiet my agitation, said, 'Nothing can possibly happen to her, ma'am, she can be in no danger. The weather is very fine; everything is so quiet; everybody is at church. I never saw you nervous before, and yet Miss A. has often been out alone, and you were never anxious about her.' 'Quite true,' I replied, 'but go directly; there is no time to be lost; go at once.' On leaving the room she told Miss O., the landlady, what had occurred, and the reason of her going out, which she thought very unnecessary.

The servant left, collected the child, and brought her back to the house. She could go out again, her mother told her – but not to the railway garden. That afternoon a locomotive went off the rails and crashed onto the rocks below, at the point where the daughter would have been playing; and three men were killed.

An even more curious case of this kind has been reported by Aniela Jaffé, told to her by a woman recalling how she had been saved from death when she was a child. She had fallen into a stream which ran by a road.

It was just afternoon when all the factory workers were already at home, and there was not a soul on the road. A friend of my father's, who lived some distance away, had hardly reached home when a telephone message came telling him to go back to the works at once. Without thinking much about it, he got on his bicycle and rode back. On his way he suddenly saw a hand coming out of the water, quickly fished me out, and as soon as he saw who I was, brought me back to my parents.

Her rescuer told her father what had happened, and said that he must hurry on back to the factory. But

it turned out that nobody had asked for him, and the factory was even closed. He made enquiries and related what had happened, but nobody knew anything about it. For the rest of his life he would laugh when he saw me, shaking his head and saying that he would never have believed he could have been rung up by a ghost . . .

Sometimes, however, clairaudience appears to be the medium for extra-sensory communication between two people who are close, not necessarily to convey a warning. 'The single most "recordable" incident of telepathy in my life – and there have been many – is that one night I was awakened by my sister calling me,' the writer Polly Devlin recalls.

She lived in London in a different house, some distance from my house there. I was disturbed enough to telephone her, though it was the middle of the night. She had indeed been calling me, in a state of high emotion, and that in response to the last sentence of a book I had written, in which I said that 'I stop calling, to hear *their* voices calling back'.

She had read the book that evening for the first time, and had called to me at precisely the time I heard her.

Far from thinking this exceptional, Polly Devlin has explained in a letter to the Koestler Foundation, she feels it is 'so entirely logical that it is unremarkable. I would have found it sad and unnatural had I not heard her cry of consolation.'

The voices which tend to make the greatest impression, however, are those which are recognised as the voices of people who have died. In most recorded cases, they take the form of warnings; one of the most macabre having been experienced by the Italian baritone Tito Gobbi.

In his autobiography he recalled that he and his brother Bruno had been very close as children, and they had continued to be, even when their different careers, Tito's as a singer, Bruno's as an airline pilot, took them apart. When Bruno became engaged to be married to a Spanish girl who lived in Malaga, Tito found to his and his brother's vexation that a radio commitment would prevent him from attending the wedding; instead, it was arranged that he would take a role in a Spanish opera, which would be broadcast so that the guests at the wedding would be able to hear. But approaching to land at Malaga airport, Bruno's plane crashed, killing everybody on board. Bruno's fiancée, who had been at the airfield to meet him, went home, put on her wedding dress and committed suicide.

Many years later there was a strange sequel to the tragedy of Bruno's death which I think I should record. Though some people shrink from admitting it, most of us have had at least one experience in our lives which is totally inexplicable by what are called rational means. In my case, I was driving one day up a steep mountain path with a cliff on one side and a sheer drop on the other. Since by that time I could indulge my taste for fast cars I was probably driving too fast. Suddenly, with a narrow corner ahead of me, I heard Bruno's voice, so distinctly that he seemed to be sitting beside me, say 'Stop – instantly!' Instinctively I obeyed, coming to a halt on a wide grass verge, practically the only spot of any width in the whole path. A few moments later, round the narrow bend came an articulated lorry out of control.

The lorry driver managed to stop by making use of the cliff wall. When Tito Gobbi went over to him, finding him slumped in his seat, he explained that his brakes had failed. Gobbi returned to his car.

Only then did the immensity of what had happened hit me. If I had not been stopped at that vital moment I would have been swept to my death as I met that lorry on the corner. Even then, the naturalness of my brother's warning and my instantaneous obedience were such that I almost expected to find him sitting in the car. Indeed, extraordinary though it may seem, I was surprised *not* to find him sitting in the car. For in those few minutes the reality of Bruno's speaking to me was more intense than the reality that he had been dead several years.

Shaking all over when the reality dawned on him, Gobbi got out of the car in a state of near collapse; it was the turn of the driver to get out of his cab to ask if *he* was all right. After a time he had recovered sufficiently to drive on. 'But I *knew* that Bruno had spoken to me and saved my life, I know it to this day — and it comforts me.'

Was it the spirit of Bruno that intervened? Or was it Gobbi's subliminal self choosing in desperation the most effective way it could find not just to warn him of impending danger, but to bring him to a stop? Whatever the explanation, it recalls Myers's plea in his essay on Socrates' daemon that although auditory hallucinations can sometimes be a symptom of disease, they could also be of profound psychological significance, representing 'a subliminal faculty to which the supraliminal may be glad to appeal'.

Mrs Grace Norris of Basingstoke would surely agree. In one of the cases sent in to the Foundation, she described how when her father was killed in a road accident she was shattered, and unable to contain her grief until he started to appear to her in her dreams, telling her he was all right and not to grieve any more over his death. She was comforted by the feeling he was still close; her grief subsided, and the dreams ceased. But a few years later, she became deeply depressed. All her family and friends seemed too busy with their own affairs and no one, she felt, cared about her; the telephone 'had not rung for weeks'. Despairingly, her thoughts turned again to her father: did he know what she was going through? Could he help? Barely an hour later the telephone rang and somebody she hardly knew asked for *her* help. Later that day her daughter rang to invite her to come to London and go to the opera. Other offers of diversion poured in from old friends; and as her social life revived the depression lifted.

Sitting in the train going to London I pondered over the phenomenon. Was it a fantastic coincidence (or series of coincidences) or had something (someone?) prompted everyone to think of me? In my mind I said, 'Was it

Dad?', not expecting an answer. Suddenly there was one single, ringing, explosive sneeze, the sort of sneeze I had only ever heard from my father, who had suffered a kind of hay fever that caused these shattering sneezes.

It could not have been anybody in her compartment, she realised. 'Was it my father's answer?'

'SMELL' AND 'TASTE'

Taste is so intimately linked with the sense of smell that in this context, they are not readily separated. Hallucinations of taste are in any case seldom reported – though 'the taste of arsenic was so real, in my mouth, when I described how Emma Bovary was poisoned,' Flaubert claimed, 'that it cost me two indigestions one upon the other – quite real ones, for I vomited my dinner.'

A few people, however, have reported frequent hallucinations of smell; in some cases, actually transmitting information. The novelist and biographer Michael Harrison described how scents would occasionally come up into his nose from the mind, and although this often had no more obvious significance than a tune floating into his mind, sometimes they carried a message.

The first time he had realised that an odour might be carrying a message to him came when, as a romantic youth living in Colchester, he was feeling deprived because the girl he loved had gone to London. One night he woke up choking, got out of bed and rushed to the window to breathe in the night air, only to find himself breathing in what seemed to be a thick cloud 'invisible but only too palpable' – of scent. He had no trouble in recognising it.

It was the famous Lilac, made by Floris of Jermyn Street, St James's – and I knew of only one of my female friends who loved this scent to the exclusion of all others. At nine o'clock on the same morning, I telephoned her.

'Good heavens! How did you know that I was back?'

'If I told you, you wouldn't believe me. But you got back at exactly three-fifteen this morning . . . didn't you?'

'I don't know about the "exactly"; but it was about then, yes. But how did you know that I suddenly got fed up with London and on the spur of the moment decided to jump in the car and come back?'

The significance of what had happened to him that night in

Colchester was that it had told him something which had proved to be correct. Or, rather, he had interpreted it correctly. Perhaps there had been messages on other occasions; but – as was notoriously the case with so many of the pronouncements of the Delphic oracle – they had come over in too vague a form for interpretation to be possible. 'One must first learn the code.'

Harrison's experience could be interpreted as the superconscious self breaking through by the most convenient route available: in his case, smell, as it was so well developed. In some cases, smell appears to break through unexpectedly to give an alarm signal. During the Second World War W. H. Sabine was working in the Ministry of Economic Warfare in Berkeley Square.

On the morning of 14 May 1940, as I was going along one of the corridors of the ministry, I was surprised to detect in the atmosphere a strong odour of antiseptic such as one encounters when visiting a hospital. I gave but momentary attention to the matter, and at 12.30, the morning's duties being completed, I quitted the building to go to lunch. After lunch I strolled along Oxford Street. The traffic was very heavy, and as I crossed the corner of Duke Street, by Selfridges, the conditions caused me (I now quote my diary) to 'think of some little suburban man, thinking perhaps of his garden or a toy for his child, suddenly knocked down, his blood mingling with the tar, and perhaps his eyes crushed into his broken glasses.' I thought how beastly, miserable and futile such things are . . .

At the time, painful though the impression was, he did not connect it with anything more than the traffic and hot tar on the road.

But no sooner had I returned to my office in the ministry building than the telephone rang, and picking up the instrument I froze with horror as an official informed me that the police had been there during my absence to inform me of an accident to my wife. She had been seriously injured, and I was requested to go at once to the hospital. My wife's face, when I saw her, was terribly swollen, her nose was broken, and she had to breathe through her mouth.

A van which had gone out of control had mounted the pavement and struck her, as she was returning from shopping, about half an hour before he had been in Oxford Street, but after his impression of the antiseptic odour. In any case, in his judgement precognition of this kind 'relates not to the event but to our coming experience of it, whether by personal participation, or by the receipt of news'.

Cases where hyperosmia (as Harrison termed it) has actually been of use are uncommon; but one was related by the composer Dame Ethel Smyth, which she had heard from her close friend Empress Eugénie of France. After the defeat of 1870 Napoleon III had fled to England where he and his family were given sanctuary; and their son – her only child – joined the British army. Nine years later he was killed in a campaign against the Zulus, and his mother determined to find his body and bring it back for burial in the family vault.

When she arrived the following year, accompanied by Sir Evelyn Wood, they found that among the native bearers were men who had actually been in the skirmish in which her son had been killed. No problem was expected in finding the grave, as it had been marked by a cairn. By that time, however, following the rains the area had become a jungle. The bearers had to admit they could not hope to find the cairn.

Suddenly the empress became aware of a strong smell of violets. 'This is the way,' she cried, and went off on a line of her own. Sir Evelyn said she tore along like a hound on the trail, stumbling over dead wood and tussock, her face beaten by the high grass that parted and closed behind her, until with a loud cry, she fell upon her knees, crying, '*C'est ici.*' And there, hidden in almost impenetrable brushwood, they found the cairn.

Her son, the empress explained, had had a passion for violet scent – the only toilet accessory he used. Simply to think of '*mon petit garçon*' was to remind her of the perfume. The first whiff had been so unexpected and overwhelming she nearly fainted; 'but it seemed to drag her along with it; she felt no fatigue and could have found her way through the jungle for hours.' She was ordinarily not in the least psychic, according to Dame Ethel – who had also heard the story from Sir Evelyn.

In *The Swan in the Evening* Rosamond Lehmann has movingly described how after the death from polio of her beloved daughter, Sally, she began to receive intimations that Sally was still communicating with her. Some messages came through mediums, but one came direct. Increasingly often, as the months went by, when I opened the door of my flat, a cloud of incomparable fragrance would greet me. What was it? What could it be? At first I wondered whether the old lady then living on the floor above me had begun to use some exquisitely perfumed bath essence whose echoes were somehow penetrating my rooms through the ventilating system. But the old lady went away, and still these exhalations pervaded all the air with an unearthly aromatic sweetness – spicy, yet delicate and fresh; compounded of lilies? clove carnations? frangipani? and something indefinable as well.

The fragrance was not for her alone, but for Sally's friends.

I remember that Laurie Lee came in one evening and after standing for a time in silence said three words only: 'Now I believe.' He had been one of the most passionately resentful of all those who loved and mourned her. I should add that the mystifying and pervasive scent I had mentioned to him was there, indubitably; I know nothing about his beliefs in the wider sense. As for myself, I don't know by whose agency this sign was given to me; much less how it was brought about. I only know that it was so; and therefore once I was sure of it, I murmured my thanks each time I came back to my empty flat.

The superconscious mind, in short, can use 'second smell' in much the same way as it can use 'second hearing' and 'second sight'; and the common assumption has been that this is accomplished by exciting the imagination so that we *think* we smell what is not actually there. But one of the case histories Dr Oliver Sacks gives in his remarkable collection, *The Man Who Mistook His Wife For a Hat*, suggests a more intriguing possibility: that hyperosmia could be redeveloped as a sense in its own right.

A gifted man of Dr Sacks's acquaintance had an accident which so severely damaged his olfactory tracts that he entirely lost his sense of smell. Much to his surprise and chagrin, he missed it badly. 'Sense of smell?' he would say,

I never gave it a thought. You don't normally give it a thought. But when I lost it – it was like being struck blind. Life lost a good deal of its savour – one doesn't realise how much 'savour' is smell. You *smell* people, you *smell* books, you *smell* the city, you *smell* the spring – maybe not consciously, but as a rich unconscious background to everything else. My whole world was suddenly radically poorer.

Some months later, to his delight, he began to pick up a faint flavour from his morning coffee; then, again, to smell something when he smoked his pipe.

Greatly excited – the neurologist had held out no hope of recovery – he returned to his doctor. But after testing him minutely, using a 'double-blind' technique, his doctor said, 'No, I'm sorry, there's not a trace of recovery.'

What seemed to be happening, Sacks suggested, was that the man was developing 'a greatly enhanced olfactory imagery, almost, one might say, a controlled hallucinosis', so that he was able to re-evoke these smells unconsciously, 'and with such intensity as to think, at first, that they were "real"'.

The implications of the recovery are startling. In the first place, it suggests that to try to make a clear-cut distinction between sensory and extra-sensory perception can be a mistake. In the case of smell, in particular – and the closely related sense of taste – there may be a psychic element. Animals in the wild, after all, and indeed to a considerable extent even domestic animals, instinctively know what they can and what they cannot safely eat. This instinct, presumably interrelated with taste and smell, has been submerged in man along with other forms of extra-sensory perception, but it may still be possible to revive it. And secondly, if it *is* possible to revive it, this holds out the prospect of finding ways to exploit hallucinations to replace other senses – sight and hearing – when they are lost.

'TOUCH'

A clergyman's wife, Mrs E. K. Elliott, told Myers and Gurney of an experience she had had some years before when she had received some letters by the post, one of which had contained £15 in bank notes (worth more than ten times that sum today).

After reading the letters I went into the kitchen with them in my hands. I was alone at the time, no one being near me, except the cook, and she was in the scullery. Having done with the letters I made a motion to throw them in the fire, when I distinctly felt my hand resisted in the act. It was as though another hand were gently laid upon my own, pressing it back. Much surprised, I looked at my hand, and then saw that it had contained not the letters I had intended to destroy, but the bank notes, and that the letters were in the other hand. I was so surprised that I called out, 'Who is here?' I called the cook and told her, and also told my husband on the first opportunity. I never had any similar experience before or since.

Her husband, the Reverend E. K. Elliott, confirmed that his wife, 'nearly fainting from the excitement caused by it', had told him what had happened at the time. Apparently 'the subliminal actually saw better,' Myers commented, 'than the supraliminal self' – the implication being that it had given Mrs Elliott a hallucination of having her hand held back.

The same explanation was given by G. N. M. Tyrrell for the experience reported by Mrs E. West in 1937. While doing the washing, she had lost a ruby out of a gold ring.

Thinking that the ruby had gone down the drain, I gave it up for lost. The next morning, while in the same room, I seemed to hear someone say: 'What about the ruby?', and without thinking that I was alone, I audibly replied: 'Oh, that's gone for good, it's no use troubling about that.' By that time I realised that I was replying to no visible person but, before I could think further, I seemed to be grasped by the shoulders and twisted round and the first thing my eyes rested upon was the ruby on the floor shining in a shaft of sunlight made by the outside door being open a crack. I do not wish it to be thought that I felt my shoulders grasped, any more than I heard any particular person's voice, but that I was aware of myself as a person inside my body, but the same shape, which heard and felt quite well without my body.

There was no need to suppose that the voice Mrs West had heard and the feeling that she was being grasped by the shoulders were other than hallucinations, Tyrrell felt; both could have come from within her.

Certainly hallucination can account for the much commoner cases of subliminal prompting which have been reported, in which people take some course of action without thinking and find themselves guided, as if by serendipity, to some goal – as in a couple of cases contributed to the Foundation. When he was editor of the *Daily Mirror* Mike Molloy came home one day when his daughter Jane, a baby at the time, was seriously ill, and found his wife distraught.

The only thing that would afford my daughter any comfort was a plastic dummy and she had lost it in the garden during the afternoon. My wife had hunted everywhere, as Jane was sobbing with pain.

I walked from the living room out into the garden, which was in almost pitch darkness because of the walls and trees which excluded the light from our house and our neighbours. Without feeling 'guided' in any sense and without any thought of a constructive search, I walked to the very end of the garden, reached down and felt beneath a plant that had very wide, fleshy leaves. Instantly my hand came in contact with the dummy.

Molloy has had a similar experience on other occasions. Once he walked along a road where a friend had lost his keys; without looking for them, he found them by the road's edge 'by reaching into pitch darkness'. On another occasion he found five people from the *Mirror*'s features department engaged on a frantic search for an envelope containing a valuable ring, which was about to be given in a formal presentation.

Anyone familiar with a newspaper office will know that after a day's work, every surface is piled with a litter of paper. Instead of a needle, it was like looking for a particular straw in a haystack. Again, without any conscious thought or any sense of guidance, I picked up the envelope immediately.

The only common factor that Molloy can discern in these experiences is the distress of the people involved; 'rather infuriatingly, this ability has never manifested itself when I have lost something myself.'

Another such experience, also sent in to the Foundation, has come from a London woman, a civil servant, recalling how in the early 1970s she was living with her daughter in unsatisfactory accommodation but unable to afford to move to something better. One night she was on her way home when she was 'prompted to cross the road and look into the window of an estate agent's office'. But was 'prompted' the word?

I debated quite how to express myself in that last sentence. I rejected 'the thought came into my mind' and similar phrases because that is not really how it was. It was exactly as if a voice whispered into my ear, 'Go and look in Finch's window' (those were the words in my mind).

There, to her astonishment, was a small typewritten notice saying that vacancies had unexpectedly occurred in a new block of flats being erected for a housing society, and it turned out that she was able to get exactly what she needed.

This was not her only experience of the kind. There had been another which she was 'a bit hesitant about revealing, but adultery is hardly shocking, these days'. About ten years later she was just finishing washing up when the thought suddenly came to her— a prompting which she had never had before, in that way – 'Why don't I get a bottle of wine from the off-licence?' Without stopping to ask herself why, without even removing her pinafore, out she went. A few doors away a neighbour was just going into his house: had she been five seconds later he would have been inside. He asked her what she was doing; when she told him, he invited her in for a drink with him. She hesitated, 'but I was so struck by the way it happened that the hesitation was only brief – it seemed to me obvious that it was "arranged" in some way.' The man's wife, she found, was on a visit abroad: 'we had a very pleasant brief affair, which we both enjoyed while it lasted.'

THE RELEVANCE OF COLOUR

It is becoming clear that hallucination is best understood in its evolutionary capacity. Primitive forms of life possessed none of the five senses; they must have enjoyed another sense before smell, sight and the rest arrived to provide specialist back-up. Later, as Julian Jaynes has shown, hallucinations of the senses helped in the transition to our present degree of consciousness. When consciousness was achieved, hallucination came to be regarded as a disorder, and the possibility that it might re-emerge as an asset has tended to be discounted.

Paradoxically it was an arch-positivist, George Henry Lewes, who suggested that hallucination might be brought back into rationalist respectability. He was worried, at first, when Dickens assured him that 'every word said by his characters was distinctly *heard* by him', because 'hearing voices', where it was not put down to insanity, was usually attributed to spirits. 'The surprise vanished,' Lewes commented with relief, 'when I thought of the phenomena of hallucination' which, he felt, could be accommodated readily into Darwinian theory. But Lewes was the exception. When Dickens further claimed that 'some beneficent power' helped him to write while he was ill – 'I don't invent it, *but see it*, and write it down' – his biographer John Forster believed him, but was reluctant to provide details for fear of what 'the vulgar may think'. And it seems only too probable that many of today's writers would also be reluctant to admit to receiving hallucinatory aid – and their biographers to record the fact, if they did.

From the accounts which have come in to the Koestler Foundation it is clear that many people take for granted that hallucinations are indicative of mental breakdown – or at least will be diagnosed as such. Describing personal experiences, the writers feel compelled to protest that they are sane: 'Not knowing me, you might think me mad or schizophrenic.' One of them even wrote, 'I am not a crank, I am a physicist.' Well, it was a physicist who tried to persuade us, more than fifty years ago, that some of the things which we most value in life are hallucinations – colour, for one. It is as well to realise that things are not always as they seem, Sir Arthur Eddington observed, 'but we do not pluck out our eyes because they persist in deluding us with fanciful colourings, instead of giving us the plain truth about wavelength.'

Mind over Matter

Hallucinations, then, can account for a surprisingly impressive range of accounts of the ways in which our senses can be fooled for our own benefit; and although the hallucinatory experience is not in itself inexplicable in conventional psychological terms, the information passed sometimes cannot easily be accounted for except on the assumption that the subliminal self cannot merely 'see' better, as Myers put it in the case of Mrs West, but can 'hear', 'smell', 'taste', and 'feel' better, if we are fortunate enough to be its beneficiaries. But there are some examples of the power of mind over matter for which hallucination does not provide a satisfactory answer. It is as if an actual psychokinetic impulse is given, with observable physical consequences.

If Benvenuto Cellini is to be believed, while he was lying helpless in a gloomy dungeon on the Pope's orders, barely able to move because his leg was broken,

I often made my mind up to put an end somehow to my life. They did not allow me a knife, however, and so it was no easy matter to commit suicide. Once, notwithstanding, I took and propped a wooden pole I found there, in position like a trap. I meant to make it topple over on my head, and it would certainly have dashed my brains out; but when I had arranged the whole machine, and was approaching to put it in motion, just at the moment of setting my hand to it I was seized by an invisible power and flung four cubits from the spot, in such a terror that I lay half dead.

It would be easier to assume that Cellini was fantasising about the episode, which he claimed converted him to a new, moral way of life, if there was not so much evidence from other sources of the temporary suspension of gravity – as it appears to onlookers. Some of it is based on legend; much of it is derived from hagiography; but some, notably the 'flights' of Joseph of Copertino in the seventeenth century and the levitations of Daniel Dunglas Home in the nineteenth, cannot be brushed aside.

There are also innumerable reports of people who have experienced a kind of weightlessness, not amounting to a total suspension of the force of gravity – among them ballet dancers. 'I often asked him how he managed to stay up in the air,' Nijinsky's widow recalled. 'He never could understand why *we* could not do it. He just took a leap, held his breath, and stayed up. He felt supported in the air.' He could even, he had assured her, 'come down slower or quicker as he wished'. By force of the soul, Isadora Duncan claimed in *Art of the Dance*, a dancer's body could be converted into what she described as a 'luminous fluid', which could possess it in much the same way as saints' bodies were possessed when they walked on water, as in the case of the miracle of St Francis: 'his body no longer weighed like ours, so light had it become through the soul.'

Lady Eleanor Smith illustrated this notion, giving it an extra twist in the process. In her autobiography, *Life's a Circus*, she described how a ballerina, Frances Doble, appeared at one late-night rehearsal to become possessed, and to perform in ways far beyond her powers. As the figure of Frances came on stage it seemed, to Lady Eleanor's astonishment, to be much smaller.

Then, as it glided into the spotlight, I caught my breath.

For the figure was not that of Frances. It had assumed the form of Anna Pavlova.

Pat (Anton Dolin, co-star with Frances) gripped my hand until I thought he would break it. I looked at him; he was ice-pale, and there was sweat on his face.

He muttered, 'This is uncanny . . . it's awful . . . what have we done? Oh, God – why did we ever bring up the past?'

The white form on the stage stood effortlessly upon one pointe; it pirouetted three times – a thing Frances could not do – and drifted like swansdown into 'Borek's' arms, as the curtain fell. I looked again at my companions. They were white and dazed.

Somebody mumbled, 'We're all very tired . . . don't let's imagine things . . .'

Somebody else said, 'We can't all have seen – what we saw.'

Pat and I ran to the pass-door. We were afraid.

Frances stood on the stage, and said to Pat in a perplexed, mechanical voice, 'Pat, I'm sorry . . . Let's take it again.'

'Take it again? Why?'

'I couldn't dance. I must be awfully tired. My mind suddenly seemed to go blank.'

Pat gave me a warning look, and we said nothing at the time.

Later he affirmed, 'We can't deny it. For a moment that particular spirit from the past took possession of Frances's mind and body.'

Shortly before the end of his life Koestler mounted 'Operation Daedalus', designed to give people who believe they can levitate the chance to do so on the Foundation's elaborate weighing machine, which measures and records 'mood-induced changes in weight' – his idea being that it will not be necessary for somebody actually to float, in order to demonstrate objectively the reality of levitation; it will be enough if somebody can 'lose' a few ounces that cannot be accounted for by any known form of physical 'lift'. But he was well aware of the problem posed by experimentation of this kind. It would be difficult, perhaps impossible, to create the necessary conditions for inspiration, of the kind Nijinsky had in his performances, to break through.

Koestler would in fact have preferred to conduct experiments of a kind where self-consciousness would not interfere. A keen watcher of football, he thought he had observed ESP and psychokinesis at work, and speculated whether it might be detectable on film. Here, again, the evidence sometimes points strongly to one or other of them being exploited by players of genius, giving them 'that extra edge of precise muscular control in a fast game', as Joseph H. Rush put it in a paper on the subject in 1964. And in *The Psychic Side of Sports* (1978) Michael Murphy and Rhea H. White provide examples of players of various games who have felt a kind of possession taking them over, giving them that 'edge'.

When Pelé first appeared in a World Cup match in 1958, he played the entire game 'in a kind of trance, as if the future was unfolding before his own disinterested eyes', according to his biographers. Dr Roger Bannister has described how he ran the first under-four-minutes mile in a trancelike state – 'I felt complete *detachment*.' Several well-known golfers have tried to describe the similar feeling which grips them when all is going well, so that they settle down to make a long and difficult putt in the absolute certainty that they are going to sink it. An entire round may be played in this condition, Arnold Palmer has claimed:

I'd liken it to a sense of reverie – not a dreamlike state but the somehow insulated state that a great musician achieves in a great performance. He's aware of where he is and what he's doing but his mind is on the playing of his instrument with an internal sense of *rightness* – it is not merely mechanical, it is not only spiritual; it is something of both, on a different plane and a more remote one.

In sport, the most remarkable example of somebody transcending normal powers in recent years has been Robert Beamon's world-record long jump in Mexico City in 1968, almost two feet further than anybody had jumped before. Over the years, records in athletics have fallen steadily, but none has been broken by so astonishing a margin. Over the preceding thirty years, to point the contrast, the record for the best distance jumped had improved by less than a foot. Beamon, trying to account for what he had done, could only say that he had felt detached, 'between time and space'.

EXTERIORISATION

There is one other variety of psychokinesis which on rare occasions has seemed to occur with the intention of providing people with help, information or protection. Technically, though not yet colloquially, it is known as 'exteriorisation': the use of mind power to influence material objects.

Its commonest manifestation, historically, is the poltergeist. There are scores of well-attested reports of what are regarded as hauntings in which furniture moves around in empty rooms, books remove themselves from bookshelves, cups and saucers rise in the air and fall on the floor, sometimes to break in pieces, sometimes, even more surprisingly, to remain unbroken. It is as if an invisible man, an inveterate practical joker, is amusing himself at the household's expense.

Most parapsychologists believe that 'recurrent spontaneous psychokinesis', as they call the phenomenon, is the product of a force emanating from a living individual, frequently a child approaching puberty. Usually it is as if some emotional disturbance is responsible, and the outbreaks are at best a nuisance, at worst terrifying. But there have been a few cases where exteriorisation has appeared to be trying to impart information; and often, in such cases, it is as if the message is being transmitted by somebody who is no longer living on earth, in order to demonstrate that life in fact continues on some other plane.

Beniamino Sirchia had made his name as a freedom fighter in the wars of liberation in Italy; and he had argued with Dr Vincenzo Calderone, a dogmatic positivist, over the issue of spirit survival. Should he die first, he told Calderone, he would prove his point by breaking a lamp which hung in the living room of Calderone's home.

In 1910, Calderone and his sister were sitting in the room when they heard sounds, as if somebody was tapping on the lampshade, which they could not account for; this went on for four or five evenings until eventually 'a loud, sharp blow broke in two the detachable cap'. It remained in its place; but the next day he and his sister, hearing a noise in the room, went to investigate. 'Strange to say – but strange though it was, I guarantee the truth of it – lying on the table, as if placed there by a human hand, was one half of the detachable cap, while the other half was still hanging in its place.'

There was no way, Calderone insisted, that the half could simply have fallen to where it lay. Later, he heard that Sirchia had died, just four days before the taps on the lamp had begun. Calderone was still a positivist, he claimed; but he had to concede 'the reality of certain mediumistic phenomena'.

Count Charles Galateri's positivist convictions were shaken in an even more ludicrous fashion. Like Brougham, he had entered into a compact with a friend, Signor Virgini, that whoever died first would warn the other – by tickling his feet. Eight years later, on the night of Sunday 5 August 1888, Monsieur Galateri was in bed, when his wife, who was beside him, said to him a trifle crossly, 'Keep still!' Her husband asked her if she were dreaming for he had not stirred. She said again: 'Keep still, I tell you! Don't tickle my feet!' Since Monsieur Galateri continued to deny doing this, they thought that some insect might have got into the bed; they lighted a candle and looked carefully. Nothing! They blew out the candle and got back into bed. But at once Countess Galateri started and cried out: 'Look! Look at the foot of the bed!' Her husband looked and saw nothing, but she persisted: 'Yes, look; there's a tall young man, with a colonial helmet on his head. He's looking at you, and laughing! Oh, poor man! What a terrible wound he has in his chest! And his knee is broken! He's waving to you, with a satisfied air. He's disappearing.'

Countess Galateri told some of her friends about her strange experience. Nine days later, a newspaper reported that some Italians had been killed in action against the Abyssinians. One of them was Lieutenant Virgini, who had been wounded in the knee and then killed by a bullet in the chest. Cesare de Vesme, who published the story, knew the count and countess and their friends personally, and vouched for its accuracy.

Although Harry Houdini became rabidly hostile to spiritualist mediums in the closing years of his life, he had earlier been far from sceptical about psychic phenomena; and he related a number of episodes which suggested the possibility that he had psychic powers. In one of them, according to his biographer Milbourne Christopher, it was as if his old friend and fellow conjuror Lafayette had literally entered into the spirit of the game. While in Edinburgh, Houdini went to visit Lafayette's grave, bringing with him two pots of flowers; jokingly, after he had placed them on the grave, he said, 'Lafayette: give us a sign you are here.'

Both pots overturned, as if a spirit hand had swept them to the ground; Houdini set them upright. Again they crashed to the ground. This time they fell with such force that the pots broke.

Houdini was inclined to put the blame on the wind which was blowing at the time, 'but it was all very strange.'

'Very strange' also applies to an experience related to the Foundation by a professor of psychology at one of Britain's older universities, not a man whom his colleagues would regard as fey. Understandably, in view of the total scepticism of many of them, he does not care to be identified.

During the Second World War, 'R.' was a junior army officer; and one of his tasks was clearing mines from the beaches at Great Yarmouth. They had been laid in a hurry in 1940, and not properly mapped; it was dangerous work.

Consequently we lost more soldiers doing that than clearing German mines. I had a friend called Perry who was the same rank as myself, and he was ordered to take his platoon down to Yarmouth to deal with the mines. Now this chap was extrovert, absolutely fearless and gave no thought to death. But before he went he changed completely. He said to several of us, including myself, that he knew he was not going to come back. Of course we all said this was absolute rubbish, but he maintained that he knew he was going to die. Anyway, he went down to Yarmouth and a week later he was blown up and killed.

'R.' was sent down with his platoon to take over. The two platoons were billeted in the Metropole Hotel, on the Yarmouth front; he and the four sergeants set up a mess in the basement kitchen, where on his first night they had the usual meal of an egg, chips and 'a cuppa'.

When we had finished I took out my pipe. I was just about to light up when Sergeant Horsham, who was sitting opposite me, smiled and said, 'You can't do that, sir.' I asked him why not. He replied, 'Mr Perry wouldn't have any smoking here.' He then pointed behind my head and I looked round to see a notice pinned on the wall behind me saying 'NO SMOKING' in large red letters. So I said, 'Well, Mr Perry isn't here now' – with all the callousness of a twenty-year-old – and turned round and pulled the notice off the wall. Then all hell was let loose in the kitchen. There were hooks screwed into the ceiling along which ran a wire from which hung some old iron ladles. The wire started to move and all the ladles flew off. Plates crashed to the floor and saucers fell out of the cupboard. This seemed to go on for eternity, although it was probably only about a minute. Anyhow the sergeants – all of whom were about twice my age – were so frightened that they would never eat in there again.

'R.' took this to indicate that there was no hoax; and this was confirmed when he investigated, and satisfied himself there was no way in which the episode could have been rigged.

To this day I like to believe that Perry was standing behind my chair saying, 'Bugger this chap taking my notice down, I'll show him', and then pulled the wire. I used to sit alone, smoking, in the kitchen afterwards but nothing ever happened again. But from that moment onwards my whole view of reality changed. I accepted the old adage that there are more things in heaven and earth.

Interventions of this kind appear usually to be prompted by a desire to put down the recipient. 'Just because I am not around in my physical body,' they seem to be intimating, 'it does not mean I have no power to tease you.' Occasionally, however, exteriorisation has appeared in the Unknown Guest's role, as protector.

In 1951, when Michael Young—now Lord Young of Dartington, founding father of the consumer movement and much else besides—was leaving his job at Labour Party headquarters, he was asked to go on a world tour – 'partly as a kind of thank you, partly because people did not know what to do with me, quite' – to collect fresh ideas for the party, following its six years in office; and after visits to Cyprus, Palestine, Singapore and India he reached his home country, Australia, where he could see his friends and relations again, in between his official visits.

The plan was that he should go on to New Zealand, and then on across the Pacific to Canada, which he thought 'a very attractive idea'. But he was also tempted to go back from New Zealand to Australia and then return to England on a boat – he had done that voyage as a child, and had nostalgic memories. 'I just didn't know what to do, at all.' Still he had his open ticket to Vancouver. On the flight to New Zealand he decided to put self-indulgence aside – 'I really ought to go on, to be serious and sensible about it and go to Canada.' He would go straight to the Auckland office of Canadian Pacific Airways. But first, he would have a wash and a shave at the airline bus terminal in Auckland, and then book a place on the flight which had been planned on his tour schedule.

My mother had given me before I left England what appeared to be a little ivory elephant – a very small, miniature one, that she had got in India when she had been there some years before, and she said this was for luck. I kept it in what seemed to be a safe place inside my washbag, along with my toothbrush and things. I looked at it quite often; sometimes I took it out and stood it on the bedside table. When I took out my washbag at the terminal I did something which was perhaps slightly strange: I looked to see if the elephant was there, where I'd put it. And it wasn't. I looked through all my possessions – very few – and I couldn't see it anywhere, I thought perhaps I'd left it behind somewhere in Sydney. Then I looked more carefully in the bag and in one corner there was just a pocket of white dust which hadn't been there before. And it was where I remembered the elephant had been. It had just disappeared – pulverised.

There could be no question, he felt, of the elephant having been crushed. The washbag was in a little leather case, in his pack, and he had had it with him on the flight from Sydney – it had not been in the aircraft hold.

It was very strange . . . Anyway, I took it as an omen: as guidance that I should not do what I had been intending to do in the next half-hour – that I should not book on that airplane to Canada, and that I should go back via Australia.

Back to Australia he duly went. He was in Sydney when he read in a paper that the flight to Canada on which he would have been a passenger had ended in disaster: the aircraft had come down in the Pacific, and there were no survivors. It has never been discovered what happened.

Synchronicity

How far does the evidence from daemon, muse and the Eureka Effect, coupled with the case histories illustrating ESP, veridical hallucination and psychokinesis, confirm Schopenhauer's idea of two different forms of causality influencing our lives, and Jung's hypothesis of what he described as acausal forces, manifesting themselves in meaningful coincidences: the principle of synchronicity?

Examining the hundreds of cases of coincidence sent to him after his *New Scientist* appeal, Arthur Koestler realised that there was no way in which they could be neatly divided into two categories, 'chance' and 'synchronous'. He sought to narrow the field by eliminating cases which not merely had no physical cause, but also resisted explanation 'in terms of telepathy and other categories of "classical" ESP' – on the ground that if ESP exists, it can be held to be quasi-physical, a kind of wireless. But if, as Jung thought, ESP is one of synchronicity's servants, this was hardly a valid omission.

Take what must be one of the commonest forms of coincidence when we think of somebody, for no apparent reason, only to encounter him on the street. Or, as Saint-Saëns told Camille Flammarion, the way in which lovers communicate: in his early days in Paris, when he was deep in composing, a girl he knew would suddenly float into his mind; moments later, the door bell would ring, and it would be her. 'The first few times I believed in chance,' he commented. 'But the twentieth time?' What more probable than that the superconscious was the prompter, on synchronicity's behalf?

It is the frequency of such coincidences that is most likely to impress those of us for whom they are a common occurrence; either that, or the length of the odds against chance, as in a case which Jenny Randles provided in her *Beyond Explanation*. In 1981 British Rail had a call from a woman who claimed she was psychic, and who had 'seen' that an engine No. 47,216 was going to be involved in an accident. Checking, BR found that she had a reputation for making correct forecasts.

A couple of years later an accident occurred of the kind she had 'seen', except that the engine number was 47,299. That might have been the end of the matter, but for the fact that a trainspotter happened to have noticed, two years earlier, that engine 47,216 had been renumbered 47,299, which had puzzled him, because that class of diesel was only renumbered after major modifications. 47,216, he knew, had not been modified. It had simply been given the number of an engine that had been. When he asked why, at the depot, he was told about the prediction, and informed that they had decided to take no chances. Questioned later, British Rail admitted the story was correct, and that it had been logged as an 'amazing coincidence'.

Hardly less extraordinary was an experience of Flammarion's. Writing about the earth's atmosphere, he was engaged upon a chapter on wind when the wind suddenly rose. Blowing through one of the windows in his study in Paris, it blew open another window, lifting the loose pages off the table and whirling them out among the trees along the avenue. A moment later the rain began to fall, 'a regular downpour', and he realised it was not worth going down to hunt for them.

What was my surprise to receive a few days later, from Lahure's printing office in the Rue de Fleurus, about half a mile away from where I lived, that very chapter printed without one page missing.

Remember, it was a chapter on the strange doings of the wind.

What had happened?

A very simple thing.

The porter of the printing office, who lived near the Observatory, and who brought me my proof sheets as he went to breakfast, when going back to his office noticed on the ground, sodden by the rain, the leaves of my manuscript. He thought he must have dropped them himself, and he hastened to pick them up, and, having arranged them with great care, he took them to the printing office, telling no one of the affair.

An indefatigable collector of experiences which could be considered psychic – he himself had coined the term, as a young man – Flammarion did not deny that coincidences, however strange, might be fortuitous; but his encounters with them, and his study of the cases sent in to him, made him feel there must be 'something unknown in the forces at work'. Some of the cases in the category Koestler called the 'library angel' give the same feeling. In a letter to him Dame Rebecca West described an occasion when she had gone to the Royal Institute of International Affairs at Chatham House to look up a reference to one of the accused in the Nuremberg crime trials, and was

horrified to find they are published in a form almost useless to the researcher. They are abstracts, and are catalogued under arbitrary headings. After hours of search I went along the line of shelves to an assistant librarian and said, 'I can't find it, there's no clue, it might be in any of these volumes.' (There are shelves of them.) I put my hand on one volume and took it out and carelessly looked at it, and it was not only the right volume, but I had opened it at the right page.

It is cases of this kind, which give the impression that the coincidence is not merely meaningful but has been laid on for our particular benefit, that make the greatest impression – even when they are of minor importance, like a case related by the American parapsychologist Rex G. Stanford. Paying a surprise visit to some friends, a New York acquaintance of his took the subway, intending to change trains at 14th Street; but when he got out of the train he absent-mindedly left the station. As his friends lived only six blocks away, he settled for walking; and on the way he met his friends. Had he stuck to his original plan, he would have missed them.

In some cases, the daemonic element is much stronger. Shortly after Commander R. N. Stanbury had been told that his ten-year-old daughter Elizabeth was suffering from an incurable form of leukemia, he was startled by the sudden appearance of a divinity notebook which he had kept at school, containing an essay on Jesus' miracles. When he was told that this daughter had no more than a week to live, he happened upon a book on the Burrswood healing centre in the local library; and by chance met a respected business man, whom he did not know, but who brought up the subject of Burrswood, and when told about Elizabeth suggested she should be taken to a healing service there. She was. 'Elizabeth is now twenty-two, and has not been near a doctor in the last twelve years.' 'Of one thing I am certain,' Commander Stanbury concluded after surveying these and other incidents. 'When events beyond coincidence occur, we should heed them very seriously.'

A remarkable experience in this category has been related by Rosamond Lehmann. Following a visit to some pre-Christian and early Christian monuments in Northern Ireland, 'said to have once been centres of spiritual power', she was reading aloud to her friends in the car to while away the journey back, and she gave them Edward Taylor's little-known 'Upon a Wasp Chilled by the Cold'. A wasp 'is not apt to be celebrated with tender observation and concern', she comments, recalling the occasion. 'In fact that poem must be a unique tribute to its beauty and its spirited hold on life'; it particularly appeals to her. When they arrived at the airport,

I opened the car door and stepped out; and amid shouts from porters of 'Look out, madam!' was met – greeted would be the more appropriate word – by a surge of wasps. I can only say that they circled before me as if performing a kind of ceremonial dance. A murmurous swarm, not buzzing but *singing*; a faintly unearthly sound which reminded me of what a professional bee man once told me: that bees sing 'a special ditty, a mournful ditty' when their swarm is taken. This was not exactly mournful, but special it was, as if acknowledging me with an unmistakable appearance of good will; as if, because of that recital during the drive, I had somehow been able to touch the spirit of the world of wasps.

Historically, one of the most often recorded forms of meaningful coincidence has been omens, linked to some notable event. 'The afternoon on which Jung died, a great thunderstorm raged over his house at Kusnacht, as if nature herself were mobilised to acknowledge the event,' Laurens van der Post noted in his biography of Jung. 'Just about the time of his death, lightning struck his favourite tree in the garden.'

At the time, van der Post was on a liner returning from a visit to

Africa. Between sleeping and waking one afternoon, he had a vision of himself in avalanche country, filled with the foreknowledge of imminent disaster.

Suddenly, at the far end of the valley on one Matterhorn peak of my vision, still caught in the light of the sun, Jung appeared. He stood there briefly, as I had seen him some weeks before at the gate, at the end of the garden of his house, then waved his hand at me and called out, 'I'll be seeing you.' Then he vanished down the far side of the mountain.

The next morning, when van der Post looked out through his cabin porthole,

I saw a great, white, lone albatross gliding by it; the sun on fire on its wings. As it glided by it turned its head and looked straight at me. I had done that voyage countless times before and such a thing had never happened to me, and I had a feeling as if some tremendous ritual had been performed. Hardly had I got back into bed when my steward appeared with a tray of tea and fruit and, as he always did, the ship's radio news. I opened it casually. The first item I saw was the announcement that Jung had died the previous afternoon at his home in Zurich. Taking into consideration the time, the latitude and longitude of the ship's position, it was clear that my dream, or vision, had come to me at the moment of his death.

Another curious example of this type of coincidence has been described by the author Guy Lyon Playfair. In 1981 he was doing some research for an American television company into the events at Fatima, in Portugal, in 1917, after three children had seen what they took to be the Virgin Mary. A huge crowd of perhaps 100,000 people who had come to the spot 'saw' the sun burst through the clouds, go round in zigzag circles, bathe the landscape in all the colours of the rainbow, and finally fall to earth. Playfair was sceptical of such tales, but his job was simply to summarise the research which had been carried out into the episode; and after examining the relevant Portuguese papers on microfilm at the British Library's Colindale branch, he went down to the cafeteria where, as he had nothing to read, he ate his sandwich 'and thought about what a Jesuit scientist named Pio Sciatizzi called the most obvious and colossal miracle in history'.

I stared at the clouds over Colindale. As I was below ground level I could see nothing else. It was a windy and overcast day and thick layers of low-lying cumulo-nimbus swirled past. I watched the peaceful and relaxing display for a few minutes, as my stomach did its best to process the unfamiliar white bread.

Then came the miracle.

The clouds parted, and the sun appeared briefly through an alignment of gaps in at least three layers of cloud, its rays reflected in sudden bright spots on their edges, and the solar disc itself visible through a protective shield of mist. The lower cloud layer was moving faster than the upper ones, and for one or two seconds the bright spots moved from one edge of the gap above to the other, giving a striking impression of a zigzag motion of the sun – a feature common to many of the eye-witness accounts from Fatima. Seen through moving clouds, I found, it is indeed the sun and not the clouds that can appear to move, as it reappears after each brief occultation. The whole effect was uncannily similar to what I had only just finished reading about; the sighting took place slap in the middle of my field of vision and the timing was exactly right. A few minutes earlier, and my attention might have been on my food and drink. A minute later I would have been on my way home.

Guy Playfair is an experienced psychical researcher. He has watched 'psychic surgeons' perform their operations in Brazil, investigated poltergeists in London, engaged in telepathy experiments, and tested mediums. Some of his experiences in the course of his research have been startling, but

the Colindale event was of an entirely different order. Although it was a wholly natural phenomenon in itself, it gave the impression that it took place when and where it did solely for my benefit. It taught me that if one applies the mind to a scientific problem with enough determination, the solution is likely to appear sometimes in the least expected ways, provided that it is in the general interest in addition to my own. This has been confirmed on a number of subsequent occasions.

It is ironical, Playfair recalls, that what could be regarded as a debunking of part of the Fatima miracle should have given him enlightenment, much as its acceptance has given to millions of the Catholic faithful. Had he been one of them, he might have put a different interpretation on his experience, 'but its effect would probably have been very similar.'

There is some, admittedly slender, evidence for meaningful coincidence operating to offer protection to members of a group –

as if a form of mass hysteria has emerged in a protective role. In *Earthworks* (1986) Lyall Watson relates how the choir in a church in Beatrice, Nebraska, used to assemble for practice on fixed dates at 7.20 p.m. On 1 March 1950, all fifteen of them were late.

The minister's wife, the one who played the organ, was still ironing her daughter's dress. One soprano was finishing her geometry homework. Another couldn't start her car. Two of the tenors were listening, each in their own homes, to the end of a sports broadcast. The bass had taken a quick nap and overslept. There were ten separate reasons to account for the unusual fact that not one of the choir turned up on time. And at 7.25 p.m. that evening the empty church was wrecked by a devastating explosion.

That all the members of the choir should have been late was improbable, Watson feels, but not very surprising. That they should all have been late on the night the boiler blew up 'begins to border on the uncanny'.

So do the results of an experiment conducted by William Cox into accidents on the American railways. He managed to obtain figures for the number of passengers involved in some accidents, and to compare them with the number who had taken the same trains on the same day for four weeks before. Invariably, he found, there were fewer passengers on the trains which had been involved in accidents.

One other category of coincidence attracted Koestler's attention: 'the practical joker'; and if the 'timid hopes' he expressed in his farewell note that there may be some form of afterlife 'beyond due confines of space, time and matter' have been realised, he will surely have been amused at an episode in the offices of the Foundation which bears his name.

Brought in to work in the Foundation fresh from university in 1984, to compile a bibliography on a subject she knew nothing about for somebody she hardly knew, Joanna Trevelyan arrived full of trepidation, wondering

if I hadn't talked my way right out of my depth, this time. The room was full of books and people with very little space for someone new. Ruth, my employer, suggested I sat at Koestler's desk, which she had recently acquired at an auction. No one had used it since his death and Ruth was far too in awe of it to do more than just set it down in a corner. We pulled the desk away from the wall, found a chair and I sat down with a pile of index cards and a biro. Now what? I opened the first drawer that came to hand. It was empty save for one white postcard, addressed to Arthur Koestler and dated 20 February 1961 – a month or so after I was born. On the other side was a short note:

> Thank you very much
> Joanna

Whether we attribute coincidences to chance or to some as yet undiscovered principle, Koestler concluded, 'is ultimately a matter of inclination and temperament'. He had found to this surprise that many of his scientist friends accepted that there is some principle, though they might be reluctant to admit it, even to themselves.

The issue, he decided, would not, and indeed could not, be settled by any appeal to conventional science; and he stressed that 'no amount of scientific knowledge can help a person to decide which of these alternative beliefs is more reasonable'. Whatever the truth of the matter, though, coincidences which appeared to be meaningful to the individuals who experienced them could have decisive consequences, prompting 'drastic changes in a person's mental outlook' ranging from religious conversion to 'an agnostic willingness to admit the existence of levels of reality beyond the vocabulary of rational thought' – the type of willingness which he had himself reached through his own experience of meaningful coincidences, and through his encounter with the oceanic feeling.

The Oceanic Feeling

Recalling in *The Invisible Writing* how the mathematical formulae he scratched on the wall of his prison cell had enchanted him, Koestler was reminded how

for the first time, I suddenly understood the reason for this enchantment: the scribbled symbols on the wall represented one of the rare cases where a meaningful and comprehensive statement about the infinite is arrived at by precise and finite means. The infinite is a mystical mass shrouded in a haze; and yet it was possible to gain some knowledge of it without losing oneself in treacly ambiguities. The significance of this swept over me like a wave. The wave had originated in an articulate verbal insight; but this evaporated at once, leaving in its wake only a wordless essence, a fragrance of eternity, a quiver of the arrow in the blue. I must have stood there for some minutes, entranced, with a wordless awareness that 'this is perfect – perfect'; until I noticed some slight mental discomfort nagging at the back of my mind – some trivial circumstance that marred the perfection of the moment. Then I remembered the nature of that irrelevant annoyance: I was, of course, in prison and might be shot. But this was immediately answered by a feeling whose verbal translation would be: 'So what? Is that all? Have you got nothing more serious to worry about?' – an answer so spontaneous, fresh and amused as if the intruding annoyance had been the loss of a collar stud. Then I was floating on my back in a river of peace, under bridges of silence. It came from nowhere and flowed nowhere. Then there was no river and no I. The I had ceased to exist.

It was embarrassing, he admitted, for somebody who aimed at verbal precision to use such phrases; 'yet "mystical" experiences, as we dubiously call them, are not nebulous, vague or maudlin – they only become so when we debase them by verbalisation.'

In his book *Mysticism* F. C. Happold has identified the most marked characteristic of such mystical states. They cannot readily be described in words. They provide insights 'which carry with them a tremendous sense of authority'. They are transient, rarely lasting for more than a few minutes. They cannot be prepared for. They gave 'a consciousness of the Oneness of everything'. They leave a sense of timelessness. And they establish the conviction that the 'I' with which we are familiar is not the real 'I'.

Although they have often been reported as occurring in a time of great emotional or spiritual tension, they can arrive out of the blue, as they did for the eminent psychiatrist Dr Alan McGlashan. In a letter to the Koestler Foundation, he has recalled that he was in a London taxi, on a summer morning,

relaxed, looking casually out of the window, on the way to my consulting room in Wimpole Street. Suddenly I was bathed in unbelievably brilliant pure white light, and I experienced an instant certainty that all the events of my life – being a doctor, writing, flying, being married – all such things were completely irrelevant to the level of being which I was touching. It was not that these daily activities were meaningless – on the contrary, they gained an added value from their transience; it was that I knew beyond peradventure that all such values could only be relevant to this moment of illumination.

McGlashan has since 'needed no other religious conviction than this'; but it is probably true to say that the great majority of present-day oceanic experiences are interpreted by those who have them as indicating the presence of the deity. Often they have led to conversions. Inevitably the religious aspect, documented in the productions of the Alister Hardy Research Centres at Oxford and Princeton, has provoked a backlash from rationalists: Marghanita Laski in her books on ecstasy; Andrew Neher, a professor of psychology, in *The Psychology of Transcendence*.

There are two possible explanations for ecstatic experiences, according to Ms Laski. 'Either they are, as many say they feel they are, from an extra-human source – supernatural, preternatural, other-worldly, divine. A second explanation, and the one I believe to be true, is that these experiences are purely human, and have no external source.' To prove her point she sets course not with a report of a mystical experience by one of the great religious mystics, like

St Augustine, or even by one of the secular variety, like Wordsworth, but with an account which appeared in *The Times* of 3 June 1974 of an episode related by Mary Wilson, wife of the prime minister.

According to this report, Mrs Wilson had been 'sick with fear' – her own words – when she had first to move into 10 Downing Street. She is a religious woman with a practice of prayer, and she had prayed for help. Then, one day, alone on a beach in the Isles of Scilly, she had what she described as 'a mystical experience . . . a most extraordinary experience as if I was dissolving'. *The Times* report went on, 'She had felt at one with the past and the future, and all the anxieties of the world seemed to disappear.'

If Marghanita Laski had contented herself with making the case that even people who are as down-to-earth as Mary Wilson can have similar experiences to those of an Augustine or a Wordsworth, and that the interpretation put upon them varies with the pre-conceptions and expectations of the individual, she would have made a valid point – even if not an original one: William James had made it in *The Varieties of Religious Experience* (1902), surveying the writings of the Christian mystics, along with such pantheists as Richard Jefferies.

The fact is that the mystical feeling of enlargement, union, and emancipation has no specific intellectual content whatever of its own. It is capable of forming matrimonial alliances with material furnished by the most diverse philosophies and theologies, provided only they can find a place in their framework for its peculiar emotional mood. We have no right, therefore, to invoke its prestige as distinctively in favour of any special belief, such as that in absolute idealism, or in absolute monistic identity, or in the absolute goodness of the world. It is only relatively in favour of all these things – it passes out of common human consciousness in the direction in which they lie.

Mystical states, James further asserted, could have baneful as well as beneficial consequences.

But the higher ones among them point in directions to which the religious sentiments even of non-mystical men incline. They tell of the supremacy of the ideal, of vastness, of union, of safety and of rest. They offer us *hypotheses*, hypotheses which we may voluntarily ignore, but which as thinkers we cannot possible upset. The supernaturalism and optimism to which they would persuade us may, interpreted in one way or another, be after all the truest insights into the meaning of life.

Unluckily the assumptions had tended to be either that they were the work of the Holy Spirit, or that they were fit only for inclusion in textbooks of insanity: 'open one of these, and you will find abundant cases in which "mystical ideas" are cited as characteristic symptoms of feeble or deluded states of mind.' This attitude is by no means extinct: the term 'mystical' is commonly used by scientists as synonymous with 'scatty', and the experiences are still sometimes attributed to temporal-lobe epilepsy. Those rationalists who are prepared to take them seriously are careful to try to naturalise them as psychological aberrations. They can easily be explained, Marghanita Laski insists, without the need to invoke 'supernatural, preternatural, other-worldly, divine sources'. So confident is she that she does not bother to discuss the evidence for possible paranormal influences.

Professor Neher believes that transcendent experiences are very important; but precisely because he is impressed by them, he is anxious to keep them in tune with conventional psychology, by demonstrating that there is nothing paranormal about them. So anxious, in fact, that he devotes more than half his book to discrediting the evidence produced by psychical research. Apart from the familiar difficulty of proving a negative, however, the sources upon whom he relies are largely unreliable, and some of them have long since been totally discredited.

For the present, the issue whether outside influences promote the oceanic sense, and suffuse it, must remain unsettled. What remains as valid as when it was written over seventy years ago by Evelyn Underhill, in her *Mysticism*, is her comment on the reports of people who have had the experience. It forms a body of evidence 'curiously self-consistent and often mutually explanatory, which must be taken into account before we can add up the sum of the energies and potentialities of the human spirit, or reasonably speculate on its relations to the unknown world which lies outside the boundaries of science'. It is as if the oceanic sense is an evolutionary device to remind us that materialism is not enough: a form of psychic shock treatment which the Unknown Guest resorts to, in appropriate cases, to jolt us out of our conditioned ways of thinking and living.

The Search for
the Superconscious

METHOD IN MADNESS

Inevitably the question arises: granted that the superconscious self has abilities and powers which all of us could benefit from – far more often than most of us actually do – are there ways in which it can be tapped more easily, without risk to the authority of the conscious self?

The main problem is that most of us are still inhibited by the fear, a hangover from positivism, that we ought to try to remain in our 'right minds' – our conscious minds; and that if we lose our hold on them, except of course for such purposes as sleep, we risk 'going out of our minds' – becoming insane. Hence the still prevalent idea that 'hearing voices' is a pathological condition, requiring psychiatric treatment.

It is true that the liberation of the superconscious self requires care. The art of dissociation – of allowing the subliminal to take over, in an altered state of consciousness – may reveal the existence of unexpected and unwelcome secondary personalities, jostling for supremacy, as in the three-faces-of-Eve case. Still, if they exist they need to be recognised, and dealt with. Whether or not they are pathological can only be determined by whether or not they render the individual incapable of leading a normal life in the community. Admittedly this can result in injustice, where a community happens to hold intolerant views of what should be considered abnormal – or, as in Russia, where the authorities brand as mentally disordered people who refuse to toe the party lines. But it is hard to think of any other method. Does the dissociation – providing trances, voices, or whatever – benefit the individual (and by extension, the community)? If so, even though the symptoms may have something in common with those of schizophrenia, it is as absurd to affix that label to them as it would be to say that everybody who has a hallucination must be suffering from delirium tremens.

Inevitably there will be borderline cases, where the benefit has to be weighed against the nuisance. In his lectures on metaphysics delivered in 1836 the Scots philosopher Sir William Hamilton drew attention to a phenomenon which he regarded as 'one of the most marvellous in the whole compass of psychology': latency – the ability of men and women to produce startling evidence of abilities which nobody knew they possessed – and which they themselves could not account for. Often they were in lunatic asylums; yet hardly any attempt has been made to study latency, except by Benjamin Rush in America. Rush had described how in his practice he had found astonishing evidence that talents 'for eloquence, poetry, music, and painting, and uncommon ingenuity in several of the mechanical arts, are often evolved in this state of madness'. A female patient of his who had gone mad after parturition 'sang hymns and songs of her own composition during the latter stage of her illness, with a tone of voice so soft and pleasant that I hung upon it with delight every time I visited her, though she had never discovered any talent for poetry or music before'; and 'where is the hospital for mad people in which elegant and completely rigged ships, and curious pieces of machinery, have not been exhibited by persons who never discovered the least turn for a mechanical art, previously to their derangement?'

In such cases, may there be method in the madness? This possibility was not squarely confronted until, in the 1960s, Ronald Laing developed his theme that mental illness is not necessarily a breakdown: it can be a breakthrough. Unluckily for the prospects of establishing this proposition, no simple way has been found to transfer individuals from one category to the other; though there have been cases where the introduction of automatic writing or drawing has enabled a disturbed patient to recover sufficient self-control to be pronounced in 'remission'. Nevertheless it seems likely that many a case of psychosis could be helped if ways can be found to release promptings from the subliminal self which are misdirected, rather than senseless or dangerous.

A few men of genius have recognised that their mental disorder can serve their purpose. George Cantor's name may not be generally familiar, but among mathematicians it stands high. His inability to solve certain problems appears to have precipitated the breakdown which in his later fifties led to his entering a mental hospital. 'During the long months of seclusion his mind was left free to ponder many things,' Joseph Warren Dauben of Harvard University has observed, 'and in the silence he could perceive the workings of a divine muse; he could hear a secret voice from above which brought him inspiration and enlightenment', and which culminated in his initiation of a whole new branch of mathematics.

DREAMS

One altered state of consciousness which arouses no fears is sleep; and dreams have been one of the commonest and most impressive ways through which the superconscious mind transmits its information. History confirms that in spite of their many disadvantages, their chaotic character and the fact that they are so often and so quickly forgotten, dreams have been the most important of the sources of information from the superconscious self. It is no exaggeration to state that they have often moulded human destiny.

In many tribal communities, dreams were relied upon for guidance about how the tribe should deal with its problems, ranging from curing an outbreak of disease to finding game. In early civilisations, dreams were assumed to be one of the devices the gods used to pass their instructions, and their warnings. Dreams had a profound influence, if the Old Testament is to be relied upon, on the prophets, and consequently on the course taken by the Israelites. It was through a dream that the identity of the infant Jesus was announced to Mary and Joseph. A dream convinced Mahomet of his destiny as one of the prophets. Dreams have since provided poets with their inspiration, scientists with their formulae. Their influence has been incalculable.

One particular aspect of dreams has excited particular interest over the past half century: the fact that they sometimes appear to foretell the future. The man chiefly responsible for reviving this belief, long ridiculed by rationalists, was J. W. Dunne, whose *Experiment with Time*, published in 1927, listed a string of dreams in which he had seen something which he was going to encounter in the next few days. Paradoxically the impact of his book was all the greater in that most of the dreams were commonplace, and the glimpses of the future of little importance except *as* glimpses of the future – they did not provide him with any Derby winners. He was insistent, too, that he was not preaching a form of occultism; it was 'merely the account of an extremely cautious reconnaissance in a novel direction'. But most importantly, as things turned out, he suggested a way in which his readers could try for themselves to find if they, too, were dreaming of the future, without being aware of it (because most of us forget most of our dreams within a second or two of waking). A pencil and pad beside the bed, he urged, were essential equipment. Dream recall should be practised every morning, and everything remembered should be written down, because often it was the trivia which would later be encountered in reality. As J. B. Priestley was to find years later, when he appealed for examples of precognitive dreams in connection with the making of a television programme, a wide range of people had evidently tried the experiment, and in some cases with remarkable results.

One of Dunne's examples was particularly significant because it prompted him to take evasive action when a crazy horse which he had seen in a dream appeared in reality. As it happened, the action he took turned out to be unnecessary; but the fact he took it went some way to supplying an answer to one of the stock objections to the idea that the future can be foreshadowed in dreams: that this would imply the future is predestined. There is now quite an extensive dossier of cases in which, forewarned, the dreamer takes a course of action designed to prevent some calamity.

OUT OF THE BODY

In *Resurrection* (1934) William Gerhardie told the tale of a novelist engaged on a book to be called by that title. In the course of a nap taken before he is due to go to a London ball, he finds himself apparently out of his body, capable of leaving it to go to another room, and eventually to visit a friend's apartment in Brighton. Waking up, back in his body, he goes to the ball, where he feels able to claim that he has himself experienced resurrection. He had 'risen', demonstrating the soul's immortality.

Research conducted since into out-of-the-body experiences (OBEs), as they have come to be called, shows that they are surprisingly common. Surveys in different parts of the world have revealed that the proportion of people who have had one or more is rarely lower than 10 per cent; sometimes much higher. But the investigations have led most psychical researchers to back away from the Gerhardie view. In *Beyond the Body* (1982), Susan J. Blackmore has forcefully put the case for a strictly psychological interpretation, in place of the theory of the 'astral body's' ability to detach itself. 'Travelling in the astral' may simply be an exploration of the contents of memory and imagination, she argues, 'brought to life by a new way of thinking in a special state of consciousness'. If this interpretation is correct 'it says nothing about survival. Nothing leaves the body in an OBE, and so there is nothing to survive.'

To reach this conclusion Susan Blackmore has to ignore or gloss over some cases where the 'travel' has apparently provided accurate information about something happening at a distance. But in the great majority of cases, the information can reasonably be accounted for without recourse to the 'astral body' hypothesis; and it seems likely that the clairvoyant component, when it occurs, is incidental to the experience, in the same way that it is incidental to dreaming. Understandably some OBEs have had a profound effect on the people who have had them, leading to a questioning of former materialist assumptions; but, for the present at least, they are best regarded as a quirky type of altered state of consciousness.

MEDITATION

Few people have the ability to exercise some degree of conscious control over their dreams – 'lucid dreaming'; but reveries or daydreams are a little easier to induce and follow up, as Kekulé did, to solve problems. And the growing popularity of meditation has thrown up indications that some of those who practise it 'come face to face with facts which instinct or reason can never know', as the Swami Vivekananda – one of the leading figures in the revival of Hinduism in the second half of the nineteenth century; in William James's estimation, 'the paragon of Vedantist missionaries' – told his followers they could expect to, if they submitted themselves to the moral discipline of the yogi.

While employed temporarily at a naval ordnance station in California, shortly after the Second World War, Elmer Green began to speculate about where he would eventually be working: and during meditation experienced 'a short hypnagogic movie' in which he saw an area of green grass, a tree-covered hill, and buildings with a tall clock tower. This vision meant nothing to him at the time, as it did not apply to the job he was about to take. If it was significant, he felt, it must apply to some future possibility; 'I merely stored it in my memory.' After finishing a course in biopsychology at the University of Chicago, he decided to explore it further, and 'saw' the place in much greater detail.

Again the institution consisted of a number of buildings spread out like a college campus over a grassy, tree-covered hill, but this time the large building with the clock tower could be seen from far away, was the more obvious feature. In one hypnagogic image I went into the clock-tower building and looked at a variety of American Indian artefacts in a small museum. There were also glass-covered cases containing manuscripts.

There was more detail, too, about the man in charge of the campus, and the work being done there. The vision so impressed Green that he and his wife Alyce decided to work their way from east to west across the United States, in the hope of finding the institution. Just as they were preparing to leave, he received a call from the Menninger Foundation in Topeka, Kansas, asking if he would like to take up a post there to bridge the communication gap between the psychologists and the biomedical team, with its enthusiasm for gadgetry. It was a job for which he was eminently well qualified, but he knew he must first inspect the Foundation. As soon as he saw the clock tower on the grassy, tree-covered hill, 'it had a feeling of rightness'; and at the Foundation he and Alyce were among those who, in the late 1950s, with the help of biofeedback, re-established the ability of the mind to exercise control over the body's automatic nervous system, a control which conventional medical training had dismissed as impossible. 'A few years ago,' Robert Ornstein, professor of psychology at the University of California Medical Center in San Francisco, recalled, 'it would have been considered "paranormal" to claim control over the blood pressure. Now a freshman in a psychological experiment can expect to learn some measure of blood pressure control in half an hour.' It was largely through the Greens' work at the Menninger Foundation, and the support they were given, as forecast in Elmer's precognitive vision, by their employer Gardner Murphy, that this revolution occurred.

Another account received by the Koestler Foundation has come from Imants Baruss of the University of Regina, Saskatchewan. After graduating in engineering science at the University of Toronto, Baruss went on to work for a master's degree in mathematics at Calgary; and while engaged on his thesis, he was working on an unsolved problem in mathematical logic, trying to show 'that a general structure, a Kripke-Joyal semantics, actually had a great deal more structure than apparent' (the technicalities, he says, would require over thirty pages of his M.Sc. thesis to elucidate). He did not think the result was possible; there was little reason to think it *was* possible. But between universities, he had learned to practise meditation.

I closed my eyes and went into a meditative state in which I formed the impression of the deceased mathematician Kurt Gödel. It was the first time that I had conjured up his image in meditation. He was standing in front of a blackboard. I asked him if the result would go through. He said yes, that it would, showing me some ways for working with the problem. Though the techniques which he showed me were too complicated for me, I think that they had some impact on my thinking. One and one half months later the result went through.

Baruss himself does not consider the experience a mystical one, 'but there was certainly a meaningful interchange with an imaginary intelligent being'.

'There is no right way for everyone to meditate,' Lawrence LeShan has explained in *Alternate Realities*, and there are various paths to it; but granted that a suitable programme is followed, meditation can bring more efficiency and serenity. 'It also does something more. As we work with it over a period of time, it leads us to a new way of construing reality – including extra-sensory perceptions.'

DRUGS

That drugs can be used to promote states of ecstasy appears to have been known to mankind from early in the development of tribal communities. The shaman, or witch doctor, would often use them to induce dissociation, facilitating communication with the spirits. Their record in more recent times has been patchy: only in one celebrated case has a work of genius been the outcome. After taking a couple of grains of opium Coleridge fell into a reverie while reading about Kubla Khan's palace. 'The author,' he recalled, referring to himself,

continued for about three hours in a profound sleep, at least of the external senses, during which time he has the most vivid confidence that he could not have composed less than two to three hundred lines; if that indeed can be called composition in which all the images rose up before him as *things*, with a parallel production of the correspondent impressions, without any sensation or consciousness or effort. On awakening he appeared to himself to have a distinct recollection of the whole, and taking his pen, ink and paper, instantly and eagerly wrote down the lines that are here preserved.

It was at this point that Coleridge was interrupted by the 'person on business from Porlock', who detained him for an hour; after which 'to his no small surprise and mortification', he found he could remember only a few scattered lines and images.

One contemporary novelist has paid tribute to a drug by naming it, in effect, as co-author of one of his best-known books. Struggling to write *The Power and the Glory*, and needing money for himself and his family to live on, Graham Greene decided to write another 'entertainment' in the mornings and *The Confidential Agent* was born. For the first and last time in his life, he resorted to taking benzedrine. 'Each day I sat down to work with no idea what turn the plot might take and each morning I wrote, with the automatism of a planchette, 2000 words' – by contrast with the 500 devoted in the afternoons to *The Power and the Glory*, which proceeded 'at the same leaden pace, unaffected by the sprightly young thing who was so quickly overtaking it'.

The Confidential Agent is one of the few books of mine which I have cared to reread – perhaps because it is not really one of mine. It was as though I were ghosting for another man. D, the chivalrous agent and professor of Romance literature, is not really one of my characters, nor is Forbes, born Furtstein, the equally chivalrous lover. The book moved rapidly because I was not struggling with my own technical problems: I was to all intents ghosting a novel by an old writer who was to die a little before the studio in which I had worked was blown out of existence. All I can say as excuse, and in gratitude to an honoured shade, is that *The Confidential Agent* is a better thriller than Ford Madox Ford wrote himself when he attempted the genre in *Vive Le Roy*.

But Greene was forcing the pace, and suffering as a result, as was his wife; looking back, he sometimes wondered whether the weeks of benzedrine for breakfast 'were more responsible than the separation of war and my own infidelities for breaking our marriage'.

The record of drugs as enlighteners has endlessly been tarnished by their side effects, ranging from irritability to chronic addiction, as in De Quincey's account. Still, the experience of exchanging the agony of facial rheumatism for the ecstasy of the effect of laudanum was to prompt *The Opium Eater*.

O heavens! what a revulsion! what a resurrection, from its lowest depths of the inner spirit! what an apocalypse of the world within me! That my pains had vanished was now a trifle in my eyes; this negative effect was swallowed up in the immensity of those positive effects which had opened before me, in the abyss of divine enjoyment thus suddenly revealed. Here was a panacea, a *Φάρμακον νηπένθές*, for all human woes; here was the secret of happiness, about which philosophers had disputed for so many ages, at once discovered; happiness might now be bought for a penny, and carried in the waistcoat-pocket; portable ecstasies might be corked up in a pint-bottle; and peace of mind could be sent down by the mail.

Aldous Huxley had a similar experience after mescalin. Ordinarily he was a poor visualiser; earlier in the morning, looking at some flowers in a vase in his study, he had been struck merely by the dissonance of their colours. 'That was no longer the point'; he was no longer looking at an unusual flower arrangement; he was seeing 'what Adam had seen on the morning of his creation – the miracle, moment by moment, of naked existence'. As for the books with which his study was lined,

> like the flowers they glowed, when I looked at them, with brighter colours, a profounder significance. Red books, like rubies; emerald books; books bound in white jade; books of agate, of aquamarine, of yellow topaz; lapis lazuli books whose colour was so intense, so intrinsically meaningful, that they seemed to be on the point of leaving the shelves to thrust themselves more insistently on my attention.

For Huxley, it was a revelation of the existence within himself of an ability to see colours in a way he had never seen them before; and this, William James had suggested in *The Varieties of Religious Experience*, was what could give drugs their justification, in this context. Some years before he had studied the effects of laughing gas, and reported his findings; and one conclusion he had reached had remained firmly in his mind.

> It is that our normal waking consciousness, rational consciousness as we call it, is but one special type of consciousness, whilst all about it, parted from it by the filmiest of screens, there lie potential forms of consciousness entirely different. We may go through life without suspecting their existence; but apply the requisite stimulus, and at a touch they are there in all their completeness, definite types of mentality which probably somewhere have their field of application and adaptation. No account of the universe in its totality can be final which leaves these other forms of consciousness quite disregarded. How to regard them is the question – for they are so discontinuous with ordinary consciousness. Yet they may determine attitudes though they cannot furnish formulas, and open a region though they fail to give a map. At any rate, they forbid a premature closing of our accounts with reality.

At best, in short, a drug can provide us with insight into what we have been missing. Inevitably the reaction will be different, according to the individual drug-taker's needs. When, to help a doctor researching into schizophrenia, Rosalind Heywood took mescalin in 1952 – before Huxley's *Doors of Perception* had publicised hallucinogenic illumination – it made the outer world seem to her 'extremely drab and boring'. She found herself 'in a world of fabulous colour, a thousand times more varied than a kingfisher's feathers', but it was an inner world. Other experimenters with drugs have simply found themselves the victims of a jester.

Determined to record his impressions when under the influence, Oliver Wendell Holmes took ether:

The veil of eternity was lifted. The one great truth which underlies all human experience, and is the key to all the mysteries that philosophy has sought in vain to solve, flashed upon me in a sudden revelation. Henceforth all was clear: a few words had lifted my intelligence to the level of the knowledge of the cherubim. As my natural condition returned, I remembered my resolution; and, staggering to my desk, I wrote, in ill-shaped, struggling characters, the all-embracing truth still glimmering in my consciousness. The words were these (children may smile; the wise will ponder): '*A strong smell of turpentine prevails throughout.*'

In a footnote, Holmes recalled that Sir Humphry Davy had had a similar experience after inhaling laughing gas: 'with the most intense belief and prophetic manner, I exclaimed to Dr Kingslake, "Nothing exists but thoughts. The universe is composed of impressions, ideas, pleasures and pains."' Holmes could not have dreamed that half a century after he wrote his indictment of materialism, *Mechanism in Thought and Morals*, these words would indeed be revealed as prophetic, when Sir James Jeans remarked that under the impact of quantum physics, the universe 'begins to look more like a great thought than a great machine'.

DIVINATION

Although in sleep, meditation or drug-induced reverie, the superconscious self can find ways to get through, it clearly still has problems. It has to use strange devices, some subtle, some importunate, to penetrate our consciousness. Throughout history, and in prehistoric times, people have sought ways to facilitate this process, by what is generally regarded as divination; either through sensory automatism, in which the information is gathered in the mind through a variety of channels – visions, say, in a drop of water, a crystal ball or the entrails of sacrificed animals; or through motor automatism, as in the use of a ouija board.

The most familiar form of sensory automatism is the one practised by spiritualist mediums; though this has come to be mainly associated with communication between the living and the dead – or, as spiritualists prefer, those who have passed on to another and higher form of life. One of the criticisms most often levelled at the contents of séances, when they are analysed, is that they so rarely give any useful information of the kind which the physically dead, if they are spiritually alive, should surely be able to supply. It is certainly true that most of their efforts appear to be devoted to establishing that they *are* still living; and very often it is trivia, such as the use of a pet name, or the recollection of a childhood picnic, which most impress the sitters. The spirits are generally disinclined to speak about their mode of life, except in vague terms; nor do they often provide the living with much in the way of guidance.

Still, there have been some striking examples of the ability of 'communicators', as the spirits are usually described, to help out. When Baron Paul Korf died, no will could be found; but in the correspondence which followed his death was a letter from Prince Emile von Wittgenstein to say that Korf had come through to him, at a sitting, to tell him that the will (which Wittgenstein did not then know was missing) had been maliciously hidden, and where it could be found. 'To the astonishment of those present,' Korf's nephew told the psychical researcher Alexander Aksakov, the place indicated in the spiritualist communication where the will would be found was precisely that in which it *was* found.

The most celebrated British medium between the wars, Mrs Osborne Leonard, volunteered to be the subject of careful and protracted trials by the Society of Psychical Research; and in the course of some of them a 'communicator' would sometimes be extremely helpful, as he was to Mrs Dawson-Smith, whose son Frank had been killed in a campaign in Somalia. In 1921, in the course of a sitting, 'Frank' insisted that his mother look for an old receipt, which was in a box-room trunk. It turned out to be a worn counterfoil of a money order; it meant nothing to her, but she felt she had better keep it. Three years later she was dunned by a Hamburg firm, through the 'Enemy Debt Clearing Office', for a sum of money which, the firm claimed, her son had left unpaid. Although she was sure that he had paid it, ten years previously, the Clearing Office Controller said that unless she could provide proof, the debt would have to be honoured. '*Then* I remembered my boy's message at Mrs Leonard's,' Mrs Dawson-Smith told the Society, 'and I hastened to look at the counterfoil.' It turned out to be the receipt for payment of the debt.

In spite of Mrs Leonard's remarkable record in her tests, mediums tended to become more suspect in the eyes of psychical researchers, and since the 1940s relatively little work has been done with them, though their popularity with the public appears if anything to have increased. An experience reported by Arthur Ellison, professor of electrical and electronic engineering at the City University, London, suggests that the joker who sometimes takes a hand in such affairs had decided to remind him that the Society for Psychical Research, of which he was president at the time, had once taken mediumship more seriously.

It was 1982, the Society's centenary year, and he was sitting at home at his desk composing his presidential address. Should he set a precedent, he wondered, by abandoning the caution customary in such orations? Should he put across his own views? While he was deliberating, the telephone rang.

It was a medium I had known very well some years ago, and had met again after her retirement some months before. She expressed some embarrassment at telephoning me, and said she did not know what my opinion would be of what she had to say. 'Anyhow,' she said, 'I have Oliver Lodge with me and he wishes to give you a message. The message is, "Ellison, do it, do it! Ellison, do it!"' She said she had no idea what this meant, and did not know whether I would know, either.

Ellison must have known very well not only what it meant, but what it implied. Lodge had been 'joint president of honour' at the Society's jubilee in 1932, along with Eleanor Sidgwick, widow of the Society's first president. Although he had spoken out in defence of spiritualism, he had not defended mediums, doubtless because he knew that Mrs Sidgwick and other senior members of the society were convinced that many of them were frauds.

Of those clairvoyants, as they commonly call themselves, who concentrate on divining the past and future of their clients without reference to the dead, a few still use a crystal ball, but increasingly they prefer cards – playing cards or the Tarot. This is a source of uneasiness to psychical researchers. Presumably, if there is a psychic component it must establish itself through the dealing out of the hands, which in effect means that the preliminary shuffling has been influenced psychokinetically – a possibility beyond the boggle-threshold of many who are prepared to accept PK in milder doses. Whatever the explanation, divination by this means can have a profound effect on the recipient: as illustrated in the account sent in to the Koestler Foundation from J. M. of Woodland, California.

In October 1985, living in Boston, Mrs M. began rather scepti-cally to read her Tarot, and found the King of Rods coming up. It meant nothing to her, but one evening she read the cards for a man whom she had met from the West, where she had lived.

I asked him to pick for himself out of the deck and he chose the King of Rods. I read his card for him and, in the 'culmination' position, was the Queen of Rods – my card. Immediately afterwards I read my cards in his presence. The King of Rods came up in my 'future' position and the Empress (married woman) came up in my 'culmination' position.

Startled, and offended, she turned away to collect some bread she had been baking.

When I turned around to set the bread on the table, I was no longer in my basement apartment kitchen. I was dressed in a long brown homespun dress (instead of plaid shirt and jeans). He was sitting at a wooden table in a wooden-beamed, low-ceilinged room. In the background there was a fireplace and fire with a big cauldron over it. As I set down the bread, the kitchen returned. He said, 'It's Tudor.' He had experienced it, too . . .

Perhaps not surprisingly, he became her husband.

If the Tarot's predictions are related to some PK effect on the shuffle, it must be classified as a motor automatism, the movement coming through the individual as if he or she were a medium – in Myers's definition, 'without the initiation, and generally without the concurrence, of conscious thought and will'. As he went on to explain, the movements are involuntary, and the medium exercises no control over the messages which emerge from the raps, the movement of the planchette or of the pen held loosely in the automatic writer's hand. 'Occasionally definite and correct infor-mation is given of facts which the medium has not, nor ever had, any knowledge,' Alfred Russel Wallace noted. 'Sometimes future events are accurately predicted.'

There have been a few remarkable instances of precognition induced in sessions, as if Fate had chosen this curious route to establish itself; one beneficiary being Sir Henry Lucy, who around the turn of the century wrote for many years the column 'Toby, MP' for *Punch*, and was also popular on both sides of the Atlantic for his articles in the *Strand* magazine.

In his memoirs Lucy described how as a young man he had experimented sceptically with table-turning, he and his three companions getting movements but no worthwhile information until,

my turn coming round, I renewed the effort. When I came to the letter C the rim of the table prodded me in the chest with evident joyous assent. Similar token was forthcoming when I got to the letter H; and so on until Charles Dickens was spelt out.

Then followed a quite friendly conversation, in the course of which the great novelist, four years dead, bade me call on his son Charles, at the time editor of *Household Words*, whom, he assured me, I should find in a friendly mood.

My companions several times attempted to join in the conversation, but Charles Dickens would have nothing to do with them, severely ignoring their existence. Whenever I spoke the table throbbed with exuberance.

Lucy was sufficiently impressed to go to the office of *Household Words* the next day, and send up his card to the editor.

My name being absolutely unknown to him, as it was to all outside a narrow circle, I expected my temerity would be properly rewarded by a message that the great man was engaged. On the contrary, I was promptly ushered into the presence of Charles Dickens, Jr, who received me in friendliest fashion, and straightway commissioned me to write an article for *Household Words*.

It was accepted, and I received a prodigiously handsome cheque – the first earned in that field of labour.

A curious feature of Charles Dickens's messages via the ouija board was that the words were sometimes misspelled and the sentences 'playfully ungrammatical' in a way that at first sight made his responsibility for them seem even more improbable. But later, reading Forster's *Life*, Lucy found that Dickens was playfully ungrammatical in correspondence, in his lighter moments; and although Lucy might conceivably have had an unconscious desire to write for *Household Words*, and transmitted it to the table, he felt that he certainly could not have been responsible 'for that singular phase of the communications'.

Automatic writing is not in itself paranormal, William James pointed out, and even when it appears to be it certainly should not be relied upon. 'Our subconscious region seems, as a rule, to be dominated either by a crazy "will to make-believe" or by some curious external force impelling us to personation' – making us write as if possessed by somebody else. Nevertheless he wanted to go on record for '*the presence*, in the midst of all the humbug, of really supernormal knowledge'.

Around the turn of the century one of the internationally most celebrated of opera singers was David Bispham; and in his autobiography he was to recall how his career was launched. In 1892 he entertained two Swedish friends to dinner, and they decided to see if they could get any messages through a ouija board. Under Baron Rudbeck's hand, the planchette began at once to write rapidly and distinctly.

I was not touching the machine, nor had I propounded any questions to it; yet it soon wrote in large letters, 'Opera, by all means'. Neither of my companions knew to what this referred or saw any connection in it with anything that had gone before, until I explained. 'It is an answer to a question I was about to ask,' I told them: 'Shall I continue in concert or make further endeavour toward opera?' Here was a direct answer to my unspoken thought.

To his first spoken question, 'What operas shall I study?', the planchette replied, 'The operas of Verdi and Wagner.' Bispham had no operatic repertoire at this time, but he was excited because he knew there were good parts for a baritone, even though he could not then sing them.

The next question I propounded to planchette was, 'Which of these operas shall I study?' The answer was 'Aida', 'Tannhäuser', 'Tristan und Isolde', and 'Meistersinger'. We sat amazed. I was pleased as well, for no better parts exist than are to be found in these works, and my next question followed almost as a matter of course, 'What parts shall I study?' There was a surprise for me at the end of the answer, which was 'Amonasro, Wolfram, Kurwenal, and – Beckmesser'.

Astonished, Bispham felt he would be wise to learn the parts –

even Beckmesser, for which he felt himself unsuited. Two months later his manager told him that if he knew the part, Covent Garden wanted him for Beckmesser; and he went to rehearsals. As it happened, the production had to be postponed; but at this point a letter arrived from Hamburg to ask if he could sing Kurwenal the following night, as a replacement for the baritone who had fallen ill. Bispham found himself taking the part without even a rehearsal.

Later, the illness of the singer who was taking the part of Amonasro at Covent Garden led to an offer to Bispham to sing that part, too; and he was subsequently many times to sing Wolfram.

When people say to me, 'What but foolishness did anyone ever get out of planchette or any other so-called spiritistic advice?' I tell them the story just narrated. My action in taking the advice I received – whence it came, I know not – resulted at the time indicated in my being fully prepared for what I was asked to do. In accepting this counsel and being ready with the parts I had been told to learn, I was undoubtedly enabled to accept the responsibilities whose execution straightway resulted in the foundation of my operatic career . . .

Some people, Bispham knew, would be inclined to put what had happened to him in the miracle category; others would attribute it to spirit intervention; others to a 'psychic flash'. 'I am content,' he concluded, 'to accept the facts as I found them, realising that there are more things in heaven and earth than are dreamed of in our philosophy.'

A few individuals have been able to exploit automatism as an everyday aid. W. T. Stead – a leading human rights campaigner in Britain a century ago in the *Pall Mall Gazette*; 'the most brilliant popular journalist of his day', in the opinion of Lord Francis-Williams – used to sit down and let his hand write letters, memoranda and reminders of appointments, as he found automatic writing more reliable than conscious writing: never, he claimed, had it let him down.

How useful the faculty could be on everyday occasions, Stead illustrated in his account of a time when he was staying in Redcar in the north of England, awaiting the arrival of a foreign journalist who did some work for him and who had said she would be arriving at Redcar railway station at about three.

It occurred to me that 'about three', the phrase used in her letter, might mean some time before three, and as I could not lay my hand on a timetable, I simply asked her to use my hand and tell me what time the train was due. This, I may say, was done without any previous communication with her upon the subject. She immediately wrote her name, and said that the train was due at Redcar station at ten minutes to three.

Stead went to the station, to find that the train was delayed. Taking a slip of paper and a pencil from his pocket, he asked 'her',

'Why the mischief have you been so late?'

My hand wrote, 'We were detained at Middlesbrough for so long; I do not know why.' I put the paper in my pocket, walked to the end of the platform and there was the train! The moment it stopped I went up to my friend and said to her, 'How late you are! What on earth has been the matter?' 'I do not know,' she said. 'The train stopped so long as Middlesbrough, it seemed as if it would never start.' I then showed her what my hand had written.

Divination – usually described as clairvoyance – has become a fashionable pastime, indulged in by well-off people for a variety of reasons, often in the hope of getting useful advice about whether to take some step which will have important consequences – accepting a new job, or asking for a divorce. Always the risk remains (apart from the possibility that the clairvoyant or medium is a fraud) that the advice given is derived from a feedback of the desires and designs of the person seeking it, either directly, if it comes through automatic writing, the crystal ball or other devices, or indirectly, picked up telepathatically by the clairvoyant. The witches in *Macbeth* might well have simply been relaying his ambitions to him, thereby precipitating his downfall.

Nevertheless, like other forms of exploration of the super-conscious mind's resources, divination can be as useful to anybody who employs it with due caution as it was to Lucy and Bispham – even if few of us can hope to get such valuable guidance the first time, or indeed at any time.

The Art of Creation

Can it confidently be said that the evidence from daemon, muse and the rest establishes the reality of that convenient abstraction, the Unknown Guest, as a force in our lives? No; but surely it is reasonable to claim that it makes the case for taking the concept seriously, and investigating it more systematically. But this raises the problem: how? The Koestler Foundation can collect some of the data, to provide the raw material, but science, as conventionally practised, is ill-equipped to make use of the material.

This is partly because the dogmas bequeathed by scientists in the past – positivism, materialism, behaviourism – still exert a powerful influence, and not just at the laboratory level: teaching at schools is still heavily affected by them, so that most of us have grown up with certain preconceptions which we find hard to shed. It is rare to find anybody who has not had some brush with the paranormal – a visit to a clairvoyant, say, or an experience in a haunted house – but it is extremely common to find that people who recall such episodes relate them as if they were of no significance, in spite of the fact that they overturn common-sense – as well as scientific – assumptions about the nature of reality.

What has chiefly been lacking is an account of the evolutionary background which will help to make sense of the Unknown Guest's baffling ways; and here, the work of W. H. R. Rivers is helpful, though its significance has sadly been missed. In the early years of the present century Halse Rivers made an enviable reputation as an anthropologist, which in academic circles he still enjoys. But his early training had been in medicine; during the First World War he joined the army as a medical psychologist, and by the end of it he was recognised as the leading authority on 'hysterical fugue' – shell shock. In the fugue state, soldiers would suddenly collapse into total immobility, or walk away behind the lines; and in the early part of the war, many were shot for cowardice or desertion. But often it was the bravest of men who were found in these conditions. Gradually it was realised they were not shamming. They had found a way out of intolerable stress – but they were totally unaware of what they were doing.

Animals threatened by a predator, Rivers knew, react in the same way. Instinct prompts flight, or absolute immobility. It is not so much that they do not move; it is as if they *cannot* move – 'playing possum' being the most striking example. Hysterical fugue ('shell shock' had been adopted clinically to provide neurological respect-ability, but Rivers realised it was a fig leaf) was an atavistic reaction – a protective mechanism.

In *Instinct and the Unconscious* Rivers developed this theme, pointing out that mass hysteria outbreaks were similarly throw-backs to the behaviour of animals in herds and birds in flocks. Naturalists, notably Edmund Selous and Eugene Marais, had been arguing that it is often as if movement is dictated by a common impulse, which cannot be accounted for except by the assumption that they surrender individual authority to some unexplained form of group control. It is the same, Rivers contended, in mass hysteria. The symptoms are introduced by suggestion, and spread by imitation. But both are *un*consciously produced. The suggestion is spread by 'the unwitting transmission of ideas from person to person'; the ideas are picked up through intuition – that is, through the unconscious mind; and they are translated into uniform action by mimesis – *un*conscious imitation.

But how are the ideas transmitted instantaneously? Rivers settled for 'thought transference' because, he explained, telepathy was still 'problematical'. He probably had in mind the then popular pastime, the 'willing game', in which somebody is sent out of the room at a party; the other guests select an object in the room, and when 'he' is summoned back, try to 'will' him to touch the object. In the 'willing game' there was no need to invoke telepathy; music-hall performers had demonstrated that the target could be traced by picking up minute, unconsciously provided signals. But as the meticulous observations of Selous and Marais had shown, group behaviour often cannot be accounted for by transmission of 'thought'. The flocks Selous watched were of birds which cannot 'think'; still less could Marais's termites. The instantaneous transmission they described had all the appearance of acting directly on the bodies of the birds and the termites – telekinetic, rather than telepathic. So it has seemed in mass hysteria outbreaks. It is as if an invisible band leader is directing the proceedings, inducing the convulsions or other symptoms.

The significance of Rivers's theory, though, and of the findings of Selous and Marais, is that hysteria is *not* inherently pathological. On the contrary, in its earlier evolutionary stage it was important development, as can still be judged from the study of insects, birds and animals. If it ceased to be of value, this was because with the development of individual intelligence and reasoning power, group control became a nuisance – as it still can be in panics, where people lose conscious control and either take to headlong flight or stay 'rooted to the spot'. Mass hysteria has become a menace, whether in its most often encountered form in schools and cults, or in induced varieties such as those the Nazis exploited in Germany.

Yet one form of induced hysteria has positive benefits, as Rivers realised: hypnosis. Hypnotised people behave in certain respects as if they were in the state of hysteria. They surrender control to a conductor – the hypnotist. Under his rule they can and do perform in ways which they would be embarrassed to demonstrate in their ordinary lives. Yet they also, in test conditions, demonstrate powers they do not realise they have. They can withstand burns without feeling pain. Even more remarkably, if it is suggested that the burns will leave no blisters or scar tissue, the body obeys the suggestion – provided, of course, that the burn is not too deep. In some cases, hypnotised individuals have shown they can detect what the hypnotist, or an observer, is seeing, or feeling, or tasting, or smelling. And there are many well-attested accounts of what used to be known as 'travelling clairvoyance' in the hypnotic trance state.

Rationalists often ask why, if in the course of evolution animals and even insects enjoyed such a potentially invaluable asset as extra-sensory communication, it should since have been lost by mankind. The evidence from hypnosis shows that it has not been lost, merely suppressed. The reason, Henri Bergson claimed, was that the brain had to develop into a filter, designed to sort out the information pouring in from the senses. The five specialist senses were offering information of a more immediate importance in the here and now. The 'sixth sense', as we now think of it – in reality the first – was squeezed into the background.

At the same time, group control had to be eased out to permit primitive man to use his new weapon, intelligence, to take over. For a while, as Julian Jaynes has shown, intuition provided a useful service with the help of hallucinations, powerful enough to break into consciousness, and in the process give the impression that gods were responsible for what was happening. But with the development of monotheism on the one hand, and rationalism on the other, hallucinations became suspect as either diabolically inspired or pathological. Hallucinations took Joan of Arc to the stake. Later, they took millions of men and women into lunatic asylums.

Hallucination should not be so necessary, if easier ways can be found to let intuition through. There is always the risk, admittedly, that the primordial element in the subliminal mind which Freud made the basis of his theory of the Id, and which Myers recognised, may become dangerous if it is let off the leash. 'Dabbling in the occult' can be hazardous for anybody who cannot handle the outcome because, as Maeterlinck stressed, the Unknown Guest can appear in many guises: friendly, facetious, terrifying. If we believe that the messages coming through a medium or a ouija board are from the spirits, they will adapt to that role; if we fear they come from the devil, they will offer diabolic advice. They can help us, but their promptings need to be subjected to the same critical scrutiny we would apply to advice from a friend or a neighbour.

But surely, some Christians will argue, this is tantamount to admitting that the Unknown Guest is simply another way of describing the age-old struggle for our souls between God and the devil? Up to a point, this is correct. It is a secular version, made necessary by the difficulty of maintaining Christian beliefs. To judge by opinion polls, the great majority of people in the Western world continue to believe in God. But they would be hard put to it to describe God. The childhood picture of an individual with a computerlike mind registering, and if necessary reacting to, our every move and our every thought has become unacceptable. Even less acceptable is the notion that God delegates functions to guardian angels, or lets Satan pursue us through his demons. Belief in God has largely been replaced by a vague belief in divine providence (though the term is now rarely encountered). Something may be looking after us, but we are unlikely to know what (or who) it is until the next life, if there is one, when all may be explained.

Perhaps it will be explained, but in the meantime there is an alternative proposition: that the Unknown Guest lies within us, in the same sense that our minds lie within us, though the evidence is beginning to suggest that they are not located in the brain. The superconscious self, on this hypothesis, has been evolving in much the same way as the human species evolved. For a time, its development was retarded by the fact that the five specialist senses made the sixth almost redundant, for practical purposes; and later, its revival was hampered when reasoning ability began to lead to a shutting-off of group impulses, leaving only the kind now encountered in hysteria outbreaks. But the superconscious has been coming to terms with our individual intelligences – or trying to. It has found ways, through intuition, to inspire artists and scientists. It has had to fall back, when compelled to, on hallucination to show us that we still have the sixth (or first) sense, and that it can be exploited without risk, if we understand its ways. But it is learning how to be a better protector, and a more efficient prompter, both of individuals and of communities.

'The words "I" and "Thou" do not cover our bodily forms and the outlines of our mind as we habitually represent them to ourselves,' Edward Carpenter, poet and social reformer, sagely asserted in *The Art of Creation*. They also cover

immense tracts of intelligence and activity lying behind these, and only on occasions coming into consciousness . . . If we could by any means explore, and realise what is meant by, the letter 'I'; if we could travel inward with firm tread to its remotest depth and find the regions where it touches close, so close, on the other forms of the same letter . . . Why then, surely, all would be clear to us, and Gladness and Beauty would be our perpetual attendants.

HAVE YOU EVER

had a premonition that has saved you from error or danger?

felt inspired to produce a work of art – a poem, composition or painting, say – of a quality transcending your everyday ability?

found the solution to a problem by intuition?

felt a powerful, unaccountable urge to take a course of action that has turned out to benefit you or somebody close to you?

had a hallucination – seeing an apparition or hearing a voice – of a helpful kind?

experienced a coincidence or a succession of coincidences so meaningful that you found it hard to attribute them to chance?

benefited from a visit to a clairvoyant, through being given an accurate glimpse into the future?

Accounts of such experiences will be gratefully acknowledged by
The Koestler Foundation
10 Belgrave Square
London SW1

Bibliography

The books listed are those which are either mainly concerned with the ideas and experiences that form the theme of *The Unknown Guest*, or contain material which is particularly relevant to it. Other works referred to in the text can be found in their relevant places in the source references. Where a work has been translated, I give the English title. The places and dates of publication in the bibliography and in the source references are those of the edition I have used – often the one which has been published most recently, and is consequently most readily available in bookshops or libraries.

Abercrombie, John, *Inquiries concerning the Intellectual Powers*, London, 1840

Æ, *The Candle of Vision*, London, 1918

Æ, *Song and its Foundations*, London, 1931

Aubrey, John, *Miscellanies*, London, 1857

Bancroft, Anne, *Modern Mystics and Sages*, London, 1978

Bazaillas, Albert, *Musique et Inconscience*, Paris, 1908

Bentine, Michael, *A Door Marked Summer*, London, 1982

Bohm, David, *Wholeness and the Implicate Order*, London, 1980

Bridge, Ann, *Moments of Knowing*, London, 1970

Bucke, Richard M., *Cosmic Consciousness*, New York, 1969

Carpenter, Edward, *The Art of Creation*, London, 1907

Churchill, Winston S., *My Early Life*, London, 1944

Cox, Michael, *Mysticism*, London, 1983

Coxhead, Nona, *The Relevance of Bliss*, London, 1985

Downey, June E., *Creative Imagination*, London, 1929

Dunne, J. W., *An Experiment with Time*, London, 1934

Eccles, Sir John and Daniel N. Robinson, *The Wonder of Being Human*, Boston, 1985

Ehrenwald, Jan, *Anatomy of Genius*, New York, 1984
Eisenbud, Jule, *Parapsychology and the Unconscious*, Berkeley, 1983
Eliade, Mircea, *Myths, Dreams and Mysteries*, London, 1960
Ellis, Havelock, *A Study of British Genius*, London, 1904

Flammarion, Camille, *The Unknown*, New York, 1900
Flammarion, Camille, *Death and its Mystery*, London, 1922

Galton, Francis, *Inquiries into the Human Faculty*, London, 1928
Ghiselin, Brewster, *The Creative Process*, University of California, 1952
Goddard, Sir Victor, *Flight Towards Reality*, London, 1975
Goethe, Wolfgang, *Poetry and Truth*, London, 1848
Goldberg, Philip, *The Intuitive Edge*, Los Angeles, 1983
Green, Celia and Charles McCreery, *Apparitions*, London, 1975
Green, Elmer and Alyce, *Beyond Biofeedback*, New York, 1977
Guinness, Sir Alec, *Blessings in Disguise*, London, 1985

Hadamard, Jacques, *The Psychology of Invention in the Mathematical Field*,
    Princeton, 1945
Happold, F. C., *Mysticism*, London, 1970
Harding, Rosamond, *An Anatomy of Inspiration*, London, 1948
Hardy, Alister, *The Living Stream*, London, 1965
Hardy, Alister, Robert Harvie and Arthur Koestler, *The Challenge of
    Chance*, London, 1973
Harman, Willis and H. Rheingold, *Higher Creativity*, Los Angeles, 1984
Harper, George Mills (ed.), *Yeats and the Occult*, London, 1975
Hazlitt, William, 'On Genius', *The Plain Speaker*, London, 1894
Heywood, Rosalind, *The Infinite Hive*, London, 1964
Holmes, Oliver Wendell, *Mechanism in Thought and Morals*, London, 1871
Housman, A. E., *The Name and Nature of Poetry*, Cambridge, 1933
Huxley, Aldous, *The Doors of Perception*, London, 1954
Huxley, Aldous, *The Perennial Philosophy*, London, 1947
Huxley, Julian, *Memories*, London, 1970

Inglis, Brian, 'Arthur Koestler and Parapsychology', *American SPR
    Journal*, July 1984
Inglis, Brian, *The Hidden Power*, London, 1986

Jaffé, Aniela, *Apparitions*, Salisbury, Wilts., 1979
James, William, *Principles of Psychology*, London, 1981
James, William, *The Varieties of Religious Experience*, London, 1902
Jaynes, Julian, *The Origins of Consciousness*, New York, 1977

Jung, Carl, *Memories, Dreams, Reflections*, London, 1973
Jung, Carl, *Collected Works*, London, 1957-79

Keller, Helen, *The World I Live In*, London, 1908
Kipling, Rudyard, *Something of Myself*, London, 1951
Koestler, Arthur, *Arrow in the Blue*, London, 1952
Koestler, Arthur, *The Invisible Writing*, London, 1969
Koestler, Arthur, *The Act of Creation*, London, 1964
Koestler, Arthur, *The Case of the Midwife Toad*, London, 1971
Koestler, Arthur, *The Roots of Coincidence*, London, 1972
Koestler, Arthur, *Janus*, London, 1978

Lang, Andrew, *Myth, Ritual and Religion*, London, 1887
Lang, Andrew, *Magic and Religion*, London, 1901
Lang, Andrew, *The Maid of France*, London, 1908
Laski, Marghanita, *Ecstasy*, London, 1961
Laski, Marghanita, *Everyday Ecstasy*, London, 1980
Lehmann, Rosamond, *The Swan in the Evening*, London, 1967
Lélut, L. F., *Du Démon de Socrate*, Paris, 1856
LeShan, Lawrence, *Alternate Realities*, London, 1976
Lodge, Oliver, *My Philosophy*, London, 1933
Lombroso, Cesare, *The Man of Genius*, London, 1891
Lyttelton, Dame Edith, *Our Superconscious Minds*, London, 1931
Lyttelton, Dame Edith, *Some Cases of Prediction*, London, 1937

MacKenzie, Andrew, *The Riddle of the Future*, London, 1974
Maeterlinck, Maurice, *The Unknown Guest*, London, 1914
Maritain, Jacques, *Creative Intuition*, Paris, 1953
Maurois, André, *Victor Hugo*, London, 1956
Medawar, Sir Peter, *The Limits of Science*, Oxford, 1985
Medawar, Sir Peter, *Induction and Intuition*, Philadelphia, 1969
Miller, Karl, *Doubles*, Oxford, 1985
Murphy, Michael, and Rhea White, *The Psychic Side of Sport*, Reading, Mass., 1980
Myers, Frederic, 'The Subliminal Consciousness: the Mechanism of Genius', *Proceedings of the SPR*, 1892, viii, 333-403
Myers, Frederic, *Human Personality*, London, 1903

Neher, Andrew, *The Psychology of Transcendence*, Englewood Cliffs, New Jersey, 1980

O'Neill, John J., *Prodigal Genius; The Life of Nikola Tesla*, New York, 1944

Owen, Robert Dale, *Footfalls on the Boundary of another World*, London, 1961

Planck, Max, *Where is Science Going?*, New York, 1932
Plato, *The Last Days of Socrates*, London, 1954
Playfair, Guy Lyon *If this be Magic*, London, 1985
Poincaré, Henri, *Science and Method*, London, 1914
Polanyi, Michael, *The Tacit Dimension*, London, 1967
Post, Laurens van der, *Jung*, London, 1976
Priestley, J. B. *Rain upon Godshill*, London, 1939
Priestley, J. B., *Man and Time*, London, 1964
Prince, Walter Franklin, *Noted Witnesses for Psychic Occurrences*, Boston, 1928

Randles, Jenny, *Beyond Explanation*, London, 1985
Rees-Mogg, William, *An Humbler Heaven*, London, 1977
Rhine, Louisa, *The Invisible Picture*, Metuchen, New Jersey, 1981
Rivers, W. H. R., *Instinct and the Unconscious*, Cambridge, 1920
Roberts, Jane, *The Unknown Reality*, Englewood Cliffs, New Jersey, 1971

Sabine, W. H. H. *Second Sight in Daily Life*, London, 1951
Sacks, Oliver, *The Man Who Mistook his Wife for a Hat*, London, 1985
Schroedinger, Erwin, *Mind and Matter*, Cambridge, 1958
Schumacher, E. F., *A Guide for the Perplexed*, London, 1978
Scott, Sir Walter, *Letters on Demonology*, London, 1830
Sheldrake, Rupert, *A New Science of Life*, London, 1981
Stevens, Wallace, *The Necessary Angel*, London, 1960
Storr, Anthony, *The Dynamics of Creation*, London, 1972

Talamonti, Leo, *Forbidden Universe*, London, 1974
Taylor, C. E. and F. Barron (eds.) *Scientific Creativity*, New York, 1962
Tchaikovsky, Modeste, *Tchaikovsky*, London, 1906
Toksvig, Signe, *Emanuel Swedenborg*, London, 1949
Trotter, Wilfred, *Instincts of the Herd*, Oxford, 1953
Tyrrell, G. N. M., *Science and Psychical Phenomena*, London, 1938

Underhill, Evelyn, *Mysticism*, London, 1912

Van Over, Raymond (ed.), *Psychology and ESP*, New York, 1972

Wallace, Alfred Russel, *My Life*, London, 1905
Watson, Lyall, *Earthworks*, London, 1986

Whitehead, Alfred North, *Science and the Modern World*, London, 1975
Whiteman, J. H. M., *The Mystical Life*, London, 1961
Wilber, Ken, *Quantum Questions*, Boulder, Colorado, 1984
Wolman, B. B. (ed.), *Handbook of Parapsychology*, New York, 1977

Yeats, W. B., *Autobiographies*, London, 1955
Yost, Casper, *Patience Worth*, New York, 1916

Source References

The words or names in parentheses refer to the subjects dealt with on the page. The source is identified by the author, the book (if it is not named in the text), the publication date, and the pages. Where the book is to be found in the bibliography, I have cited simply the author, the date of the edition I have consulted, and the page. The letters 'p.c.' indicate personal communications.

THE OPEN QUESTION

1 (Koestler): Hardy *et al.*, 1973, 170–1.
2 Schopenhauer: Hardy *et al*, 1973, 234.
    (Jung): Storr, *Jung: Selected Writings*, 1983, 293.
3 Myers, *Proceedings SPR*, 1892, viii, 333–403.

DAEMON

6 (Socrates) Plato, *The Last Days*, 1985, 74; *Theages*, 413–14; *Five Dialogues*, 1949, 6–7; *Phaedrus*, 43. Myers, *Proceedings SPR*, 1889, v. 522–47.
8 (Joan) Lang, *Proceedings SPR*, 1895, xi, 198–212.
10 Churchill, *The End of the Beginning*, 1943, 207; *My Early Life*, 1944, 294. Lady Churchill, 1963, 160–1.
12 (Koestler) Inglis, 1984, 263–72 (a fuller account, with the sources)
16 Heywood, 1964: 'Orders', 80; 'Julia', 148–51; Victoria, 47–9.
19 Guinness, 1985, *passim*; Hardy *et al.*, 1973, 172–3.
21 Jung, 1973: table cracks, 125; Freud, 178–9; daimon, 368–9, 389.
25 (Hitler) dream, de Becker, *Understanding of Dreams*, 1968, 79–80; magician, Ehrenwald, 1984, 194; plots, Manvell and Fraenkel, 1966, 53, 98–9; Trevor Roper, *Last Days of Hitler*, 1947, 81–8. Goethe, 1848, ii, 159.
28 Maeterlinck, 1914, 318.
    Goethe: Eckermann, tr. Dennis Stillings, *SPR Journal*, Jan. 1986; *Autobiography*, 1932, 683.

29 Maeterlinck, 1914, 320
   Huxley, 1970, Introduction.
30 Lélut, 1837, 11–13.
   Lombroso, 1891, Preface, 336.
31 Holmes, 1871, 66–7.
32 Jaynes, 1977, 342.

THE MUSES

34 Downey, 1929, 155.
   (Freud) Storr, 1972, xi.
   (Watson, Skinner) Koestler, 1978, 166–9.
36 Ehrenwald, 1984, 242, 192–205.
   Kipling, 1933, *passim*; Birkenhead, 1978, 353–67.
40 Myers, 1903, i, 222.
42 Cross, *George Eliot*, 1985, iii, 424–5; *The Lifted Veil*, 1985, Introduction.
43 Guyon, *Autobiography*, 1897, ii, 90.
   Lombroso, 1891, 339.
44 James, Ghiselin, 1952, 6–7.
   (Benson) Langdon-Brown, *Thus We Are Men*, 1938, 126–8.
45 Wolfe, Ghiselin, 1952.
   Miller, *Black Spring*, 1963, 51–67.
   Stowe, 1889, 154–61, 184–6.
46 (Blyton) G. R. Taylor, *Natural History of the Mind*, 1979, 223–4.
47 Daudet, *Alphonse Daudet*, 1898, 82.
48 Cleeve, p.c.
49 Roberts, 1971, i, 15.
   Yost, 1916, *passim*.
51 Collis, *Somerville & Ross*, 1968, 177–222.
52 Maurois, *Victor Hugo*, 1956, 343–7.
53 Thackeray, *Works*, 1899, xii, 375.
   (Robertson) Eisenbud, 1983, 187–207.
54 Ellman, *Joyce*, 1983, 599, 677.
   Bates, *The Blossoming World*, 1971, 67.
55 (Nietzsche) Ghiselin, 1952, 209.
   Housman 1933, 48–50.
56 (Milton) Lyttelton, 1931, 225.
   (Longfellow) Underwood, *Longfellow*, 1882, 258–9.
57 (Rilke) Hudson, *Night Life*, 1985, 76–99.
   (Howe) Richard and Ellcott, *Reminiscences*, 1899, 103.
58 Sassoon, 1945, 140–1.
59 Masefield, *So Long to Learn*, 1952, 185–9.

60 (Keats) Lyttelton, 1931, 226.

(Blake) Wilson, *Life of William Blake*, 1948, 69–70.
(Yeats) Ellmann, 1961, 70–97; Harper, 1976, 114–21. Hyde-Lees:
   Ellman, 222.

62 Jung, *Modern Man in Search of a Soul*, 1933, 187–8.
Oakes, p.c.

63 Myers, *Proceedings SPR*, viii, 363–4.
(Bird) Maine, *Elgar*, 1, 117.
(Puccini) Harman and Rheingold, 1984, 35.

64 (Stravinsky) BBC3 broadcast, 9 April 1982.
(Elgar) Maine, *Elgar*, 1933, i, 117.
(Mozart) Holmes, *Life*, 1912, 254–8; Jahn, *Mozart*, 1891, ii, 415.
Tchaikovsky, 1906, 274–307.

67 (Wagner) Newman, *Wagner*, 1937, ii, 361–2.

68 (Schumann) Flammarion, 1922, iii, 109.
(Saint-Saëns) Flammarion, 1922, i, 89.

69 (Brown, Lill) *Psychic News*, 23 August 1980.

70 Parrott, p.c.

71 (Blake), Gilchrist, 1863, i, 59–60.

72 Hazlitt, *Essays*, 1949, 158, 230.
(Moore) U. O'Connor, *Celtic Dawn*, 1984, 59.
(Picasso) Ghiselin, 1952, 50; Auty, *Spectator*, 20 Sept, 1986.
(Cézanne, Klee, Breton) Haftman, *Klee*, 1954, 137–40.

73 (Ernst) Ghiselin, 1953, 61.
Bacon, BBC3 broadcast, 18 September 1966.

74 (Le Brocquy) Walker, *Le Brocquy*, 1981, 67–9.
(Pollock) Potter, *Pollock*, 1979, 207–223.

75 Manning, 1974, 77.
James, p.c.

76 Weisberg, 1986, 17.

77 Æ, *Candle of Vision*, 1918, 50; 1932, 42.

79 Priestley, 1939, 42–3.
(Geley) de la Mare, 1939, 607.
Lodge, 1933, 42.

EUREKA!

81 (Ampère) Koestler, 1964, 117.

82 Koestler, 1964, 105–6; (scientists irrational), 146.
(Gauss) Hadamard, 1945, 15.
(Hamilton) Hankins, *Rowan Hamilton*, 1980, 293–4.

83 (Wundt) Koestler, 1964, 153.
Poincaré, 1914, 52–64.

85 Hadamard, *passim*; Hadfield, *Faraday*, 1931, 25.

87 (Kekulé) Koestler, 1964, 118.
(Kelvin) Thompson, *Kelvin*, 1910, ii, 1096, 1126.
(Nicolle) Hadamard, 1945, 19.
(Einstein) Hadamard, 1945, 142–3; Ehrenwald, 1984, 119–29; Reiser, *Einstein*, 1931, 116–17.
88 (Galois) Hadamard, 1949, 119–20.
89 (Tesla) Harman and Rheingold, 1984, 63–70; O'Neill, 1944, 40–56.
90 (McClintock) *New Scientist*, 1 September 1983, 632.
91 (Swedenborg) Wilkinson, *Swedenborg*, 1849, *passim*; Toksvig, 1949, *passim*.
93 Wallace, 1905, i, 361–3; Marchant, *Wallace*, i, 116–17; ii, 242–3.
94 (Berger) Krippner, *Advances in Parapsychology*, 1977, i, 1.
Hardy, 1965, 234–61.
Myers, *Proceedings SPR*, viii, 351.
97 (Lodge) Hall, *Lodge*, 1932, 52.
99 Sacks, 1986, 185–203.
101 (Banting) Stevenson, *Banting*, 1947, 67.
Medawar, 1969, 11–12.
102 (Newton) Keynes, *Essays in Biography*, 1961, 310–11.
Wilber, 1984, Introduction.
103 (Einstein) Ehrenwald, *Science*, 30 September, 4 November, 1977.
Planck, 1932, 159–65.
(Pauli) Wilber, 1984, 158–63.
104 (Penfield) LeShan, *Light*, Summer, 1985, 53.
(Sperry) Harman, 'Transcendent Experiences', Institute of Noetic Sciences, California, July 1985.
Eccles, 1985, 36.

THE SUPERCONSCIOUS MIND

105 Lyttelton, 1931, *passim*
106 Holmes, 1871, 40–1.
(Wilberforce) Ashwell, *Life*, i, 397.
107 Whitehorn: p.c. Katharine Whitehorn.
108 Varley: Flammarion, 1900, 299; Lodge, *Proceedings SPR*, xxxiv, 316.
(Whitaker) Playfair, 1985, 126–7.
109 Sinclair, 1930, 208.
Owen, 1861, 332–5.
110 (Tallmadge) Sabine, 1951, 65–6.
111 (Wait) Myers, 1903, ii, 108–9.
113 Hearne, *SPR Journal*, February 1982, 210–13
Rhine, 1981, 114–15.
Cooke, 1968, 31–2.

114 MacQuitty, p.c.
116 Chaplin, *My Autobiography*, 1954, 376–7.
    Guirdham, *We Are One Another*, 1974.
117 Rees-Mogg, 1977, 5.
118 Zschokke: Howitt; *History of the Supernatural*, 1863, i, 96–7.
119 Bentine, 1982, *passim*.
121 Lyttelton, 1937, 120.
    Hudson, 1922, 44.
122 Gurney, *SPR Proceedings*, v, 305–6.

HALLUCINATIONS

125 James, *Principles of Psychology*, 1891, ii, 115; Van Over, 1972, 50.
    Galton, 1928, 58.
    Flammarion, 1900, 1922.
126 Goddard, 1975, 23–7.
128 Yeats, *Essays and Introductions*, 1961, 36–7.
    Goethe, *Autobiography*, 1932, 439.
129 (Dutch engineer) Green and McCreery, 1975, 77.
    (Wilmot) *Proceedings SPR*, vii, 41–3.
130 Smyth, p.c.
131 (Schopenhauer) Flammarion, 1922, iii, 7.
    (Smith) Barrett, *On the Threshold of the Unseen*, 1917, 141.
132 (Johnson) Boswell, *Johnson*, 1935, ii, 381.
    Bennett, 1939, 134–9.
134 G.P.: p.c.
    Jaffé, 1979, 165.
    Brougham, *Autobiography*, 1871, 202.
135 Aubrey, 1857, 78.
    Kerner, *The Seeress of Prevorst*, London, 1845, *passim*.
136 Perovsky, *Proceedings SPR*, xvii, 385–7.
137 (Erskine) Lady Morgan, *The Book of the Boudoir*, 1829, 123–4.
    (Warren) *SPR Newsletter Supplement*, August, 1985.
    Mitchell, I have mislaid the source of Silas Weir Mitchell gave of his
        experience (p. 138), and would appreciate a reminder if anyone knows
        it.
139 Jaynes, 1977, 85–6.
140 Myers, *Proceedings SPR*, xi, 411.
    Hodgson, *Proceedings SPR*, xi, 481–3.
141 Rhine, 1980, 92.
142 Symes, *SPR Journal*, May 1889, 326–7.
    Myers, *Proceedings SPR*, xi, 339.
143 Hodgson, *Proceedings SPR*, xi, 424–6.

144 Flammarion, 1922, iii, 214,
   Koestler, 1973, 173–4.
   Paul, p.c.
145 Green and McCreery, 1975, 187.
146 *SPR Journal*, March 1897, 45–9.
147 Jaffé, 1979, 35.
   Devlin, p.c.
148 Gobbi, 1979, 88–9.
150 (Flaubert) Downey, 1929, 219.
   Harrison, *Zetetic Scholar*, 1982, ix, 98–107.
151 Sabine, 1951, 101–3.
152 Smyth, *Blackwood's Magazine*, November 1921, 582.
   Lehmann, 1967, 114–21.
153 Sacks, 1985, 149–53.
154 Elliott, *Proceedings SPR*, viii, 244.
155 (West) *SPR Journal*, March 1938, 180–7.
   Molloy, p.c.
157 (Dickens) Forster, *Dickens*, 1928, 719–20; H. House, *All in Due Time*,
   1955, 187.
   (Eddington) Wilber, 1984, 198.

MIND OVER MATTER

159 Cellini, *Life*, 1920, 236–7.
160 (Nijinsky) Fodor, *The Riddle of Nijinsky*, 1914, 24–9.
   Duncan, 1928, 51.
   Smith, 1939, 238–9.
161 Murphy and White, 1980: Rush, 42; Pelé, 21: Bannister, 16; Palmer,
   26.
163 (Sirchia) Bozzano, *Discarnate Influences on Human Life*, 1942, 152.
   (Galateri) Flammarion, 1922, iii, 60.
164 (Houdini) Christopher, *Houdini*, 1969, 165.
166 Young, p.c.

SYNCHRONICITY

   Jung, *Works*, viii, 421; Storr, *Jung*, 1983, 337–41.
   Koestler, 1978, 259.
   Saint-Saëns: Flammarion, 1922,
169 Randles, 1985, 166–7.
   Flammarion, 1900, 192–3.
170 (West) Hardy *et al.*, 1973, 161–2.
   (Stanford) Isaacs, *The Unexplained*, vii, 81 (n.d.)
   Stanbury, *Light*, Spring 1985, 24–7.

171 Lehmann, *Light*, Spring 1984, 17–18.
     Van der Post, *Jung*, 1976, 263.
172 Playfair, p.c.
174 Watson, 1986,
     Cox; *American SPR Journal*, July 1956, 98–109.

THE OCEANIC FEELING

176 Koestler, 1969, 429.
176 Happold, 1981, 45–50.
177 McGlashan, p.c.
     Laski, 1980, 9–12.
178 James, 1975, 410.
179 Neher, Preface.
     Underhill, 1912, 3.

THE SEARCH FOR THE SUPERCONSCIOUS

181 Hamilton, *Metaphysics*, 1861, i, 341–6.
182 Dauben, *George Cantor*, 1979, 288–91; Grattan-Guinness, *Psychology
       in the Foundations of Logic and Mathematics*, 1983, 104–8.
184 Blackmore, 1982, 240–52.
185 (Vivekananda) James, 1902, 386.
     Green, *Beyond Biofeedback*, 1977, 1–20.
186 LeShan, 1976, 83.
187 (Coleridge) Hanson, *Coleridge*, i, 259–60.
     Greene, 1982, 69.
188 De Quincey, 1960, 179.
     Huxley, *Doors of Perception*, 1954, 10–13.
189 James, 1902, 374.
     Heywood, 1964, 205–13.
190 Holmes, 1871, 54–5.
     Jeans, *The Mysterious Universe*, 1937, 122.
191 (Wittgenstein) Myers, 1903, ii, 493–5.
     (Dawson-Smith) *SPR Proceedings*, xxxvi, 299–310.
192 Ellison, *SPR Newsletter Supplement*, Aug. 1985.
193 Wallace, *Miracles and Modern Spiritualism*, 207.
194 Lucy, *Sixty Years*, 1890, 89–90.
195 James, 1902, 321–2.
     Bispham, *A Quaker Singer's Recollections*, 1920, 110–16.
196 (Stead) Vyvyan, *A Case Against Jones*, 1966, 68.

THE ART OF CREATION

198 Rivers, 1923, *passim*.
202 Carpenter, 1907, 203.

Index

LAURIE TAYLOR AND BOB MULLAN

UNINVITED GUESTS

– CALVIN (40): 'I don't think I've ever once seen an Arab in Dallas. I know America has got its own oil industry but they must have to collaborate with the Arabs from time to time. I don't think I've ever seen an Arab negotiating.'

Previous studies of Britain's viewing and listening habits have been dry sociological surveys. In UNINVITED GUESTS it's the audiences themselves – rather than the academics – who give their views on the programmes which are such an integral part of our popular culture. Their comments – perceptive, knowledgeable and often very funny – form the basis of this highly entertaining account of the *real* effects of television and radio on us all.

POST A LITTLE HAPPINESS

Post·A·Book

A Royal Mail service in association with the Book Marketing Council & The Booksellers Association.

Post-A-Book is a Post Office trademark.

BOB WOODWARD AND CARL BERNSTEIN

THE FINAL DAYS

Bob Woodward and Carl Bernstein's THE FINAL DAYS is the international success story of the decade, with millions of copies already sold. Here the final desperate days of the Nixon administration are brought vividly to life, with the same behind-the-scenes investigative reporting and devastating novelistic style that made ALL THE PRESIDENT'S MEN one of the greatest international bestsellers of all time.

'A book which is impossible to put down'
Financial Times

'This is history-as-it-happened and immensely readable'
Daily Mirror

HODDER AND STOUGHTON PAPERBACKS

ANDREW SINCLAIR

THE RED AND THE BLUE

Cambridge University between the wars: a clash of two cultures — Science and Art.

On the one hand, the brilliant Cavendish Laboratory physicists who split the atom and later discovered the genetic secrets of life.

On the other, the visionary intellectuals, epitomised by the Apostles, the secret society which so profoundly influenced the economics, literature, politics and philosophy of this century.

THE RED AND THE BLUE provides a fresh insight into the activities of the Cambridge spies, tracing the development of the 'two cultures', their eventual conflict and how it led to startling changes that have transformed our world.

'Brilliant and disturbing'

The Sunday Times

'His book is both useful and entertaining — useful in that it compendiously summarises and brings up to date much other work on the Cambridge traitors, and entertaining because of the sharpness and elegance of his writing'

Daily Telegraph

HODDER AND STOUGHTON PAPERBACKS

JUDITH COOK

WHO KILLED HILDA MURRELL?

The body of Hilda Murrell was found on March 24th, 1984.

Aged 78, still-vigorous, Cambridge-educated, a rose grower of international repute, she had been attacked in her own home in Shrewsbury, abducted in her own car and left to die in a small copse several miles away.

A straightforward, if particularly nasty crime; the police expected an early arrest. But then came the doubts, coincidences and different stories.

Her house had been expertly searched. Her phone had been tampered with. As had that in her Welsh cottage – which later, inexplicably, burned down. She had been scared that something might happen to her. Why?

Was it connected with the missing draft of her paper on nuclear waste disposal for the Sizewell B enquiry? Or with the fact that her ex-RN nephew had handled the vital signals traffic from HMS *Conqueror* at the time of the *Belgrano* sinking?

Now journalist Judith Cook investigates the disturbing case of the killing of Hilda Murrell – a death that raises alarming questions about the activities of this country's security services.

HODDER AND STOUGHTON PAPERBACKS

ANTHONY SAMPSON

THE MONEY LENDERS

'Sampson is in a class by himself as a chronicler of power: who has it, how it works, who wins, who loses. The story of international bankers has never been better told'

Studs Terkel

In this updated edition, THE MONEY LENDERS reveals the personalities, the motives and the tragic mistakes which helped to bring about the current global debt crisis. Anthony Sampson vividly traces the development of bankers and lending from the Medicis, the Rothschilds and the Barings, through to Barclays, Citibank and the global money-machines of today. And he traces how the debt-ridden countries like Poland, Zaire and Brazil were first indulged and then pressed into the predicaments which face them today.

'An excellent, clear, well-written guide to the universe of money'

The New York Times

HODDER AND STOUGHTON PAPERBACKS

ALSO AVAILABLE FROM
HODDER AND STOUGHTON PAPERBACKS